Money Enough for the Winter

Adrian and Susan Vaughan

3P
PUBLISHING

First published in 2022 in the UK
3P Publishing
C E C, London Road
Corby
NN17 5EU

A catalogue number for this book is available from the British
Library

ISBN 978-1-913740-64-1

Cover design: Rebecca Vaughan and James Mossop

Dedicated to our dear daughters,
Rebecca, Connie and Beatrice
— a gift from the past.

Authors' Note:

We relied upon letters, diaries and other records as well as our memories to write this joint memoir. Other people's recollection of events may be slightly different. Any mistakes are ours alone. Some names have been changed.

Editor's Note:

Adrian's words are written in regular text. Susan's words are written in italics.

Photographs:

Apart from the 'wedding group' all photographs were taken by Adrian (and occasionally Susan) on his Rolleiflex camera. Front cover: The first harvest. September 1976. Back cover: Killorglin town seen from Faill na Gabhair: Cliff of Goats.

Contents

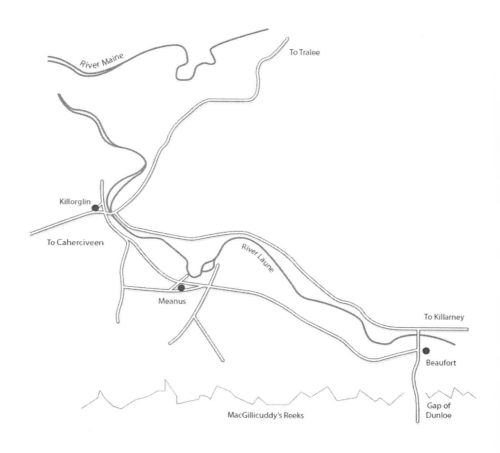

Meanus and the surrounding area

Chapter One
Serendipity

That 7th September 1970 was a very ordinary day for me. I had finished the early shift in Hinksey North signal box, gone back to my lodgings in Abbey Road, Oxford, eaten, washed and set out at four o'clock to drive to Childrey, to the west of Wantage, to see my parents. It was just something to do. I turned right at the end of Abbey Road, over Osney Bridge and headed west along the Botley Road. The sky was overcast, rain was due.

The 'Bishop's Move' removal company's warehouse was 150 yards away when I saw the girl thumbing a lift. I pulled up alongside her. She stopped and turned towards me. I leaned across the eternally empty passenger seat and wound down the window. She was seventeen or eighteen. She was slim and tall. Her face was fine. An intellectual, aristocratic face, high cheekbones, a slightly hooked nose, all framed with glorious auburn hair.

'Where do you want to go?' I asked.

'Wantage,' she said.

'That's where I'm going – get in.'

She got in clutching a carrier bag from a boutique in the city centre and we set off. The car was exhilarating up Cumnor Hill, pulling hard. I glanced sideways at the lovely profile. Oh what a beautiful girl! I blathered on about how well the car was making it uphill. Wantage was only fifteen miles away, twenty-five minutes and she would be gone.

She had been in the car six minutes, I hadn't stopped chattering – she hardly said a word. I was nervous. I was worrying. In twenty minutes she would disappear from my life. I turned onto the Wantage road and accelerated away. How silly you are, I thought. She's seventeen or eighteen at most and you're twenty-nine so why should she be bothered about you? She just wants to get home. But I didn't want her to go away. Down the straight now towards the Frilford crossroads and the golf course. The greens were on both sides. I glanced at the mileometer: 45 miles. Panic!

'Oh no! I'm afraid we're going to run out of petrol.' I spoke as the wide open spaces of the golf course surrounded the car. Her head snapped round, furious. I took the full force of wonderfully blazing green eyes, haughty nose and freckled, pink blushed face. '*No we are not!*' she snapped.

'Yes we are,' I said quietly as the engine struggled and died. I braked and turned to her to explain. She was glaring hard, ferocious green eyes.

'It's OK,' I said. 'I'm measuring how many miles to the gallon the engine does. I only put one gallon in at a time and I have a spare gallon in the back for when it runs out.'

'Well, you'd better have!' she said.

I pointed to my brass-cased GWR locomotive vacuum gauge. 'Look, this is what I have to tell me if...' She looked at the dial and now her face relaxed as she realised she was not in the company of a dangerous sex fiend but simply a dotty nerd. I got out to get the petrol.

I was only seventeen. I had had a few boyfriends – in fact, I had a date with one on that very evening. The boys I had gone out with were mostly sixth formers from the local grammar school. There was a whole gang of them who fooled around King Alfred's Statue in Wantage market place whenever they didn't have anything better to do, and my best friend Marilyn and I hung out with them. We all went to 'The Swan' together on Friday evenings to listen to the latest hit single and where the girls all danced and the boys propped up the bar. We attended endless parties on Saturday nights thrown by various boys whose parents went away a lot. The parties invariably ended in grubby orgies with couples all over the place and a few lone males, usually the party holders, tanking it up on the stairs. I remember one occasion when I was fourteen: two of the boys tossed a coin for me! The butcher's-son-

made-good 'got me' and I was so pathetically pleased. I blush to think that I should condone such behaviour as perfectly acceptable. In those days, at that age, getting a boyfriend was all that mattered. We spent the rest of the evening groping each other on the floor in the dark. It was very uncomfortable. I had the weird sensation that I was floating above it all, detached from what was going on and slightly perplexed. What was all this about? The butcher's son and I went out together for a whole year afterwards until I was able to assert some independence of spirit and fancied someone who was a little more exciting: fabulous, flamboyant Pete. With his long red hair and ankle-length greatcoat he swanned around the market town radiating hippiness. He was definitely tut-tut material for all the mums and dads and I liked him all the more for it. I still have his boxed Valentine card bought from Woolworths in which he promised his undying love.

Later when I was sixteen or so I had a blind date with a Muslim boy. I really fancied him because he seemed so exotic. We went out for a bit but I was taken aback when he didn't want to have sex with me, because by then I was desperate to join the ranks of my gang of friends in the sixth form, all of whom had triumphantly lost their virginity. Farid told me that he could not have sex with someone who wasn't a Muslim, and in any case he would have to be married first. I was very puzzled, knowing nothing about Islam. Regretfully, because we did like each other, we went our separate ways.

So that was more or less my experience of the opposite sex when I climbed into this slightly old-fashioned grey car with its dazzling array of brass dials on the dashboard and a rather handsome young(ish) man at the wheel. He spoke in a strange clipped way with a broad Wantage accent but he had lots to say and I was enthralled. That is until he told me that we were about to run out of petrol and for a horrible second or two I thought I was in real trouble, but his easy, if eccentric, explanation put me at my ease once more.

We drove on. She was calm but I was in a great state of nerves. I felt I simply had to hang onto her. She could not just get out of the car in Wantage and disappear from my life. She seemed to me to be very special. But I was so old and she was so young. But then again, that was merely a matter of arithmetic. I wasn't anything like as experienced in these matters as my years might have suggested. I knew that I wanted to find a beautiful girl with whom I could make love and be with forever. Unfortunately I had been brought up to believe that thinking such thoughts was a mortal sin that needed to be confessed before I died or I would be consigned to Hell for ever.

I chattered with shyness. Extolling the fineness of my adjustment of the position of the distributor for advance/retard position, then onto current affairs, the Labour Party shutting down the railway and all the while thinking 'Ask her to come out with you when we pass the 'Noah's Ark',' but the words never came. At Venn Mill. At Hanney crossroads. At Wantage Road station. All these became critical points. 'Ask!' But I didn't. We slowed down at the edge of Wantage. Harcourt Way was on the left.

'You can drop me here,' she said.

'No, no. I'll take you to your house. Where do you live?'

She told me that she lived in Aldworth Avenue. Her voice was music, her accent educated, unlike my Old Berks twang. We drove through the Harwell estate in silence. Panic rising. 'For goodness sake, ask her!' I ordered myself. Left into Aldworth Avenue, and I stopped the car outside her house. She had her hand on the door handle.

'Well, thanks for the lift,' as she opened the door. She had one foot on the road.

'Will you come out with me tonight?' I blurted it out.

'Yes, OK,' came the instant, yet casual reply. 'What's your name?'

'Adrian, Adrian Vaughan. What's yours?'

'Susan O'Sullivan,' she said.

We agreed a time for me to pick her up, she slammed the door and dashed indoors. I was bowled over. The effect was similar to shoulder-charging a door that was not locked. But bursting through that door would change my life forever.

I had never met anyone like him. He never stopped talking but he had so much of interest to say that I said he should write a book about it all. He was sexy! Not like the immature boys I had been hanging around with. I liked his golden velvet cord flares. The thought went through my mind that he must be married, but I quickly dismissed it as a bigger thought consumed me: I wanted to see him again. As we reached Wantage I was relieved when he offered to take me to my door and I dared myself to ask him for a date but the words wouldn't come and we spent the final part of our journey in silence. There was a tension in the car. We came to a stop outside my house. I still hadn't said anything – it felt cheeky and improper somehow, especially as I thought he was married – but as I was getting out of the car he asked if he could see me that night! My heart leapt with pleasure and gratitude and I said 'Yes' almost before he had finished speaking.

The tension that drove the mental effort of asking to see her again and the quite unexpected answer made me feel elated. As I drove towards Childrey I felt as if I was flying. I was miles high. What a beautiful girl. What a fantastic stroke of luck. No, it was a miracle. If I'd have left Abbey Road a few minutes earlier or later I might never have seen her. And she wanted to see me again! I decided it was too good to be true and, preparing myself for the inevitable collapse of my dream, I told myself she would chuck me within two weeks. And there was so much I was interested in that I wanted to share with her. Never mind. Enjoy the fortnight.

I collected Susan from outside her house at around seven o'clock. The twilight deepened as I headed for the 'Blue Boar' inn, on the Newbury road, high up and lonely on the Berkshire Downs. Where the motor road crosses the prehistoric trackway – the Ridgeway – east and west from Lincolnshire to Dorset, I pulled onto the grass and suggested we walk along the famous old grass track to the Lord Wantage Memorial. We were high above the Vale. There was a half moon, the planet Venus and the brighter stars were visible as the sun dropped glowingly below the horizon of the western Vale. The lights of Wantage town and the scattered villages burned small and yellow far below.

This was my country, the Vale of the White Horse and the Berkshire Downs. I had a lifetime's acquaintance with White Horse Hill – I'd broken my leg up there as a child, running down the grassy flanks and putting my foot in a rabbit hole. From up there I had watched the trains steaming through the Vale on 'Brunel's billiard-table' railway. For three winters, 1953-56, I had the privilege of a fine, dapple-grey pony to ride and had hunted the fox through the Vale on winter Saturdays with the Old Berks hounds. I had ridden through the Vale on the footplates of the steam engines. I had once *driven* the Didcot-Swindon stopping train from Challow to Swindon and I had signalled the express trains from the immaculately polished Challow signal box. The Vale and the Downs were beautiful and magical for me. I felt free up there. I had for years wanted to share my love of the countryside with the love of my life – and now here she was – for a couple of weeks anyhow.

She will probably tell you that I talked my head off. I might well have pointed out the beauty of the evening but – the beauty of the view apart – she was wearing a close-fitting, pleasantly short, white silky sort of dress with red and blue lines slashed here and there – the one she had bought in Oxford that day. My right arm was around her narrow waist and my right hand rested on her hip. She moved closer to me and I felt enormously happy.

I couldn't get over my luck. I had a date with a man who was probably married but I was so excited that I didn't even think of the consequences of such a liaison. I was much more concerned about what to wear that night. Luckily I had just bought a silky new mini-dress. As for my unfortunate prearranged date – I rather cruelly stood him up. Adrian called for me in his car and we drove up onto the Downs – he talked so much about everything, all the adventures he had had with his little grey pony and on the railway. He was obsessed by the railway – I had never come across anyone with so much passion for anything. I gathered during the course of our conversations that he was not married, which came as a relief, but apart from asking him the odd

6

question I don't think I had very much to say. After all, I could hardly admit that railways had barely entered into my consciousness and compared to his life, mine seemed mundane. But I do remember talking about a little adventure of my own when a couple of years earlier a crowd of us from school had taken part in a sponsored walk along the Ridgeway past the Lord Wantage Memorial. I thought that we had walked as far as Reading, and Adrian was gallant enough not to contradict me, because, having consulted the map in later years, that seems unlikely. I did not take too much notice of the scenery during our money-raising walk. I was too busy having a laugh with my friends, but we grew quiet as we realised that our feet were beginning to suffer from the lack of proper footwear or any sort of preparation for our ordeal, and my overriding memory of the occasion was my painful limp to the finish, then gingerly removing my plimsolls to reveal several huge blisters on my feet, some of which were already weeping.

I had come this way so as to eat at the 'Blue Boar' inn, to show Susan to Marianne. Marianne was a petite, blonde German woman. I met her in 1960. She then lived with Peter Rawsthorne, a white South African, in a solitary house a few yards along the Ridgeway above Childrey. He was a tall, slim, thirty-something man, stubbly chin, a cadaverous face, and very bright, brown eyes. He wore a circular white headgear of the sort US Navy sailors wore and had the look of being 'mad, bad and dangerous to know'. Then Peter disappeared. Upped and went, never to be heard of again. I went to see Marianne. There was a log fire. She sat in an armchair and I sat on one of its arms. She was like a statue. I put my arm around her. We sat in silence. I hadn't a notion of her situation. Eventually she broke the silence, saying quietly and sadly, 'I'm sorry Adrian, I've nothing to give – let's go down to Lambourne and have a drink.' So, now I had found this wonderful girl, I wanted to take her to meet Marianne.

The 'Blue Boar' was solitary beside the high road across the Downs. I swung the car onto the gravel space in front of the inn. The windows threw bright yellow light onto the gravel, and over to the right a big old Scots pine with strangely contorted branches made a raggedy silhouette against the starry sky. Marianne, serving behind the bar, looked up as the door opened. Then she recognised me and came hurrying round – arms outstretched. I had come here for this, her affectionate approval. If I had taken Susan to see my parents in Childrey I knew there would have been only restrained, English, *Catholic*, politeness. Susan needed a better reception into my life than that.

Adrian introduced me to this rather sophisticated German woman who kissed me on both cheeks, a completely new experience that left me feeling somewhat shy and gauche so that I could find nothing to say to her. Thankfully she was called away by one of her customers, leaving us free to find an empty table, and we made our choices from the chalked menu at the bar. Adrian bought himself a pint and a gin and tonic for me and ordered our meal. As the evening went on, he regaled me with stories of his encounters with various people including Marianne and her lover, Peter. I became intrigued and yearned to be a part of this other world full of interesting people, which seemed so far away from the world that I inhabited.

We finished our meal and, taking affectionate leave of Marianne, we went outside. It seemed natural to put our arms around one another as we walked towards the car in the silvery blue starlight. The chemistry was flowing and before we knew it we were locked in a long passionate kiss.

Chapter Two
Anglo-Irish Relations

If Susan's father, John O'Sullivan, was concerned about me, a twenty-nine-year-old man courting his seventeen-year-old daughter, he did not show it. Maybe my cheerful chatter charmed him. He loved a lively conversation. In fact, he went so far as to say to me one day, 'You're more Irish than you realise,' which, however inaccurate, I took as a compliment.

John had been born in 1926 at Cahirciveen, a small town and fishing harbour on the south shore of the Valentia River in the 'Kingdom of Kerry'. His father and mother went to America to make their fortunes, leaving John and his brother with his grandparents. They came back from the USA a few years later with their third child, a daughter, and little else.

Sometime in 1947 John decided to go to England to earn what, in Kerry, were regarded as very high wages. He travelled by train and ferry from Cahirciveen to London, arriving at Euston after a twenty-four-hour journey. He told me what I had never heard before – what it was like to be an immigrant. He was transported from a run-down little town in the back of beyond – where he'd walked barefoot, except on Sundays – to London, the hub of the Empire. He was totally confused. He found it difficult enough to get out of the station, but outside, through the big stone arch and onto the street, he had no idea which way to go. There were so many people and so much traffic. He gave me an example of how confused he felt. 'I was seeing all these red vans marked 'Royal Mail' and I was wondering at the amount of mail the King must be getting – only days later did I realise they were Post Office vans. That's how it was – I didn't know anything.'

He started as a labourer with the Watford Gas Company and spent a short while there before moving to Scammell Lorries in Watford. He said this was the happiest industrial job he ever had. He worked in a gang with five others to erect an entire tractor unit. It was not an assembly line – they drew the parts from the stores and built the whole lorry. It was in Watford that he met Pamela Ashby, who became his wife.

It is a mystery to me how my parents ever fell in love, but I suppose they must have done, because they married and it was not a case of a shotgun wedding as I didn't appear on the scene for another three years.

My mother's parents were captivated by the tall, dashing Irishman who courted their daughter. He seemed to be hardworking too, as most Irish men were, but my grandmother issued a warning, 'He's a Catholic, so I hope you know what you're letting yourself in for.'

Her words were prophetic, but my mother shrugged them off – clearly then, she must have been in love. My parents did not have a thing in common: he was an Irish Catholic, she was an English Protestant. They had what in those days was called a 'mixed marriage'. Not a good start. They had to be married in a Catholic Church and my mother had to vow to bring their children up as Catholics although she staunchly refused to convert to Catholicism herself. The first penalty she had to pay for falling in love with this Irishman was to forfeit a second marriage ceremony in her local Protestant church – my father said it wasn't allowed. She was bitterly disappointed.

My mother was brought up in a modest, mid-terraced council house in Bushey, near Watford. My grandmother worked as a cleaner and kept her own little house spotlessly clean and tidy, whipping out a special dark grey blanket to cover the table whenever they played cards in the evenings. My grandfather 'Pop' had served in the Bedfordshire & Hertfordshire Regiment during the Great War and had been gassed. It was only a slight whiff, enough to incapacitate but not kill him. He lived to smoke roll-ups for the rest of his long life. He worked as a gardener for Lord Bethel at Bushey House and during the Second World War smuggled home rare delicacies such as asparagus and nectarines for his family to enjoy. He also had a beautiful, productive garden of his own.

My mother had been an enthusiastic Girl Guide. She enjoyed the annual camp and the games. She was a good sport but she was not adventurous. For her, being grown-up meant getting married, 'settling down', having a nice home of her own, and having a family. She was very 'proper' and disliked gossip and avoided acrimony of any kind. She enjoyed shopping and she liked everything spanking new. In an ideal world she would have been an Aldous Huxley's 'Brave New World' sort of girl, but in the real world of being married to my father she had to make do and mend. Under no circumstances would she bring herself to buy second-hand, so when she could not afford new clothes for herself or her children she made them. She was an excellent needlewoman and could knit well too, but I always got the feeling that making clothes was done out of necessity rather than pleasure. She endured years of making and mending, skimping on her own wardrobe to clothe her children, and never had the money to buy the High Street clothes she desired until well into middle age when most of her family had left home.

My father was completely the opposite: he couldn't care less about shopping or clothes. He wanted adventure. He fantasised about living and working in the great outdoors, about survival in extreme conditions, living off the land, raising chickens, keeping bees. His great hero was Ernest Shackleton, who had been accompanied on his great adventure to the South Pole by the Kerry man and seaman, Tom Crean. My father's most enduring fantasy concerned the sea – he wanted to go back to Ireland to earn a living as a fisherman. He was young, energetic and enthusiastic and, unbeknown to my mother, his plan to go back home underpinned everything he did.

They married in 1950 and started their life together in a caravan. Although my mother rarely had any say in decisions that were made, she did insist that they have their own house before their first child was born. My father bought a nice little terraced house in Fern Way, Watford. I was born there in 1953, and my sister Karen came along three years later. Much to my mother's consternation my father kept chickens in the garden. She hated boiling up the potato peelings and leftovers for the chicken mash because it soiled her spotless kitchen with its mess and permeated the house with its odour, but luckily she did not have to endure cleaning out the hen house. My father did that. He worked hard, saved hard and then, without my mother's knowledge, he and one of his brothers hatched a plan to set themselves up as fishermen with a small trawler back in Caherciveen.

In 1959 the house was sold and my mother was whisked away from her family and her cosy, 'all-mod-cons' home to 'the back of beyond' on the west coast of Ireland. Now the experience of immigration was reversed and my mother found herself with two small children living with her in-laws in a remote south-west corner of Ireland. Seven people, including my teenage Uncle Tadhg, were squashed together in the pebble-dashed, Corporation-built, terraced house, which was situated in a sort of square, a quarter of a mile away from the pier where the newly acquired trawler the 'Sancta Lucia' was moored.

My mother hated everything about her new life. The inside of the house was even drabber than the outside, with badly painted, brown gloss woodwork, scraps of linoleum on the floors and a couple of uncomfortable grubby armchairs. The kitchen where she prepared our meals in between my grandmother's preparations was dirty, tiny and freezing cold in the winter. For sleeping, our family were squashed together in a small double bedroom containing a large wardrobe, a double bed and a three-quarter-sized bed with a sagging mattress, which is where my sister and I slept. It was my mother's worst nightmare in terms of living conditions – a horror she had first glimpsed when my father had introduced her to his family several years back and she had seen some bloody rags soaking in the bathroom sink. It was a real challenge to her respectable English working-class sensitivities when she realised that they were menstrual rags belonging to her mother-in-law. My mother would rather have died than to have such things on display.

Living conditions apart, there were other problems too. My paternal grandmother was warm and kindly towards us but my grandfather was cold and unwelcoming. His relationship with my father *had always been difficult and he clearly detested the fact that my father had married an Englishwoman. He was a hard, brave man who had been a member of the IRA during the Irish War of Independence and had tried to blow up the railway viaduct high up on the hillside going into Caherciveen to try and stop the Black an' Tans from reaching the town. But he was arrested and spent time in Cork Jail where he went on hunger strike for a bit. I remember him as a big, dour man who brought an atmosphere of fear into the house. At night time, if I needed to use the bathroom I would hurry past the door of my grandparents' bedroom with a feeling of horror to think that 'he' was sleeping in there, so close to us. I can remember my grandfather speaking to me only once. My grandmother, sensing that he was in a good mood, encouraged me to approach him and he suggested that I sit on his knee. I registered the hard man's black leather wristband on his outstretched arm and squirmed away in distrust and fear. My mother avoided my grandfather by spending much of her time in our bedroom looking after my little sister and furiously knitting or reading romances that I chose for her from the library.*

To avoid the atmosphere in the house, I spent my time out of doors when not at school, and have wonderful memories of being wild and free. I explored the streets of Caherciveen and the stinking alleyway where men from the pubs took a leak. My mother forbade me to enter this alleyway so it always held a fascination for me and I used to run through it holding my breath so as not to inhale the stench of stale urine, but it always seeped into my nostrils somehow. I made bonfires on the hillside one summer with a gang of unruly boys, cooking chips in lard in an old battered frying pan. They were greasy, rank-tasting and only half-cooked. We pretended they were delicious.

I liked the pier best, especially on stormy, squally days, when the gulls circled, squawking and swooping for the tiniest morsel. I remember gazing with fascination at huge ghostly white skate lurking at the bottom of the muddy sea by the quayside when the tide was low and the boats were out. I spent hours watching the fishermen at work mending their lobster pots and making nets outside the large black-tarred, pungent fish and sea-salt smelling shed, which housed huge coils of rope and other fishing paraphernalia. A small gang of us children played in the shed when the weather was wet, screaming and leaping from one great mound of nets to another, neither considering the rats that made their homes there, nor the damage we might be doing, but we were never told off.

One day, though, our exuberance got the better of us. When no one was about we decided to explore the trawlers that were moored at the quayside. We clambered down onto the first trawler and leapt from one to the other until we reached the outermost boat, which was the 'Sancta Lucia', where it felt like we had permission to muck around for a bit, then we made our way back to the pier. Just as we reached it a girl slipped into the deep, dark water between the boat and the quay.

An older boy, whose name I forget, immediately took control of the situation and instructed the rest of us to keep the boat clear of the quayside. This we did by standing on the sides of the trawler, pushing it away from the quay with our hands until we were almost horizontal, watching in horror as the girl, who couldn't swim, surfaced spluttering in the water beneath us, then sank again. The brave boy threw a rope, but it was too slippery for her to grasp and she sank for a second time. The boy had the presence of mind to tie a knot in the end of the thick, stiff rope and threw it into the water once more. This time she managed to hold onto it and we hauled her to safety.

By now we were all trembling with shock and I assumed the responsibility of taking her home to her father (I seem to remember that her mother was dead). I put my arm around her and we walked slowly, she squelching and dripping, back to her house a few doors up from my place. I knocked on the front door. It seemed an age before anyone answered, but eventually her father appeared and I explained what had happened. He was furious and said that it was all my fault. I was taken aback by his reaction. I felt he should be thanking us, especially the brave boy who had saved her life. I tried to tell him about this heroic deed but the man wouldn't listen. He angrily ushered his wet and trembling daughter inside and waved me away, muttering something about the 'bloody English'. I felt for the first time the injustice of racial prejudice. A feeling that many Irish men and women had experienced in

England. A feeling that my mother instinctively understood and that for the most part kept her isolated from the community in which she lived.

If my mother was suffering, my father was having difficulties too. The business partnership with his brother was under strain. My father and uncle were working the 'Sancta Lucia' under some arrangement with An Bord Iascaigh Mhara, the Irish Sea Fisheries Board. It seems that my uncle then became ill and could no longer work the boat. My father had to hire an extra man to help crew it. My father's accounting records from that time are on scraps of undated paper, but show that my uncle was being paid a wage, which I can imagine irked my father as my uncle was not doing any work. But presumably it was only fair if my uncle had made some financial investment in the business. However, all through the last six months of 1959 my father's bank book shows that his income matched his outgoings so all appeared well financially.

Then disaster struck. The 'Sancta Lucia' was a typical fifty-foot wooden fishing boat with a wheelhouse amidships, a sail fore and aft and a single-cylinder Gardner diesel engine. In December 1959 she was coming into Wexford with Dad at the helm. They had a huge catch of herring, and she was well down in the water when, just as darkness was falling, one of the crew managed to get a rope around the propeller and the boat went ashore on some rocks. They had hopes of being rescued at first, but a storm brewed up the next day and huge waves pushed the 'Sancta Lucia' further onto the rocks. The men stayed below trying to keep warm. That night they heard the sound of what appeared to be footsteps crunching on gravel going round and round the deck of the boat. My father and a deckhand went up with a torch to see what was making the noise, but they found nothing. Dad later attributed this experience to his grandfather keeping watch over him, as he had done when he was a boy, doing his rounds of the remote little house last thing at night.

My father and the crew were rescued from the stricken trawler, but that was the end of my father's involvement with the boat. Years later Pat O'Shea, skipper of the steel-hulled trawler 'Pato's Wish', who had worked for my father as a teenager, told me that the 'Sancta Lucia' had been salvaged and had operated out of the port of Wexford for many years afterwards. My father went on to skipper another fishing vessel, the 'Ros Brighde'.

John spoke to me of being out on the ocean on his little trawler, when the ocean swells were so high and troughs so deep that the tops of the masts of the accompanying boats absolutely disappeared from view. These swells, he said, were the Atlantic's version of ripples, the final end of some furious storm far away out there beyond the horizon. He set pots for lobster around the Skellig Rock and, as the shoals of herring swarmed northwards up the west coast of Ireland, he fished for them from Bantry to the Aran Islands.

One story he told me – which he promised faithfully, insisted, had happened to him – is very hard to believe. He was lifting his lobster pots. When he went to lift this one it was too heavy and he called for assistance from his deckhand. They heaved on the rope that was attached to the lobster pot until a large plate of steel broke the surface. It was a piece of a ship. There were rivet holes all around – *but the rope from buoy to lobster pot passed through one of the holes.* I suggested that an underwater diver had undone the rope from the buoy and threaded it through the rivet hole before re-tying the rope to the buoy. While this was rational it still was as unlikely as the idea that at once came into their minds that a mermaid or water sprite had done it. John said how disturbed, how shocked, he and his deckhand were by this event.

While my father was having his adventures at sea, my mother came out of her shell a little with the help of a lovely family called the Martins who lived a few doors away from us. Mr Martin was a photographer. His wife Moira and my mother became friends while my sister Karen and I played with their three children. We spent one Christmas day with them: it was such a relief to be out of my grandparents' house and for once I could see Mum relax and actually enjoy herself. It was only a little respite, however, as things were going from bad to worse in the paternal home. My mother was always being picked upon, until one day my grandfather pushed her out of the way in the tiny kitchen. My

16

mother, who had kept her mouth buttoned up until then, complained to my father, who confronted my grandfather on the stairs and there was a fight. Real fisticuff stuff, with the neighbours gathered around the front door and my mother cowering in her bedroom.

After that, we moved into a two-roomed flat above a betting shop in Main Street, Caherciveen. My mother, who had never stepped foot inside a betting shop, found this sordid and distasteful. Shabby looking men came and went, torn up betting slips littered the pavement. It was not very salubrious, and once a rat scuttled into the dingy hallway from the street. My mother screamed and screamed until at last a passer-by managed to tease it out of its hiding place with the help of a little white dog and the crack of his blackthorn stick. But at least she had her own space, and was free of the bad feelings in the house down below near the pier.

One of the rooms in the flat was converted into a kitchen/living room with a makeshift work surface along one wall, holding a tiny two-burner gas cooker, washing-up bowl and pots and pans. We all slept in the other room, which had two double beds, and shared a grimy, grey bathroom with the other occupants of the house. My mother would never use the bathroom at night, preferring a chamber pot in the bedroom. The young woman who lived in the rooms above didn't like to use the bathroom either, and emptied her night-time chamber pot out of the window. We often glimpsed the contents as they swooshed past our bedroom window into the courtyard below, mother tut-tutting and saying, 'Now you know why I won't let you play down there.'

I thought the woman was rather exotic because she wore the most fascinating shoes – black espadrilles with a wedge heel and black ribbons, which laced up her legs. I would lurk in the dingy corridor waiting to catch a glimpse of her strange footwear as she hurried up and down the stairs. She had two tiny children who were hardly heard, let alone seen, and there may have been a man but I cannot remember him. Her hair was black and her skin rather dark so maybe she was Spanish, but we knew nothing else about her. My mother was not the sort to invite conversations.

It was while we were living in the flat that a young, handsome, Irish

Catholic priest befriended my mother. I think he understood that she felt isolated in this remote Catholic community and he acted with kindness towards her, often calling to see her, especially as my father was away at sea for days or even weeks at a time. Once he brought me the gift of a doll. I was thrilled, but my mother was a little put out that he hadn't included my sister in his largesse. Perhaps he visited in the hope of converting her to Catholicism, but there was no chance of that. She felt bitterly let down by the Catholic Church and her sense of injustice grew after my sister Bernadette was born. My mother was recovering from the birth in St Anne's Hospital when her new-born was whisked away to be 'baptised'. My mother was distraught to think that her new little daughter was being 'christened' in her absence, but babies had to be 'baptised' immediately in Catholic Ireland because if they died without being 'baptised' they would spend eternity in 'limbo' and could not be buried in consecrated ground.

Meanwhile, my poor father (gosh, my loyalties will forever be divided) struggled to make things work financially with the 'Ros Brighde'. And with the strain of the various family feuds getting to him, he eventually capitulated and told my mother that they would have to return to England. It was the happiest day of my mother's life.

And so, in the autumn of 1962 the O'Sullivan family, now augmented with Bernadette, and hundreds of pounds poorer, returned to England for salvation. Now, from the great cliffs of Kerry and the vastness of the Atlantic Ocean, John went to work on the assembly lines of the British Motor Corporation at Cowley, Oxford. I always admired him for the way he adapted to the necessity for change from the great ocean to the conveyor belt. For Susan's mother Pam, of course, it was a huge relief to be back in England, even though they were living in a static caravan in Grove, a satellite village of the Betjeman town of Wantage. They stayed there all through the bitterly cold, freezing winter of 1962/63. At night the warm breath of the sleeping family rose to the metal ceiling, condensed, froze and created icicles. John had been prudent enough to buy a plot of land in Caherciveen, so when this was sold and the money put together with his savings from hard, monotonous work at Cowley, he was able to put down a deposit on a bright, new house in Aldworth Avenue in an estate on the eastern edge of the town of Wantage.

Chapter Three
The Red Threat

I dropped Susan off at Aldworth Avenue. We agreed to meet up again the following evening – Sunday – and after a passionate kiss we parted. I had never experienced anything like this. Susan and I were clearly no fleeting fortnight's friendship. Was this for real? Had I, without even trying, fallen in love? Surely this girl was in love with me?

On Sunday I drove over to Childrey and had some lunch with my parents. I didn't mention Susan to them. Desiring a woman for one's friend had sinful connotations, or so they had always told me. At last dusk crept over Childrey and off I went to collect this amazing girl. We went to 'The Lamb' to meet her sixth form friend Jane. Sitting there with drinks, the awful news came out that Susan and her class were off to Minehead on Monday for a Biology 'A-level' field trip – for a *week*. I was devastated. I'd only just met her. She had bewitched me – and now she was going away till next Saturday. What a gap. An abyss. I drove back to Abbey Road feeling so lonely – more than when I had, in fact, actually been lonely.

It was a blow to be going away so soon after meeting Adrian, but my disappointment was offset by my new-found status amongst the school party of girls at the Leonard Wills Field Centre in Somerset. Don't ask me what we learned during the course of the week because I can't remember a thing, but the highlight – receiving letters from two different boys (well a man and a boy) on the same day – is firmly imprinted upon my memory. Never a popular girl, I found myself suddenly to be the centre of attention. The girls crowded around me in the brown, drab dormitory, giggling and begging me to read out the contents of the letters. To my shame I did, giggling with the best of them, and shared Adrian's touching endearments expressed in a letter now lost to posterity. The other letter was from Grant, the boy I had stood up. I took the mickey out of him because he was a mod. Not at all my inclination – I was much more a hippie type! I am not sure why I went out with him in the first place except that Marilyn and I had been foot loose and fancy free at the Shepton Mallet Music Festival in June and had somehow ended up in the tent of a pair of mods.

On Monday I worked a twelve-hour day shift in Hinksey North signal box. I got back to my Abbey Road lodgings just after six to discover that over the weekend the Man of the House had done a wife swap and the two little children had a new 'mother'. The Man of the House had swapped his plain, dark-haired, capable wife for a tall, blonde, imitation of Marilyn Monroe. 'Marilyn' was clearly no cook. She had a boil-in-the-bag dinner waiting for me, and as I sat down she told me, very kindly and with evident embarrassment, that she was very sorry but she couldn't manage to look after the two children, her Man of the House and me – so I would have to go, as from the end of the week.

All that week I was on duty from six in the morning to six in the evening. It was hard to go around looking for lodgings after that, and I did not try too hard. On Saturday afternoon I packed up my belongings – mostly railway memorabilia – and took them over to my parents' house, and that night I parked the car on the grass track alongside the Osney Town allotments. I would sleep in my Wolseley until I found lodgings. I had some tinned food, milk, tea bags, a primus stove, a pair of army mess tins, a knife and fork. I undressed and got into my ex-RAF Air-Sea rescue sleeping bag, which made me look like the 'Michelin Man'. I slept well and in the morning I had a cold wash in the public lavatory by the taxi rank close by the station before going to work.

Adrian turned up at my house on Sunday afternoon and I was rather taken aback to find that he had spent the night in his car and that this was to be his home until he could find some new lodgings. He showed

21

me the 'Michelin-man' look-alike, ex-RAF sleeping bag he had slept in and the little primus stove on which he had heated Campbell's meatballs. The whole car and his clothes stank of stale cooking, which was not in the least bit romantic and decidedly off-putting. Momentarily, I wondered what I saw in him. While on the one hand I admired his unconventionality, on the other hand I regretted that he was not remotely like a hippie and he certainly wasn't in any way trendy in spite of the golden flares he had worn when I first met him. Adrian was definitely 'square', a person to be avoided and even giggled at by my circle of friends. But he charmed me once again with his interesting stories, this time about the 'wife swap' that had taken place at his lodgings – this was the stuff of 'The Sunday People' and 'The News of the World', which my father sometimes bought, but didn't like me to read. I was fascinated.

I introduced Adrian to my parents, who were watching Sunday afternoon television. He didn't stay long but I could sense that he had woven his magic spell and that my father in particular was charmed and fascinated by this new boyfriend. My mother told me in later years that although they both took to him immediately, they were alarmed by the discrepancy in our ages, especially as I was only seventeen, but they were wise enough not to say so.

I found a tiny room at the top of No 6 Polstead Road. This was a very dignified area of wide tree-lined streets and three-storey houses. No 6 had large rooms except on the third storey. In my room the ceiling, following the roof, sloped down to two feet above the floor. There was just enough vertical wall against which to push the single bed. I stood against the far wall to dress. The room had a window overlooking the road. There was a cupboard-sized space 'off' with a 'Baby Belling' electric cooker and above that a skylight in the sloping roof. I shared a bathroom with the two other occupants of that floor.

Of those two I only ever saw 'Cissel', a Bristolian who worked as a refuse collector in Oxford. He spoke Bristolian out of the corner of his mouth, hardly opening his lips. He was very familiar with classical music and was a member of a BBC Third Programme 'Panel of Listeners'. He had been a keen cyclist all his life and cycled back to Bristol for weekends.

'Thur's a foine concert in th' Col'son all this weekend, Adren', he would tell me through his barely opening lips.

In the 1930s he and a friend had made annual cycling holidays in Baden-Württemberg, in the Black Forest. The last one was in 1938. 'We wuz at this little beer garden 'avin' a meal on the tables outside and these 'itler Youth turned up. Arrogant they were, Adren – very unpleasant. We 'et up quick an' left. Never went back.'

I have gained much history from eye witnesses, over the years.

The owner of No 6 was a sweet old Jewess, a widow – Mrs Morgenstern – *Morning Star*. Her stature and dress always put me in mind of a woolly tea-cosy. She told me that she had been brought to Oxford, from Vienna, by her father and mother in 1938, when Hitler took over Austria, and thus they saved themselves from the gas chambers. She had the front room of the house for her sitting room, the door of which opened onto the hallway and the stairs bottom. If she heard me coming downstairs she would come out to open the front door for me. I remember one day when she opened the door, as I passed through she said brightly in her Austrian accent, 'Goodbye – a Free Man in a Free Country.'

The Polstead Road house was an easy fifteen-minute cycle ride from Hinksey North signal box. I could cycle to work down the Woodstock Road, through St Giles, swinging right at the Martyr's Memorial, into Beaumont Street, between the expensive Randolph Hotel and the Ashmolean, where King Alfred's Jewel lay, down to Worcester College, swinging left past Gloucester Green where there was a 'British Restaurant' at the scruffy bus station. Going through St Giles for the two o'clock shift, I sometimes cycled past a flock of bicycling undergraduates, wicker baskets full of books, gowns flying out behind. How I envied them their education.

When going to work for six in the morning, and most probably for a twelve-hour shift, I went along Walton Street, because of the need to buy a pint of milk from Mr Wiggins the milkman of the

Walton Street/Jericho area. Henry Wiggins drove a three-wheeled milk float, which he had built before the Second World War. If I did not accost him on Walton Street or down one of the side streets, I'd have to take a pint of milk from some doorstep further along the journey – and leave a two-bob piece behind. It was unthinkable to incarcerate oneself in a very busy signal box for eight or twelve hours without the 'makings' of constant cups of tea.

I wanted to show Susan Hinksey North signal box and took her there one Sunday when the line was much quieter and the box was 'switched out'.

Adrian looked left and right and, seeing that it was safe, ushered me across the line. In my mind's eye I can see us negotiating vast swathes of railway track, dodging around stationary goods wagons and stepping over points until we reached the safety of the signal box on the other side. He opened the door and we climbed a long staircase to reach the operating room. The signal lever frame stretched along the length of the signal box, with sixty-nine red, black and blue levers gleaming in full glory, some of them pulled over to set the signals so that the trains could pass while the signal box was 'switched out'. A number of antiquated-looking instruments occupied the shelf above the frame and there were bells and buzzers and telephones as well as an intricate diagram of the tracks controlled by the box. I was over-awed and Adrian, full of enthusiasm, began to explain how it all worked. He pointed to the home signals and the distant signals, this set of points and that set of points, and explained which levers worked which bit and in which sequence, but it all went over the top of my head. It was far too complicated for me – and it seemed so full of danger. A grown-up working person's world – and yet it was romantic, too – ensuring the safety of the trains and the passengers as they journeyed towards their various destinations. What a wonderful job to be a signalman. My admiration was complete.

After the tour of the signal box, Adrian took me to meet his parents who lived in the village of Childrey, which nestled on the edge of the downland not far from Wantage. I was apprehensive about meeting them because Adrian had spoken of them in less than complimentary terms, and they seemed always to be having arguments. They were Catholic converts who had remained loyal to traditional Catholicism after the Latin Mass had been abolished in the early sixties. A far cry from the situation in my home, because by 1970 my father and the vast majority of Irish Catholics had embraced the ecumenical changes wholeheartedly – much better to listen to the Mass in a language they could understand rather than in incomprehensible Latin. Adrian tried to reassure me by telling me that his parents were all right if you kept away from certain subjects such as religion or politics and various other things that might trigger an unhappy response. Very reassuring! We drove into the village and parked just off the roadway by a converted pub. We got out of the car and I followed Adrian up onto the pavement, which led past a low-slung, pretty black and white cottage on the left, its cedar shingle roof swept like eyebrows over the top of the two upstairs windows, with chocolate box charm. He turned in at the second gateway and I was astounded. Was this it? My trepidation increased. In my experience, which admittedly was very limited, posh people lived in places like this. Oh dear, what was I letting myself in for?

The front door was opened by a portly, elderly lady, slightly shabbily dressed but with a sweet face crowned by a precarious-looking silvery-grey bun. Adrian introduced us and his mother, Edith, smiled and said that she was pleased to meet me. We squeezed into a tiny sitting room, heavily beamed and full of antique-looking furniture, blue and white china and polished brass. There was a miniature, bottle green and brass steam engine occupying a shelf alongside the fireplace. On the chimney breast there was a picture of the Sacred Heart – something I was used to seeing in the homes of people in Ireland, but not in this country, and we didn't display religious pictures at home because my mother was a Protestant. There was also an ornate brass and wooden Jesus on the Cross in all his crucified glory and a painted statue of a saint unknown to me. Adrian told me later that this was Blessed Edmund Campion – one of the most famous of the English martyrs in Elizabethan times.

Edith pulled up a wheelback chair (the same one that now occupies a place at my kitchen table) and positioned it in front of the fire for me to *sit down, and as I did so Adrian's father, Owen, came into the room. He was a gaunt-looking man, slightly stooped and dressed in trousers that were far too short for him. He shook my hand in welcome and we all sat down. Edith made us tea and brought the tea things into the sitting room on a tray lined with a starched white tray cloth. The tea was poured from a pretty teapot into delicate porcelain cups and we were each handed a teacup and saucer and a piece of fruit cake on a matching plate. Then, once we were settled down, sipping our tea and eating cake, the Vaughans started to hold forth. I can't remember what they talked about, but I do know that I could barely get a word in edgeways and I was petrified lest they stray onto contentious subjects. Apparently they did not – well, at any rate they avoided an argument, and the tea party was broken up when I finally plucked up the courage to intervene and asked to be shown around the garden.*

Adrian's parents took great pleasure in directing me around their lovely garden, which surrounded the long cottage – their cottage at one end, the other half let to tenants. The lawns were a uniform green and closely cut with neatly kept edges along the beds and borders. Most of the flowers were over apart from a few lingering roses, clumps of blue and mauve asters and two rows of staked and regimented chrysanthemums. There were several huge, gnarled old apple trees and dozens of windfall apples scattered and squashed beneath them. There was a lingering scent of apple in the autumnal air, and for ever more I would associate fallen apples with Edith and Owen's garden in Childrey. I had always been interested in gardening and as a child had loved my Granddad's garden with its colourful dahlias and whitewashed containers of cascading fuchsia. I had even helped my father on his allotment until more important teenage interests had got in the way, but seeing this traditional cottage garden really inspired me and I knew that I wanted a garden of my own.

We took our leave shortly after. The visit had not been half as bad as I had imagined. Adrian's parents were certainly eccentric and I still felt a little fearful of them and all those possibilities for arguments, but his mother in particular had been very sweet to me. She had come across as a little pretentious but not that posh, and that in itself was a great relief.

Ever since I'd passed my driving test in March 1959 I'd explored the countryside, starting with a succession of three 1935 Morris Eights. Now I had found a beautiful friend, I wanted to share all my discoveries with her. At weekends we drove over the Downs, along green tracks that led past Iron Age burial mounds and out again onto tarmac roads. We admired the ruins at Minster Lovell, the twin villages of Eastleach Martin and Turville, one on each side of the River Leach. Bibury, Hatherop, Quenington and Coln St Aldwyn, beautiful villages with poetical names. We talked non-stop, or maybe I talked and she listened. It was not very long before a monster of contention arose.

When I took Susan to see my parents I was — except for their anti-semitism — still in the frame of mind inculcated by them. They were devout Catholic converts. My father was a great enthusiast for the villages of West Berkshire, the Downs and the Vale of the White Horse. The village of East Hendred, barely altered since mediaeval times, was a favourite place. The village had been owned by the Eyston family since 1100, and at Hendred House there was St Amand's, the private chapel of the family who had clung to Catholicism right through the Reformation and later centuries of persecution. While still 'C of E', my mother and my father (a Baptist!) had, one afternoon in 1936, attended a service of 'Benediction' in St Amand's. My mother told me how, as the gilded monstrance — container for the white wafer that was the 'Blessed Host' — was raised above the congregation, she did not bow her head. The Monstrance flashed as it was caught by sunlight through a lancet window and she said she was *pierced* through her heart by this sudden brilliance. With that she knew that God wanted her for a Catholic.

This was unfortunate enough, but to make matters worse she had, years earlier, developed a passionate hatred of '*Jewish* Communism'. She had read just one book on the subject of Communism, *The Red Terror in Russia*. It was an illustrated book of

27

Communist atrocities against the religious in Russia, with illustrations. As a great reader from an early age, I had read it too. The horrors depicted had the same effect on me as on my mother. The book did not say anything about *why* the religious were attacked or anything about *why* the people of Russia rose up against their Establishment. She made up her mind about vast subjects such as the evils of the Russian Revolution and the rightness of Catholicism on the strength of one book and a trick of the light. This fear and hatred of Communism led her to admire Hitler because, she told me, 'If he's against the Communists he must be a good man.'

She passed all her fears and prejudices on to me. By the time I was ten years old I would go – literally – *hot* under my collar at the sight of the Anglican clergyman of Earley St Peter's walking down our street – St Peter's Road in Reading. 'They killed our martyrs.' 'The Jews killed Christ.' I had it all.

In 1945 my older sister and I had sat in our front bedroom window and had looked down longingly on the VE Day street party. We were forbidden to take part. My parents solemnly informed me, aged four, 'Now that Hitler is dead the Reds will come and cut our throats.'

When I met Susan I was in the process of learning proper history. I learned the truth about the Nazi Holocaust of the Jews from eye witnesses in the Army and elsewhere. Many were the furious rows I had with my parents because they refused to believe eye-witness accounts of the extermination camps. 'The people telling you these things are Communists,' they would say. I knew they were not. However, Communism itself was still a phobia with me.

So there we were, Susan and me, happy as could be, driving along a country lane when the subject of the Vietnam War came up. Almost certainly it was me who brought it up. The noble Americans, bravely fighting the hydra-headed evil of Communism. I had absolutely no idea of the history of Vietnam. These were strange people who objected to being governed by the civilised French. In 1954 the Vietnamese had ejected the French after the

28

siege of Dien Bien Phu. Now the gallant Americans were obliged to fight the Vietnamese because they had chosen to be Communists. Clearly the Vietnamese were a bad lot. Susan objected to my view of the Vietnamese situation – and I was astounded. My old, Catholic-fascist hackles rose. Susan was a Communist sympathiser! 'Well, if that's the way you think, there's no point in continuing this,' I said bitterly. 'I'd better take you home.' And that's what I did.

I felt totally dejected as I stepped out of the car back at Aldworth Avenue. We could barely say goodbye to one another, such was the ferocity of our disagreement. I went indoors, rushed upstairs and flung myself onto the bed like any truculent, disappointed teenager. I couldn't understand how he could think like a fascist and speak to me with such venom in his voice. I could not cast aside the socialist principles I had been brought up with and the idea of 'freedom for small nations' that my father preached, especially, of course, in relation to Ireland. I could not turn my back on the anti-Vietnamese war movement and the hippie slogan: Make Love not War. I cried myself to sleep.

The next morning I went into school and talked with Marilyn about this dreadful falling-out. When I got home a letter was waiting for me – it was from Adrian. I opened it with trepidation, but also with some hope – perhaps this was an apology? No such luck – the spleen, the anger spilled off the pages and Adrian wanted to bring an end to our relationship. He didn't think there was much point in our continuing as we had such opposing political views. I was devastated and realised that, no matter what, I wanted to be with this man. I loved him. Simple as that. I decided that I would skip school the next day and visit Adrian in the signal box to try to retrieve our love, which had fallen into this great black hole of hatred.

I had savaged Susan in a letter and posted it. I had unloaded my anger and calmed down. Then the regrets rose. What had I done? I'd rejected the best thing that had ever happened to me! She loved me. I'd never been aware of *anyone* loving me before – to be loved had been my one great desire, always, and I loved her in return. The

'Red Threat' belonged to my past life, to my parents and all the misery that their religious fanaticism had caused in our family. I had discovered that their religion and their politics were rubbish and a cause of ignorant hatred. I had been learning not to hate. The tolerant kindness and explanations I had experienced in the Army from my Second World War veteran instructors and from my railway friends had helped. But now the old poison had done its work. I had destroyed the long-awaited, first and probably only chance I was going to have of a properly civilised life. My shame, the horror of how my letter would make her feel, prevented me from composing a letter of apology because nothing I could say would bring her back.

A couple of days after the posting I was working in Hinksey North. Walking to the Oxford end of the lever frame to 'pull off', I saw Susan walking up the narrow path from the riverbank to the signal box! I heard her knocking on the signal box door as I clanked the levers over, and I clattered hurriedly down the stairs and opened the door. The door to a second chance.

Chapter Four
Married!

A couple of days after Susan had come to the signal box, forgiving me after all my rudeness, I came back to my lodgings to find a letter from her on the hall table. I read it with increasing amazement. She never actually used the word – but what she was proposing – was marriage! This was a dream come true. I knew she was changing my life. But I was thirty years and nine months old without any education worth mentioning, wedded to a lifetime on the railway. She was not yet eighteen, but not far off. Was the age gap too wide? Would marrying me drag her down? She had a great education ahead of her, maybe even a university degree and a professional career. She swept all that aside. So I took her advice. We became engaged on her 18th birthday.

After the exams – the Summer Holidays! I took two weeks annual leave from the railway for a camping holiday in France. On Saturday 24th July I was away to Wantage at one o'clock with a full tank of petrol, the tent, my air-sea-rescue sleeping bag, a gas stove in the boot and 970 francs in my wallet. They cost £50. In 1971 £50 was the most cash that one could legally take out of the country. Susan was ready at Aldworth Avenue with food and cooking utensils. We set off for Dover in the Wolseley 1500 brimming with a pleasant excitement and good cheer.

The ferry arrived at Boulogne at twelve thirty the following morning. The rain was coming down so hard it overpowered the windscreen wipers. That was made worse by the spray from the tyres of hundreds of French cars whizzing past, the drivers knowing exactly how to get to where they were going. Vast roads sign were hardly legible. By sheer luck we caught a sign directing to the Bois de Boulogne camp site. The site was a Flanders of mud beneath the

31

dripping trees. Tents were pitched everywhere, in no order. We sloshed about the camp site and marvelled at the variety of people parked around in all manner of conveyances, motorised and not, from all nations of Western Europe. There was a very happy teenager who had cycled from Amsterdam on an ice cream seller's tricycle. He intended to cycle all over France before going home.

Next day the weather was pleasantly warm and sunny. Knowing nothing we set out to see Paris. We went down side streets, saw shop windows laid out in an astonishingly artistic, beautiful way. Elegance was natural. England suddenly seemed rough-hewn and crude. We bought pistachio nuts from market stalls, and nougat from sweet shops of stupendous temptation. We wandered lost, unable to ask directions but eventually found the Boulevard Haussmann, followed that to the Arc de Triomphe, then retraced our way to our tent in the swampy *Bois*.

The camp site was hopeless. So we drove away, heading for Bordeaux. Bordeaux outskirts suggested a vast city so we drove on and miles further down the 'N10' road we saw a seaward turn and took it. We came to La Teich. It was after ten o'clock. We followed the signs to 'Camping' and drove into an orchard – lit only by our headlamps. The following morning the owner knocked on the tent and charged us Fr3.60 per day for as long as we stopped. After him came a man in a small van with fresh produce, seafood and wine. We bought fresh sole, tomatoes, peas, grapefruit and peaches. The good man came each morning.

A short walk took us through tall pines to a wide lagoon of warm water stretching away north into the distance. Beyond the enclosing dunes was the Atlantic Ocean. The weather was unvaryingly a blue sky and blazing sun. We swam in the warm lagoon. We had the orchard almost to ourselves. We sat around eating fruit and gorgeous bread and cheese that the van man brought. Nearly every evening we went to the village and ate a five-course meal for Fr16 each. The experience changed the way Susan and I thought about eating and cooking. English cooking that we were used to, seemed unimaginative. Roast beef and Yorkshire pudding heavy. The

French made delicious food with less, so it seemed. The wine was better too. Travel broadens the mind. On Thursday 5th August we reluctantly struck camp and set off on the long drive for Boulogne and home.

In August, exam results were announced. Susan had gained both A-levels with enough marks to qualify her for a place at a teacher training college – Canley near Coventry. She was to move there in September. I drove the road from Oxford to Canley in daylight and in darkness according to my shifts. Her time was taken up with lectures during the weekdays but her nights and weekends were always free. When I was working early turn at Hinksey North I had to be away very early in the morning. I was not the only one. The memory of the sounds of furtive footsteps along the corridors of the hostel and the rustle of the clothes of departing boyfriends at the crack of dawn still raises a smile. Once we went to a party outside the college. Several couples ended up sleeping together on the floor and I remember an astonished female voice from across the room saying, 'Oh! It's gone all limp!'

At weekends we explored the Warwickshire countryside. The Hatton flight of locks on the Grand Union Canal was a favourite place. One weekend I arrived at Canley when there was a funfair in Warwick. Susan wanted to go and when we got there she insisted we boarded some whirling contraption while the chair we paid good money to sit in spun round on its own axis. A sadistic member of the crew of the fair came and spun our chair all the more. It was unbelievably dreadful. When the horror finally became stationary I was reeling and staggering like a legless drunk and Susan had to help me off. I was so dizzy I reeled around the pavement until I could grab hold of some railings. It took several hours to cast off the terrible nausea. Susan enjoyed the 'ride' and even more my highly demonstrable weakness. Very cruel.

I have to confess to laughing at Adrian's terrible discomfort, and looking back it seems such a horrible thing to do. I have no excuse but callow youth. In the meantime I had my own nausea to contend with at Canley

College itself. I had never been that keen on teaching but had been pushed into it by my Headmistress. She said that I was not university material and that the best career for me was teaching. I presume she said this because I had failed my 11 plus and gone to the local Secondary Modern School. I gained enough O-levels to get into the sixth form at Faringdon Girls Grammar School but I was only 'allowed' to take two A-levels – university entrance demanded three.

The Biology A-level course was very interesting, delivered by an enthusiastic and inspiring teacher. I was fascinated by dissection and during my two years in the sixth form had dissected frogs, rats, dogfish and earthworms to display the nervous or circulatory system, or some other internal structure. I liked the intricacies of dissection, reproducing every detail in a carefully executed pencil drawing and labelling the anatomical parts that had been so meticulously displayed and pinned out. I chose Biology for my main subject at Canley College only to find that there was no laboratory work just indescribably boring lectures on the chicken and the egg. In drama, the lecturer had all of us crawling about in the dark on the gymnasium floor groping at each other. This seemed so very weird, infantile and irrelevant that I began to seriously question whether Canley College was the place for me.

Then there was my first teaching practice in a school in a disadvantaged area of Coventry. I enjoyed working one-to-one with the children, but a whole classroom of them utterly defeated and exhausted me. I did not feel comfortable in my role and quickly became disillusioned with the whole idea of teaching.

The only bright times at college were hanging about in the evenings with a bunch of students, drinking and listening to rock music in someone's bedroom. We played Neil Young's album 'After the Gold Rush' over and over until it became forever associated in my mind with Canley College. Those evenings apart, I was only happy when Adrian visited. One day I told him about my disappointment with the course and my lack of vocation. He advised me to cut my losses and get out. My parents were disappointed when I told them I wanted to leave college and my father's first thought was that I might be pregnant but I quickly disabused him of that idea! I left the college at the end of term

34

and moved back home.

In January I went to work for Pergamon Press in Headington, Oxford, as a sub-editor. After some training I was put into a smoky, open-plan office and given the task of sub-editing three scientific journals, one of which was written in Cyrillic script! Our next-door neighbour at home took me into work every day, and when he was on the right shift Adrian would be waiting at a convenient location so I could change cars and he would take me on into work. We often met up at lunchtime too. We found it very hard to be apart.

It wasn't long before we started looking for a house to buy. We looked at several houses in the Oxford area but they were way out of our reach financially. Eventually we found an attractive Victorian terraced house in Wantage that we thought we could afford. The location wasn't ideal. It was on a busy road and just three doors up from 'The Royal Oak' where I used to drink vodka and orange illicitly with the boys from King Alf's. But we liked the house well enough to put in an offer and agreed to buy it at the asking price of £4,750.

Adrian approached the building society for a mortgage but he was turned down. The vendor's agents advised that we might be able to get a mortgage from the local Council so we put in an application, but they were so slow in processing it that we were 'gazumped' in the meantime. We were very disappointed but in fact the 'gazumping' was to change the course of our story infinitely for the better.

We reported our disappointment to my parents. My father, who was himself contemplating moving back to Ireland, said, 'Well, why don't you go to Ireland? You could get a place over in Kerry for what you've got in your pocket. It might not be much of a place — but at least it would be yours.' The idea lodged in our minds as a real possibility for the future.

A few weeks after I had been so incredibly lucky to meet Susan, I had a stroke of luck in meeting another person who brought about a significant change to my life. Finishing at two o'clock at Hinksey North, and having nothing to go 'home' to, I went to see Sid Mumford in Oxford Station North Box. I'd been up there an hour when Sid noticed a civilian 'poking around' in the ruins of the old LNWR engine shed of Rewley Road station. He pointed this chap out to me and suggested I go and see what he was doing.

I went down and asked the man why he was looking around in the ruins. He said he was interested in railway history and we walked off together along the canal towpath. His name was Colin Judge. He was working for the BMC at Cowley, in the advertising department, and wanted to become a publisher of railway history books. I said I had a collection of glass negatives showing the Great Western Railway between Paddington and Oxford taken by my friend W. L. Kenning between 1913 and 1921. He jumped at the idea and so it was that I got my first book contract, *Great Western Portrait*. I printed the negatives and wrote some very weak captions and the book was published in November 1971. It was the second book published by Colin's 'Oxford Publishing Company'. The first was *Great Western Era* by my father's old friend, M. W. Earley.

It was Colin Judge who suggested that I could get a job working for 'Parchment the Printer'. I had become exhausted by weeks of alternating twelve-hour day and night shifts in the signal box. Rashly I handed in my notice and worked my last shift – nights – finishing at six in the morning on 22nd January 1972.

'Parchment the Printer' was a family concern run by Don Parchment. He was a born Cockney, an ex-paratrooper Company Sergeant-Major. Short, stocky and grizzled. He employed four or five people and printed pamphlets and single sheets as posters for events or advertising in what had been a house in that network of streets between the Iffley and Cowley roads. The printing machines were in a cramped, gloomy, ink-fumed basement. Next to the 'machine room' was the cramped space of the hydraulic guillotine room. I was put to work on that, cutting great wads of bedsheet-sized paper down to the standard sizes the print machines needed. I never did get the hang of it and destroyed a lot of paper by cutting it the wrong way.

Don tried me serving customers. This was a bit better for me – in so far as I was in clean air and daylight. Unfortunately I spent too much time talking to the customers, too much time turning round in circles looking for a customer's order, not correctly filling the customer's requirement form and giving the wrong change. The only thing I could do properly for Don was to drive him to places he had to visit.

Susan and I were to be married on 3 June 1972, just short of her nineteenth birthday. The ceremony was to be conducted by Fr James Wicksted in St John Vianney's Catholic Church in Wantage. A church wedding was arranged out of consideration for Susan's father's feelings. Left to ourselves we would have opted for a civil marriage. Neither of us liked the priest. In spite of his English-sounding name he was a Limerick man and not quite sane. John, a staunch Catholic, would have been very upset if we had not been married in a Catholic church.

Susan had been brought there to Mass each Sunday by her father. When I was introduced to him in 1970, I remembered his face as the man who handed round the collection plate. She and I shared vivid memories of the priest's red-faced rants, which he delivered while striding to and fro along the communion rail thumping it with his fist to emphasis his words. My parents stopped attending at St John Vianney's in 1965 when the Latin Mass was replaced by a liturgy in English. My parents, the devoutest of Catholic converts, despised Wicksted for obeying the Pope and using the new liturgy. Getting married at St John Vianney was an uncomfortable thing for Susan and me.

I had spent the night before the wedding at Ken Fuller's place, the one-time Station Master's house at the one-time Wantage Road station. Ken was a friend, a signalman and now my best man. On the wedding morning his wife, Pat, made us a grand breakfast and we played with an air gun in the garden until it was time to get changed.

At midday Ken and I walked to the front pew of the church. My mother and father were in the row behind. They had faces on them that would have curdled milk. They looked as if they were awaiting their own execution – possibly by a thunderbolt from God Himself.

My mother prayed a lot at home and was absolutely certain she had a hotline to the Creator of the Universe. What a wait that was for Susan to arrive. I sat rigid, hardly hearing anything around me. Then John Burgess struck up 'Here comes the Bride' on the harmonium. My heart leapt – throwing me into the standing position. Everyone stood. Then my gorgeous girl came up alongside me – softly, gently, silently. We looked at each other. She was quite breathtakingly beautiful even through the netting veil over her face. Everyone was stunned. Everyone was in love with her. I was without a doubt the luckiest, happiest man in the world.

The reception was held at 'The Bear' in the Market Place. We were horrified to see that John had invited Wicksted, an Irish courtesy. I made some sort of speech – neither Susan nor I can recall a word of it – then Ken Fuller made a brave attempt to crack the conventional best man jokes, and finally Susan's father took the floor. He was too overwhelmed with emotion. He said a few words ending in something like 'I love you both', then, close to tears, he turned to his parish priest and invited *him* to 'say a few words'. Susan and I were totally horrified. We would never have done such a crazy thing.

The silence that descended as Wicksted came to the front was not necessarily that of politeness. There was my Uncle Harold and his wife Grace – they were Baptists. Then there was my Uncle Peter and his wife – she was a Jehovah's Witness. My sister Lalo detested Catholicism. Susan's Uncle Stan was an ex-paratrooper from the Second World War who would have put himself down on his army form as 'C of E'. Wicksted launched into a totally inappropriate, utterly unwelcome, full-blown sermon on the Blessed Virgin Mary. My heart was pounding from the start and it only grew worse as the priest got into full flow and seemed to be enjoying himself. Even the Irish family members were uncomfortable. Restless coughing and shuffling began. People were staring down at the tablecloths, fiddling with teaspoons. No one wanted to be rude but it had to be stopped. After about five horrible minutes I broke in, started clapping and said loudly, 'Thank you very much, Father, that was lovely.'

He did not stop! He bored on ignorantly – arrogantly. I gave him another couple of minutes and tried again. This time everyone took the cue. They drowned him out with a huge round of sarcastic applause. Defeated, he glared around angrily, then, red-faced, reluctantly sat down.

My memories of my wedding day are hazy – it all passed in a glorious light-headed whirl. My mother said afterwards that I was all 'sweetness and light'. Apparently she had thought that I was going to behave like a spoiled brat and be horrible to my sisters who, along with Marilyn, were my bridesmaids. Wherever did she get that idea from? But no, I behaved serenely and sweetly as befitting a young bride. The wedding was not a sophisticated affair. My mother and I made the bridesmaids' dresses for my younger sisters Bernadette and Siobhán – who had been born in 1966. They were made from lilac seersucker and adorned with a deep purple velvet ribbon that tied in a bow just beneath the chest. They looked quite sweet on the two little girls, but the contrast with the flowery blue and mauve maxi dresses worn by the older girls was startlingly horrible. I wore an empire line wedding dress with a high neckline and leg-of-mutton sleeves, stylish for its day but now seeming terribly dated. I chose a traditional veil with a long train and went to the altar on my father's arm with the blusher veil covering my face, to stand by the side of my beloved husband-to-be.

The reception was marked by Father Wicksted's outlandish behaviour but not marred by it. I remember moving gaily from one group of guests to another, chatting and laughing and having my photograph taken – I had a wonderful time being the centre of so much attention. I have no memory of the food but, judging from the photographs, it was quite clearly an abysmal, unimaginative 'finger buffet' – bridge rolls, vol-au-vents, sausage rolls and scotch eggs – food that you would not find at an event in a village hall now, but in those days it was standard English fare for a budget wedding.

After the reception we went back to my parents' house as we were not planning to go on our honeymoon for a few days. We were eager to continue with the convivial celebrations rather than escape back to Adrian's little garret for some private wedded bliss. My father's family dominated the little house and it reverberated with loud, inebriated conversations.

I felt more relaxed than normal whilst talking to my uncles. I reasoned rightly that on my wedding day they would not embarrass me yet again by asking me to declare my loyalty to one county or another. I had never given them the satisfaction of the answer they were looking for and remained stubbornly loyal to both my parents by saying that I liked them both equally. It was such a daft question to ask a child, but it was connected to the deep feelings of injustice and resentment they felt as a result of the horror stories handed down through centuries of English rule and the Troubles that the Irish had endured in getting rid of the English, now renewed in the North in the aftermath of Bloody Sunday.

Perhaps they thought I had declared my loyalty by marrying an Englishman. They must have been perplexed then, when finally taking our leave of the wedding party, with all the relations and neighbours gathered around, Adrian suddenly burst into a loud and tuneful rendition of 'The Garden Where the Praties Grow', a cheerful tribute to the Irish contingent. The first verse went:

Have you ever been in love me boys
Or have you felt the pain
I'd rather be in jail myself than be in love again
For the girl I loved was beautiful, I'll have you all to know
And I met her in the garden where the praties grow

They were all startled, but quickly understood, joining in to a roaring conclusion and sending us off to Oxford with their resounding cheers ringing in our ears and the car smothered in shaving cream and loo paper.

Chapter Five
Honeymoon and house-hunting

The next day we were both floating half in, half out of our bodies. We drifted outside to clean the wedding mess off the car and I remember trimming Mrs Morgenstern's hedge! That evening Susan cooked an inspired dinner, with me falling easily into the role of vegetable preparer and washer-up. We had rolled bacon, roast chicken, broad beans, green peppers, new potatoes. A bottle of red wine followed by cake and oranges. We drifted all the next day. My best man Ken brought us his tent – reminding us that it was considered normal to have a honeymoon. We were perfectly happy where we were, but our friends seemed to expect it. So the following morning, Tuesday 6th June, we packed the tent, a primus stove and various helpful bits of kit in the boot of the car and set off for what the GWR Publicity Department had called 'The Shire of the Sea Kings'.

We broke our journey at the home of my elder brother, Keith. He was a nurse serving in the Royal Army Medical Corps with the rank of Warrant Officer Class 1 – a Regimental Sergeant-Major in infantry terms. He was living in a new army married quarters house with his Spanish wife, Aracelli, at Perham Down, near Ludgershall. After dinner he got out his albums of photographs. He had kept away from the military strictness and boredom of Aldershot by volunteering to perform a nursing role in remote places around the world. He had been posted to Borneo for three years, living with the Dyak Indians in jungle villages and in the Malayan jungles. His photos were good and the stories he told of the excellence of the people he was caring for were very interesting, but as the hands of the clock crept around towards the midnight hour and Keith's enthusiasm continued unabated, Susan and I felt we were entitled to call 'time' and head for bed.

After a couple of hours sleep, I was woken by an awful feeling of *fear*. I lay motionless. I thought someone, or something, was just outside the door, standing there, waiting. Then I thought that the curtains were moving as if the window was open. I forced myself out of bed. The curtains were moving but the window was shut. I had a feeling of terror. Something was in the room. I actually looked in the wardrobe and even under the bed. Nothing. Of course not. I went to the bathroom and slipped back into bed without waking Susan. I lay there motionless and eventually the feeling eased and I fell asleep.

I didn't say anything to Susan first thing but I could see that she was as keen as I was to get out of the house and away. Immediately in the car I launched into a description of the previous night's weird event. I was astonished, because I thought that Susan had been asleep all the time, when she replied, 'I know – it was the scariest thing ever. I was too frightened to move and I just lay there holding the covers tightly over my face, even when you got out of bed and started looking around.' Houses that produce those kind of effects on people are conventionally old, with a history. That one was brand new.

After Perham Down our next port of call was to be Plumer Barracks, in Crownhill, on the Tavistock Road, a few miles north of Plymouth. I had lived there from 6th March 1956 to 8th August 1958. It had been the home of the Infantry Boys' Battalion, renamed 'Infantry Junior Leaders Regiment' in 1957. It was a Regular Army training regiment for the 'NCOs and Warrant Officers of the Future'. I followed the road signs for Crownhill and became lost. I couldn't recognise the area. Where once there had been ordinary late-Victorian streets lined with little shops there was a bewildering network of ugly dual carriageways, concrete fly-overs and curving complicated intersections with ordinary roads. Towering blocks of offices completed the horrible scene. I should have realised that nothing we were going to see was as it had been in 1957.

I wanted very much to take Susan to Tintagel. The regiment had a cycling and youth hostelling club. One summer Saturday morning in 1957 half a dozen of us had set off for Tintagel, forty miles away through Callington, around the north of Bodmin Moor to Altarnun, where we turned north into remote, narrow lanes, where streams were running along the wall tops and where I was seized with painful cramps in the back of my thighs. We came at last to what seemed to be the end of the world in the magically named Tintagel. A remote and ancient village, with grey stone-walled cottages under crooked roofs and medieval architecture in every building. The youth hostel at Tintagel was then the single-storey, once upon a time office of a slate quarrying company. It was built on an excavated flat area, at the end of a path down the face of the cliffs. The day following our arrival in 1957 we had gone walking along the cliff tops. The coast was dramatically ravaged by millennia of wind and waves. Deep ravines with the waves roaring far below, a huge ball-shaped headland jutting out like a buttress to fend off the ocean, the ruins of a very ancient fort atop. Eventually we had come to a slag heap of slate coming down the hillside from our right, to the very edge of the dizzying drop. We had been chatting, in line abreast, admiring the astonishing coastline, not taking notice of what was underfoot. After a few paces we were startled awake, as plates of slate shifted downhill under foot. If we had been carried closer to the cliff edge we would have gone over. We stopped stock still and looked at each other. The cliff edge was now maybe twelve feet to our left and the safe grass was thirty feet behind us. There was certain death in panic. Ever so carefully we had turned and inched our way back to safety. So Tintagel was very special to me!

Susan and I drove into the village in June 1972 to find a cottage tourist industry in place: a pixie well with attendant gnomes in every garden and an ice cream stall at every corner. Cars everywhere. It was a real let-down, but people have to earn a living. We left heading south. Somewhere in the lane beyond Lostwithiel we found a meadow of field flowers surrounded by a nice stone wall on three sides and bordered on the fourth by a fast-flowing brook lined with

43

a fringe of trees. There was a five-bar gate through which we drove in. We set up the simple tent, got the primus stove going and Susan cooked supper.

Waking at six next day Susan and I crawled out. There was a summertime mist floating above the grasses and a clear blue sky above. Susan went off to pee in a corner of the field. Kneeling, I started the primus, boiling water, sorting out breakfast. I glanced across at her as she walked across the field. Walking slowly in her long, white Victorian nightdress, she seemed to be gliding through the misty grasses. With clear sun on her lovely auburn hair, which was in some disarray falling over her shoulders, she looked like a Millais painting. As I watched, a man came walking around the corner of the lane, and his line of sight would have been across the field. He stopped dead. Stiff and upright. He took half a pace backwards, relaxed and walked on. He thought he'd seen a ghost.

Homeward-bound we stopped at Newton Abbot. I needed to take some photographs of signals and signal boxes for the book I was writing for OPC, *A Pictorial Record of Great Western Signalling*. The station had two large signal boxes and some fine, historic signal gantries. I parked, left Susan in the car reading a book, and jumped down onto the track to start my photography. I forgot Susan as soon as I got down onto the track and started to photograph everything signalling. I had no idea of the passage of time. I eventually arrived at Newton Abbot East Box, which contained 206 levers. I went in, got into conversation with the signalman and so did not hear the station announcer broadcast a message asking Adrian Vaughan to 'come to the Station Master's office'. Finally tearing myself away from the kind signalman and his signal box, I went back to the station.

A railwayman came up to me. 'Are you Adrian Vaughan?'

'Yes,' I replied.

'Well, you'd better come quick – we've got your wife locked in the waiting room for trespassing.'

Susan, getting bored with her book, had followed me onto the track and, being young, slim and mini-skirted, immediately attracted the attention of the station staff. But *locking* her into a waiting room seemed a bit much. Still, once I'd arrived to claim her, she was released and we went off without further ado. And that explains the dedication in *A Pictorial Record of Great Western Signalling*: 'To my wife Susan, to make up for being arrested at Newton Abbot Station'.

I continued 'working' – hopelessly badly – for Don Parchment. Don was good company when we were out in the car, but my work at the shop was miserable. Try as I might, I could never carry out properly what I was being paid to do. And yet Don never asked me to leave. He put up with my uselessness and I struggled with my embarrassment while I took his wages. At the end of July I felt so guilty about taking Don's money that I handed him my resignation, saying, 'I think I owe you an apology.' He simply said, 'All right, me duck.'

I had written to District Inspector Jones at Oxford station asking if there was a signalling vacancy, but so far no reply. Becoming unemployed, I went to 'sign on' at the Labour Exchange only to discover that I was not entitled to any unemployment benefit because I'd left work voluntarily. I got back to lodgings to find a £75 royalty cheque from Colin for *Great Western Portrait*. It hadn't occurred to me that writing books was 'work'. I also had my savings and my time was my own. I had lots to do. There was a picture book for OPC called *Kenning Collection* to finish as well as the much larger *Great Western Signalling* to research.

Shortly after becoming unemployed, Susan and I moved into more expensive accommodation. That was a move we had applied for while I was still in work – out of the Victorian servant's tiny garret room costing £4 a week and into the 'Middle Flat' costing £10.50 a week. That would have been nearly half my take-home pay had I been working on the railway. Susan offered to be the cleaner of the ground floor hallway, the three-storey stairs and the two bathrooms, and Mrs Morgenstern's agent reduced the rent by a pound. The Middle Flat had two big rooms with large windows and high ceilings. The last tenants were a theatrical couple who owned a parrot. The bird had been free to fly around the sitting room from a

45

perch on a stand in one corner. The carpet below the stand was encrusted with months of parrot shit, while all around the room were lesser accumulations – including on the curtains. It was very hard to get off.

It was worrying to have to pay so much extra in rent, but Susan was still employed at Pergamon Press and I assumed that I would eventually be accepted as a signalman. On 21st August 1972 a note arrived from D. I. Jones inviting me to go to see him. I went at once and was told to go to Hinksey South, Class B, and learn the job. I brushed up on the Rules and Regulations and was ready a week later to take the job on, but it was another week before Mr Jones had me in for the examination. I passed that and had to wait another week for the exam by the Chief Inspector at Reading. I passed and returned to the only job I could do properly, earning my wages for being useful.

Now that Adrian was back on the railway he was happy again, but I was at a bit of a loss. I wasn't sure what I wanted. It never occurred to me to go to evening class to study for another A-level for university entrance. That idea had been knocked firmly on the head by my headmistress. I was married but I had no interest in starting a family and having a 'career' didn't appeal to me either. Teaching had been a disaster and I found working at Pergamon Press increasingly stultifying. I could not imagine spending the rest of my life working up the career ladder in publishing. I wasn't interested in earning lots of money, although I wanted to pay my share and I wanted to live in a nice house in the countryside and have a garden. Wishful thinking, or perhaps there was another way?

Shopping in Oxford one day I came across The Eastgate Gallery in the High Street, near Magdalen Bridge. I went inside to look around. The gallery specialised in porcelain and Japanese art. The owner, Mrs Hopkins, was at least 70 and needed someone to help her in the shop and with book-keeping. She offered me a part-time job – I jumped at the chance. It didn't pay much but it felt much more civilised than working in the smoky office at Pergamon Press, and it was infinitely more interesting. Dear Mrs Hoppy had owned and run the gallery for several decades. She was an expert in her field – an institution in Oxford – and she kindled in me a lifelong interest in Oriental and English porcelain.

As for a house in the country, I thought we could find somewhere rent-free in return for some work. We could save up the money we would have spent on rent to put towards buying our own house. Adrian was sarcastic. 'Oh right – that's clever. A free house? There's no such thing.'

'There is – actually,' I said, loftily, 'I've been looking in 'The Lady' magazine and there's lots of free houses on offer in return for work. We could move to the countryside. We could have a lovely cottage with a garden. We could grow our own vegetables! I could work in return for a house and maybe you could get a job in a signal box somewhere nearby – there are vacancies all over the place – you've said so yourself.'

Adrian said that so long as he could work as a signalman, it would suit him.

Enthusiastically I set about answering advertisements: 'A free cottage in return for...' Visiting the advertisers was an education in itself, and it was a surprise to discover that in 1972 there were plenty of people who were still living in 1922. We went to see a couple in Wendover and discovered that the cottage they were offering in return for work was in fact a hut. A couple in Redditch wanted help in the house in return for a free three-bedroomed house. It was then revealed that while I did the housework, Adrian would be expected to work a 49-hour week in the gardens and also undertake driving a 7-ton lorry, for £27 a week gross. This wasn't exactly the sort of situation or adventure we had envisaged, even if it did save us rent. But then we had an encouraging response from some people who lived in Rutland, inviting us for an interview at their expense. We drove 176 miles to view a beautiful stone house offered in return for some caretaking and cleaning. We fell in love with the house and garden and thought that Adrian would easily find work on the railway locally. Unfortunately the owners did not fall for us – they said we were 'too intelligent' to take on such lowly occupations as cleaning and caretaking. They were surprised that Adrian wrote books and said that with my A-levels I should be *looking towards a proper career. It was the sort of advice one normally gets from parents, not that I took any notice. We were both hugely disappointed and couldn't understand why they thought they knew what was best for us. But perhaps it was more to do with knowing what was best for them – they wanted more traditional tenants.*

In February 1973 my parents moved back to Ireland. My mother didn't want to go but she had no choice in the matter. She didn't want to break up her family and she was financially dependent upon my father. At least this time, though, she was consulted and she insisted that they move to somewhere 'civilised' rather than the 'back of beyond' like before. And this time they would move into a home of their own. My father sold the house in Aldworth Avenue and bought a very similar house in a brand-new housing development on the west side of Limerick City. He found himself a job in a factory called Farenka, which produced the steel cords for car tyres.

It must have been tough for my mother, uprooting herself and her family yet again, to go back to the country that held so many unhappy memories for her, and to leave behind her newly married eldest daughter. It must have been difficult for my sister Karen too – she was taken out of school just before she was due to take O-levels – my father couldn't or wouldn't wait until she had completed this stage of her education. He also refused to let her stay with the family of a school friend, who had offered to put her up and look after her until the exams were finished. Over in Ireland Karen was unable to slot into the education system and it took her decades to recover her academic self-confidence, eventually gaining an honours degree in Ceramics. My father could be a very selfish man, yet I have another image of him as a warm-hearted, generous person always there for us, especially when we were ill or in trouble.

John admitted that England had been good to him, but from him I gathered that the Irish had a standing grudge against English governments. He did not make a big thing about it, but it was from him that I realised it. I had no idea that Irish people had cause for a grudge against my country. After the astounding events of 'Bloody

Sunday' in Londonderry in 1972, he told me something about the political system in Northern Ireland. He told me that the people who were murdered by British soldiers in Londonderry were members of the 'Northern Ireland Civil Rights Movement'. I associated 'Civil Rights' movements with the oppression of black people by white people, and asked, 'Why is there a civil rights movement in Northern Ireland?'

'For the same reason that they have them in the US and South Africa,' John replied. 'The Protestants in the North of Ireland are the whites and the Catholics are the blacks.'

'I am not a British citizen', he went on, 'yet I am allowed to vote in all British elections, local and national, regardless of whether or not I am a property-owner. If I was living in the north of my own country – which the British say is part of their country – I would not have a local vote unless I was a property-owner or paid rent above a certain amount. If the laws of England applied to Northern Ireland, there wouldn't be any of this trouble.'

I was astonished and found it hard to believe this was the truth, but John's explanation, I soon discovered, was a simplified description of an institutionalised system of outrageous discrimination and inequality against Catholics in Northern Ireland. Talking to Susan's father was an important lesson in British and Irish history.

John took Pam, Susan and me to see the house he had bought in Limerick on 28th December 1972. This was my first ever trip to Ireland. The only other place in the British Isles to which I had been that required a ferry was the Isle of Wight. So I envisaged Ireland as an Isle of Wight type of place but just a little further across the water. The ferry, the *Innisfallen*, was only three years old and had a top speed of twenty-four knots, but she was no match for the Irish Sea that night. A south-westerly gale roaring in off the Atlantic whipped up enormous waves that were hitting her at an angle to her course. The remarkable thing was that she was able to hold that course. The *Innisfallen* rose slowly over successive walls of water, higher and higher, then just *fell* into the trough as the wave

49

passed. The sensation produced within the ship was like hitting a concrete floor: there was a 4,848-ton *thud,* a shudder and then *up* we went again. In the dimly lit lounge passengers were sitting in seats like on a bus; the groans began after an hour and developed into almost screams.

Invocations were rife from females as well as males – crying out loud for God, the Virgin and all the saints to help them. In the dimmed saloon lighting, twilit figures began rising from the seats heading for the lavatories, swaying, tottering, nearly falling, as the ship writhed and rose and crashed and shuddered. Eventually I joined the exodus to the lavatories, only for a pee. The carpeted passageway outside the lavatory door was squelchy. I opened the door and stepped inside. The room was crowded, the urinals and cubicles were overwhelmed. Men vomited involuntarily on the floor, pissed on the floor. The floor was *awash* with semi-liquid food, half-digested chips and sausages, rolling in a wave, up and down, side to side, following the movement of the ship. The stench was conveyed on the shoes of the men back to the saloon. After a couple of hours everyone who had so unwisely partaken of a fried supper washed down with pints of beer had emptied their bellies and bladders and now sat quietly or even slept. The ship continued to behave like a wild mustang for the five hours of our crossing. We eventually reached the shelter of the River Blackwater estuary, blessed stability was restored and that is how I learned how far Ireland was from Wales.

John and Pam's bright new house was in a new estate on the edge of Limerick. We did a few things in the house in preparation for the family's move and returned home on 31st December, celebrating New Year's Eve on board ship. Thankfully the crossing was calm.

Chapter Six
The end of the hunt

John's suggestion that we could easily buy a place in Ireland had lain dormant as Susan and I pursued daily work, but now that her parents were over there, the dormant idea awoke. We travelled by train and arrived in Limerick on April Fools' Day 1973. Susan's Uncle Michael had found a few Kerry cottages for us to view. John still had the bread van he had used to move his furniture from England and we borrowed it to drive down to Kerry. The cottages we looked at were all single-storey, long-abandoned buildings without piped water, electricity or sewage disposal. They had rusting corrugated-iron roofs, covering a simple, rectangular ground plan enclosing three or four rooms. One we were taken to see was high on the side of Knocknadobar, a great hill towering over the north side of the Killorglin-Caherciveen road. The cottage was built on a ledge along the contour of the hill with nothing to mark the boundary of the property. The back door, directly opposite the front door, across the width of the central room, opened to a view of the steeply rising hillside. The floor was concrete and decades of water, running down the hill, under the back door and out by the front door had worn a slight but visible depression in the floor. We decided against paying £2,500 for this very exposed place with built-in running water.

The next day we went to see a small cabin one and a half miles east of Killorglin, in the townland of Meanus, on the Beaufort road to Killarney. We met the auctioneer, Tom Moriarty, and a man who said he was the owner. The cabin was built parallel to the road, forty foot back, on a level patch of land. There was another triangular piece of land at a higher level to the right-hand side of the cottage, in all measuring '29 perches', which according to an online calculator is 877 square yards, facing south, and sheltered by trees on three sides. The cabin was four walls and a roof. The central part was very old with extensions at each end: the west end room had a slate roof, the rest was under rusty corrugated iron. It had a useful porch – a little concrete room four feet by five feet – to keep storms off the inner door. There was no back door. It had not been lived in for years. It was derelict. But it smiled in a weary kind of way at me and Susan. It suggested happiness to us – if we were to take the trouble to make *it* happy.

I asked the weather-beaten vendor how much he wanted for it. He looked at me thoughtfully for several seconds and said, 'Sixteen hundred pounds.' He read my thoughts. That was the entire amount of my savings – but I have never over-loved money, and if that figure was the key to the ownership of this promising little place – well, the shabby little man looked as if he could do with the cash.

'Done,' said I.

The man was clearly taken aback by this way of doing business, but we shook hands on the deal and he hurried away.

Tom Moriarty settled himself into his rusty, black Morris Minor and, looking up, said to me, 'What the *hell* did you do that for?'

'Do what?' I said, puzzled.

'Agree to his price just like that. The man has gone away furious. He thinks he should have asked three grand.'

'But,' I said, 'he asked me for sixteen hundred and that's all I have so he's welcome to it for the cottage.'

The auctioneer had never come across anything to compare with my ignorance. 'But man – you *never, ever,* accept the asking price. You could have had the place for a thousand if you'd *bate him down* and he'd have been happy with that. But to close it like you did – he thinks 'twas worth double what he asked and he's very unhappy.'

'But I gave him what he asked,' I protested. 'But if I'd argued and got him to accept less, he would have gone away happy?' I was astonished!

And that was my first lesson in the ways of rural Ireland.

We were thrilled that we were about to become the owners of a dwelling and went into Killorglin to celebrate with a meal at the Bianconi Inn. We had some vague notion that we would restore the cottage and have it as a holiday home. We were about to *own* a property, that was the big thing. It was only when we arrived home – twenty-four hours away from Kerry – that the impracticality of the purchase dawned on us. I had spent all my savings simply to enable us to become house-owners. But we were actually further away than ever from solving the problem of how to put a roof over our heads where we needed it – in England.

We left for home on 7th April but such was our enthusiasm that we were back in Limerick a fortnight later. We drove down to Kerry in the bread van and, taking the coast road, stopped for a picnic by the Shannon. We brewed tea on my father's primus stove. The air was warm and moist, full of sweet, almost sickly gorse scent. It was intoxicating and we talked excitedly about our plans for renovating the cottage almost as if we were drunk. The roof would need replacing, an extension built for a bathroom, a bore drilled for water, electricity connected... We knew nothing about building or renovation, but that didn't stop us from thinking that we would do most of the work ourselves during our holidays. Anything was possible. We called in to a builders' merchant in Tralee to find out the cost of bathroom furniture – cheaper than in England – then drove down to Caherciveen to see our solicitor. He told us that he was waiting for the arrival of a document from Dublin before he could proceed with the sale, but that all was in order. He asked us to leave a cheque for the deposit which we did.

We then went to the vendor and asked him to let us use the cottage as a holiday home until the sale was completed. That sounds more than a bit cheeky in retrospect! But he agreed providing that we returned the keys to him at the end of our stay. That first time we just 'camped out' for a couple of nights and thought some more about our plans to restore the place and the equipment we would need to begin work. On our last evening we went to The Forge in Killorglin for a drink and met the vendor's daughter. She told us that they had had three higher offers to buy since we had made the deal with her father. We thought this unlikely. More likely was that the vendor was sitting at home, gnashing his teeth in frustration at having charged us too little, thinking of ways to put pressure on us to part with an extra few hundred quid.

We were back in Kerry again on Midsummer Day, this time in our VW Beetle, laden with tools and equipment. We bought a wheelbarrow, sand and cement and, having collected the key from the vendor, went to the cottage and – I can hardly believe this now as the place wasn't legally ours – quickly got to work smashing damp and crumbling plaster from the walls in the room that was to become our kitchen. This created a filthy dust that gave Adrian a pain in his chest. Then he removed about sixty cubic feet of wet earth, roots and stones that over the years had filled the space between the back wall of the cottage and the bank that formed the boundary of the farmyard next door. Now the back wall of the cottage could start to dry out. The spoil was barrowed round to the front and dumped along the eastern boundary to make a bank between us and the field next door. Meanwhile I rubbed down and painted some window frames, Snowcemmed the front of the cottage and cut the grass. One day Mrs Clifford from next door came to see us with gifts of gooseberries and eggs and later that evening came with four roasted pink-fleshed trout freshly caught by her husband from the River Laune. They made a delicious supper.

Towards the end of our stay the vendor came round. He explained that a snag had been found in the deeds that would slow down the house purchase. At least that's what we think he said. It wasn't easy to understand him. His announcement didn't worry us unduly but obviously it worried him. He said he was worried that the sale might fall through, worried about the work we were doing or might do. Worried that the cottage would be broken into and that our stuff would be stolen. Worried about the length of time the Land Commission was taking to sort out the paperwork, and concerned that he might have to pay two solicitors. Why two?

Our attitude, rightly or wrongly, was that we had made a deal, paid our deposit and the house would be ours sooner or later. What we didn't realise then was that the 'snag' in the deeds was that the vendor did not have any – he had no legal title to the property he had agreed to sell us!

In mid-July I received notification that early in October I would be redundant as mechanical signalling at Oxford would be replaced by an electric control panel taking over the work of several signal boxes. I applied for a vacancy at Clink Road Junction at Frome on the Wiltshire/Somerset borders, and on 5th August I set off from Oxford in pouring rain to visit the box. The weather was sunny by the time I reached the outskirts of Frome. I turned left at 'The Vine Tree' pub and along Clink Lane to a bridge over the railway cutting. There was a stile in the fence and a path leading down the cutting side to the box. I went down and entered. The signalman was taken aback at the invasion of his privacy, but after I had introduced myself as a prospective candidate for the vacancy, he got to his feet in a rush, and, as his head hit the bottom of the hanging Tilley lamp, stretched out his hand and with a roar said, 'I'm 'Tiny' Fred – and I'm welcoming you here!'

I spent a while chatting to Tiny, then set off to walk the track out to the Distant signals in each direction to familiarise myself with what I would be controlling. I hadn't gone far when I saw a man sitting on the grass on the cutting side. He had a camera round his neck, so I climbed up to speak to him. That's how I met Ivo Peters, the well-known railway photographer. I invited him to visit the signal box when I took it over and we became firm friends at once.

About this time I began to research a very large book on the architecture of the Great Western Railway. This was organised as a 'Joint Venture' with British Railways Western Region. Keith Montague, at Paddington Public Relations Office, was most helpful, and nearly fifty years on we are still good friends. Leslie Soan, the Chief Civil Engineer (CCE) of the Western Region, gave me unlimited access to the architectural drawings collection of the Western Region going back to 1835. I also had the cooperation of Mr McDonald, Head of the CCE's Photographic Department, who gave me access to tens of thousands of superb prints. On 29th August I went to Westbury (Wilts) for an interview with the

Assistant Area Manager, Mr Hopkins. He agreed to take me on at Clink Road Junction when the boxes at Oxford closed.

In mid-September we received two months' notice to quit the flat in Polstead Road because the house was to be sold, and at the same time Susan replied to an advertisement in *The Lady* looking for a person to manage some rented properties in Bath in return for £10 a week and a rent-free cottage in the grounds of Midford Castle, not so far from Frome. Shortly after, we received an invitation to appear for interview at Midford Castle by Susan's prospective employers, Mr and Mrs Briggs.

The turning into the place, off the Bath-Frome road, was enclosed by splendid beech trees. A gravel drive led through the trees and suddenly the plantation stopped and there it was! An 18th-century fairy-tale folly castle – three semi-circular battlemented towers, pierced with Gothick windows looking south over a precipitous valley. The drive curved downwards, an elegant retaining wall rose on our right and into view came a row of two cottages with an archway between them and a Gothick pinnacled tower rising at the far end. Susan entered the castle through a double door in a mock-medieval porch crowned by a coat of arms and flanked by battlemented octagonal towers. She emerged after the interview saying the result was one of 'don't call us, we'll call you'. We drove away thrilled with the place and yet hopeless – we could never be so lucky as to live there.

But I got the job! We moved to The Old Chapel, Midford Castle, on 20th October 1973 ready for me to start work on the 22nd. We hired a removal firm to move our few pieces of furniture and the removal van detoured to Uffington on the way to collect a beautiful, brass, Art Nouveau double bed that had been given to us on permanent loan by Adrian's sister Lalo together with two friendly tabby cats: Baby Cat and Uncle Tolly. We arrived at Midford Castle ahead of the removal van and collected the keys to our new home. The Old Chapel included the mock Gothic tower. It had a large kitchen and a sitting room. A stone spiral staircase rose from a corner of the sitting room to a corridor giving access to two bedrooms and a bathroom at the far end. We settled into the cottage over the weekend, but Adrian had to go back to Oxford for another week's work.

On Monday morning Mrs Briggs outlined my responsibilities. She introduced me to her two youngest children, whom I would drive to and from their prep school each day. Then she drove me down into Bath, to Lansdowne Place West, and showed me the flats I would be managing, and introduced me to some of the tenants. My mind was occupied busily every day, but the lengthening autumn evenings were tedious and silent, with only the two cats for company. I quickly discovered that the cottage was very cold and the antiquated central heating system hardly took the chill off the place. The sitting room was freezing, no matter how much I banked up the fire. I couldn't relax in there, so spent most of my evenings sitting reading at the kitchen table. At night I snuggled down with my hot water bottle in the gloriously comfortable brass bed but I felt strangely ill at ease and did not sleep well. I put it all down to missing Adrian. The week dragged by, but what a celebration we had when he finally joined me in our new home.

On the day we moved to The Old Chapel, Susan and I got out of the car in the driveway and stood in silent admiration. I think we almost disbelieved that we were coming to live here. I looked up to the silvery tower, pinnacled and romantic against a clear blue sky, and said, 'Look at the lady waving to us from the tower.'

'What lady?' asked Susan.

'Oh, nothing,' I said, because there was no lady. 'It's just a beautiful place.'

But some instinct had brought the words out. The year after we'd moved in, Susan's parents came to stay with us. As they got out of their car John looked up at the sunny tower and said, 'Look at the lady waving at us from the tower.'

The proverbial tingle ran down my spine.

I suggested to Susan that she ask the Briggs about the history of the place, and they gave her an essay from the 3rd March 1944 issue of *Country Life*. The design had been built for Disney Roebuck – an extremely wealthy man with estates in Somerset and Nottinghamshire – in 1775. In 1808 the estate had been sold to an exceedingly unusual person, a wealthy Catholic Irishman, Charles Connolly. He was a son of Thomas Connolly of Castletown House, a vast Palladian mansion near Celbridge, Co Kildare. Charles Connolly and his Italian wife – Louisa Brancaccio, Marchesa di St Agata, otherwise known as Lady Connolly – caused to be built the chapel with its tower, the stable block and servants' living quarters. Those two were joined by an archway through the depth of the buildings to a handsome, Bath stone carriage shed. Of the Chapel, only the tower remained, but there were some gravestones in the space where the nave would have been.

When we knew that there had been Catholics at the Castle, Susan decided to make an inquiry to the archives of the Diocese of Clifton. From that source we learned that the Connollys had established a school and an orphanage at the Castle and there was a resident priest – his room was over the archway. At the end of our corridor upstairs there was a walled-up arch where a door had been. Lady Connolly must have walked along there hundreds of times to discuss matters with the priest. That explained why I thought I felt the presence of a smiling woman in there – the presence of the warm-hearted, philanthropic Lady Connolly.

On 12th April 1975 at ten past eight in the evening, I was eating supper in the kitchen preparatory to going on night shift. Baby Cat was sitting on the step, facing into the cold sitting room, washing her face. Suddenly she was on her feet, back arched, fur extended, and her tail like a bottle brush. She stood there, rigid, hissing as cats do when they are defending themselves. Susan and I looked into the sitting room. It was faintly illuminated by light from the kitchen. There was nothing to see. Uncle Tolly jumped off the top of the dishwasher to look at what was frightening his friend. Hitting the floor, he instantly turned into hissing mode, walking backwards. Baby Cat was also walking backwards, still hissing, then both cats turned, ran to the kitchen door and wailed to be let out.

58

Life at Midford Castle settled into a quiet routine, Adrian driving backwards and forwards to the signal box, often working twelve-hour shifts and continuing to research and write in his spare time. I was often on my own. Seemingly it was a fairy-tale place in which to live – it certainly looked that way – but underneath, like all fairy tales, there was a sinister element. I did not feel happy there. I felt frightened being on my own, especially at night, so there must have been something in Adrian's feeling of a 'presence'. He thought it was a friendly presence, but my feelings were overwhelmingly of fear. Adrian's sister Lalo put it into words when she pronounced that a 'Death Wish' hung over the place.

I found my work was stressful and unsatisfying. Tenants kept phoning up at all times of the day and night to complain that the roof was leaking or the heating system had broken down or the pipes had frozen. I had to deal with the aftermath of a house fire in one of the top flats, which meant that all the tenants in the house had to be temporarily accommodated elsewhere due to either fire or water damage.

But the biggest problem was that I didn't have a garden. There was an area at the back of the cottage that had once been the chancel of the chapel, now ruined and laid to grass with a few gravestones and parts of the perimeter wall left standing. It was completely unsuitable for growing vegetables as the depth of soil beneath the grass was too shallow. I asked the Briggs if there was somewhere in the grounds where I could have a garden. Midford Castle was set in extensive gardens, yet apparently there was nowhere in all that space for me to have a little garden to grow some vegetables. The kindly, drunken cook who brewed his own beer and lived in the 'dungeons' of the Castle encouraged me to grow tomatoes and herbs in pots lined along the sunny wall of the ruined chapel. He also suggested that we dig up a bit of the farmer's land that adjoined the boundary wall of the Castle. He said the farmer wouldn't notice, so we dug up a piece of ground and sowed some vegetable seeds and planted potatoes.

By this time I had caught the self-sufficiency bug thanks to John Seymour and his book 'Self-Sufficiency'. This was really an instruction manual on the art and science of food production and preservation. Seymour and his wife Sally, an Australian potter, had brought up their family on a rented smallholding in Suffolk, later moving to Wales. They produced much of their own food and used their crafting skills to make and mend the things they needed. During the 1970s there was a growing interest in the self-sufficiency movement, which encouraged and inspired people to live more sustainably, be self-reliant, produce their own food, use natural energy and revive and use old crafts and skills. The idea of self-sufficiency as a way of life was popularised in the Television sitcom 'The Good Life' first broadcast in April 1975, although we were not aware of it at the time.

I spent my spare time making jams, preserves and wine from anything I could gather in the woods or the grounds of the Castle. We had crab-apple jelly, blackberry and apple jam, sloe gin, dandelion wine and rose-petal wine. I tended the vegetables growing in the farmer's field, but it wasn't a satisfactory arrangement. A clandestine garden was no substitute for a proper garden of my own where I could grow whatever I wanted without fear of getting into trouble.

We began to think seriously about moving permanently to Ireland. We could renovate the cottage, grow vegetables in our own garden, keep animals and be as self-sufficient as possible. We were not naive enough to think we could 'live off the land'. We would need to earn money, but surely I could find some work and Adrian could continue writing? Excitedly we talked through all these ideas. Adrian was as enthusiastic as I was. We both needed change, an adventure, an opportunity to live a simpler, more satisfying lifestyle.

Chapter Seven
Moving to Kerry

I had worked Clink Road Junction for nearly a year when a vacancy arose at Witham, a busier box, six miles further west. I applied and started there a month later in September 1974. The signal box operated on the same main line as Clink Road but it also controlled the single-track branch line to Merehead Quarry and Cranmore. By a most curious coincidence, the area of Witham village in which the signal box stood was marked on the Ordnance Survey map as 'Kerry Croft'. Occasionally a couple of policemen from Bath, patrolling in a van with a police dog, used to visit me in Witham signal box. They were interested and I arranged for them to have a cab ride in a 'Western' diesel up the branch to Merehead Quarry and back. A few years later this old acquaintance proved very useful.

On 30th October 1974 we received notification from our solicitor that the cottage was now the legally registered property of the vendor so that the process of the sale could move forward. The letter also informed us that the vendor was of the opinion that the property had so greatly increased its value since we handed over our deposit in April 1973 that he wanted to be paid interest on the whole purchase price from the date we shook hands on the deal until we finally signed the deeds, which would be some long time in the future, judging by the way matters had been proceeding. Of course I wrote back at once to say that I would not pay any interest. Our solicitor did not reply to that until 3rd December, when he wrote asking me to send him the balance of the purchase – £1,200. I at once sent a cheque, drawn on my building society.

The next letter we got was on 2nd January 1975 informing us that the vendor had dropped his demand for interest and instead was demanding £200 because he said we had promised him this to

61

compensate him for what he said was the rise in the value of the property. This seemed to me to be the same as asking for interest and I refused. One month later we received a letter *via* our solicitor from the vendor's solicitor saying that the vendor would sue us if we did not pay – though on what possible grounds we could be sued was beyond me. However, the letter continued, the vendor would be satisfied if we paid him £100 extra. So for the sake of clearing up our business with him as soon as possible, we agreed to pay that and I sent off the £100 cheque the next day. We set out for Ireland on 10th March 1975 for a twelve-day stay and we signed the contract to buy the cottage and land at Meanus West on 19th March 1975. It would take us another seven years to get our title deeds.

I worked at Witham for thirteen months. There was a seventeen-mile drive each way from Midford and increasingly I worked twelve-hour shifts. In the high summer of 1975, with all the windows open, the temperature inside the signal box exceeded Health & Safety Regulations. We had been given an H&SE thermometer and the law was that when the temperature in our 'work place' exceeded 70 degrees we should stop work!

In the middle of July, Susan and I were in deepest Dorset, in our VW Beetle, driving along an eight-foot-wide lane lined on one side with a dry stone wall, and a barbed wire fence on the other. About 100 yards ahead the lane took a ninety-degree turn and went uphill. I saw the roof of a car above the stone wall coming down the hill – fast. I recognised a boy-racer and there was nowhere for us to pass. I stopped 50 yards from the bend. He skidded around the bend, saw our car at last and braked, but the gravelly road was like ball bearings under his locked wheels and he hit us head-on. We were unhurt but the accident forced us to make up our minds to move to Kerry as soon as possible. We needed a better life.

Then in the heat of August my nemesis took place. I was on twelve-hour shifts, day after day, night after night. I became exhausted but soldiered on like the rest of the chaps in temperatures of 90 degrees plus. The steady grindstone, where even going home to sleep seemed like part of work, wore me down and caused me to be involved in two incidents at the end of August. In the first I thoroughly lost my temper with the Bristol 'Chief Passenger Train Controller', for which I was put on a charge. The other, which happened the following day, could have derailed a passenger train. I have written the full account of these elsewhere, but suffice to say that in the first case the Chief Passenger Train Controller at Bristol interfered with the signalling regulations, thereby delaying the 'Cornish Rivera Express', and had I not intervened with some proper railway work the 'crack' train of the day might have been standing there for several hours and of course delaying following trains.

The afternoon following that a down express stopped and the driver reported 'a buckle in the Up Main track near Blatchbridge but it isn't so bad that you can't get over it at walking speed.' That wasn't a proper message, but I was so hot and tired I simply could not think of the question I should ask to pin down exactly where the buckled rail was. That sounds ridiculous now, but at that moment I just couldn't think, after fourteen years as a signalman. I went out to the driver and asked him to repeat his message, which he did precisely as before. I was thoroughly confused and embarrassed so I told him I understood and off he went.

An up express was on its way to me from Castle Cary. I stopped it and told the driver to proceed with caution from Witham to Blatchbridge looking out for a buckle in the track, which might be passable at walking speed. He went off and found nothing up to Blatchbridge Junction signal box. He had just put on power when he saw the buckled track and stopped. The driver went back to Blatchbridge and, naturally enough, complained that I had given him a wrong warning message.

I was absolutely mortified, humiliated and alarmed by this. I would not allow overwork to bring the passengers or myself into that situation again, so I handed in my notice on 8th September. On 1st October I took a last ride up to Merehead Quarry on a 'Western' Class diesel. Friday 3rd October was my last shift as a Western Region signalman. I was on the late shift. I saw on the roster sheet

63

that my name had been crossed out and 'Vacancy' written in. I don't remember who relieved me at ten. All I remember is walking down the box exterior steps and red-hot tears welling up. I knew it was time for me to leave but, in spite of everything that had made me take this step, leaving the railway was like a divorce.

On 4th October 1975, with all our savings – £1,350 – in the bank, we said goodbye to Midford Castle, our friends, our way of life and set off for a precarious new beginning in Ireland. Adrian's signalman colleague at Witham, Sean Bolan, helped us load the hired van with what was left of our possessions after we had given away or sold things like the dishwasher, which was not much use without electricity or running water. Sadly the beautiful brass bed went back to Uffington and we took with us instead a big, heavy mahogany bed that we had purchased from Bert Haines's scrapyard in East Challow. Adrian drove the van and I drove behind in our little white VW Beetle with the cats in a home-made cage on the seat beside me, crying piteously. Their fearful cries and the sight of the overloaded yellow van swaying somewhat as it sped along the road in front diminished my enthusiasm and accentuated my fears for our unknown future.

But the journey was uneventful and we arrived safely if much too early at the Swansea port. Adrian drove the van to the freight depot and I settled in the car to await embarkation. The cats were quiet now, the sedative prescribed by the vet having taken effect. I poured myself a cup of tea from the thermos and switched on the radio. Paul Jennings was on Desert Island Discs just at that moment requesting Purcell's 'Come ye Sons of Art', a beautiful piece of music that we had recently discovered. Adrian had opened up a whole new world for me with his love of classical music, and this seemed like a good omen, doubly blessed as he admired Paul Jennings. Jennings's book 'Just a Few Lines', about his love of railways, was packed away in a tea-chest in the van. The book was a present from Penelope Betjeman with an inscription that read 'To the Vaughans, railway lovers. Just take care. From Penelope. 1970.'

Adrian was the first to be beckoned onto the 'Innisfallen'. I watched as the yellow van disappeared from sight and thought, 'This is it. There's no turning back now.' The cars began to move forward and soon it was my turn. I bumped the Beetle over the ramp, waking up the cats, and rattled along its iron ridges into the gaping mouth of the waiting ship. As I parked, Adrian walked towards me grinning, pleased that we were on our way at last. The cats cried out feebly as we transferred them to one of the cages for domestic pets, situated at the rear of the ship. The roaring and booming in the car deck was deafening and would have been frightening for the cats so I was glad that we had thought of sedating them. As we stroked them back to sleep a couple of young Frenchmen came along with a lovely yellow retriever. The poor dog was very frightened by all the noise and commotion and refused to go into a cage. We gave them a spare sedative and, leaving them to administer it, made our way to our sleeping berth. Surprisingly we slept well that night and, like the cats and the golden dog, were oblivious to the voyage until the following morning when the stewardess rapped on the cabin door to announce that breakfast was being served.

The 'Innisfallen' docked at Cork, on schedule. Down in the car deck the cats were crying horribly. We took them back to the car where they quietened down in more familiar surroundings. Adrian took up his position in the van. I watched eagerly as the front of the ship opened, exposing our first glimpse of Ireland. The van, first in the queue, moved slowly forward followed by a multi-coloured snake of cars, and we made our way across to customs. The window of the car was wound down. I could smell turf smoke in the air and knew I had come home. The French guys and their dog were waiting by the exit gates preparing to hitchhike. They wanted to go to Macroom so we offered them a lift. We all stood about waiting for customs clearance, stamping our feet in the cold and chattering away in a curious mixture of schoolgirl French and broken English. Marc was a sweet, shy boy in his early twenties and the owner of the dog, Yoko. Pascall was older, definitely chilled out, and when we couldn't understand him he would say 'Phut … it's OK.' He volunteered to make us tea on a little gas stove produced from his capacious rucksack. The tea was strong and black with no sugar, barely drinkable, but the morning was so chilly that I forced myself to swallow a couple of mouthfuls to warm up. After waiting for two hours, a

65

customs official sauntered towards us, glanced casually at the van and gave us the all clear. Marc, Pascall, Yoko and two large rucksacks squeezed into the front of the van with Adrian and we set off. At Macroom we waved goodbye to our new friends and resumed our journey.

My mother and father were waiting at the cottage for us to arrive. They had kept themselves busy by sweeping the dusty concrete floors, brushing away the cobwebs, cleaning windows and lighting turf fires in the two fireplaces. My mother had prepared a meal for us and, after the excitement of our arrival subsided, we were each handed a plate of mutton stew. We were too jiggy to sit down, so with plates in our hands we wandered about admiring this and that, telling my parents about our plans. My father was so proud that we had bought into his beloved Kerry and he was quite sure we would make something of the ol' place. But my mother was bewildered and clearly couldn't see the delights we could see in this barely habitable cottage.

We put the cats' home-made cage onto the grass in the garden and opened the door to let them out. Baby Cat, the female, braver than her male companion, sniffed around with interest and curiosity, but Uncle Tolly remained in the cage and, when finally he ventured forth, headed straight for the car and spent the rest of the day crouched beneath it. Baby Cat became very brave after a while and made several circuits of the garden to establish her territory before going inside to casually wash herself in front of the fire.

We unloaded the van and stored the tea chests we couldn't unpack in the west end room of the cottage. We set up a makeshift 'kitchen' in one of the middle rooms. With the cottage we had inherited an old, battered wooden table about three feet by two feet, upon which we put a five-gallon, copper tea-urn with a nice brass tap to be used for water storage, a washing-up bowl, and a wooden plate rack on a tray to drain the dishes. We had a small fridge with a custom-made, wooden capping making an extra work surface, but of course there was no electricity to run the fridge. For cooking there was my father's primus stove and a couple of camping gas cookers that would have to make do until we could buy a Calor gas stove. Food, crockery, pots and pans jostled for space in a small pine cupboard, the bottom half of a little country dresser. One of Adrian's very first jobs would be to make a dresser top with shelves to fit onto this cupboard to take our crockery and display plates. The cutlery went into a large mahogany and brass cutlery box that found its home on the wide windowsill together with the pottery bread crock. Finally we brought in our 18th-century pine settle given to us by the Briggs in exchange for work we had done at The Old Chapel, a table and two chairs. 'Et voilà', our kitchen was complete!

I was interested in the fate of the potatoes and onions we had set in the spring. I was disappointed to discover that the onions, neglected over the summer, were enmeshed in a tangle of weeds. They had hardly matured from the sets we had planted; there were just a few bigger specimens, which I laid out on a small straw mat to dry. The potatoes had fared better and I dug up a plant that yielded about a pound in weight. Just perfect for our supper.

My parents left for Limerick at around tea-time and darkness fell by seven o'clock. We lit the Tilley lamp and ate supper sitting on the kitchen chairs in front of the fire. We felt very pleased with ourselves and our dear little cottage. There was a knock on the door. It was my Uncle Michael – come to welcome us to Ireland. This was cause for a celebration and, rooting around in the tea chests, I found a bottle of home-made rose-petal wine. I poured the wine into two cups and a mug. My uncle raised his cup to wish us good health, and we cried 'Sláinte' in unison.

The next day Adrian set off alone to return the empty van to England. After I had seen him off, my first task was to fetch the water. The nearest water supply was a stream that we called the 'little river', situated about a hundred yards away, which flowed into the River Laune. To reach this little stream we went through the gate into the field adjoining our garden and trudged across very broken ground – old drainage ditches and worn-down cattle tracks, covered with prickly gorse, rushes and the knee-high, sword-like leaves of Montbretia clumps, to a grassy bank where it was possible to lower the buckets into the water without falling in. From the field I could see the mountains of MacGillicuddy's Reeks shimmering in a bluish haze in the distance, and the early morning sunlight slanted across from the east, sparkling on the dew-drops in the hedgerows. The cats scrambled up trees and cavorted about in front of me as we made our way down to the stream. Sitting on the damp grassy bank, sunshine filtering through the hawthorn and hazelnut trees, I watched the clear bright water tumble and splash over the boulders and stones, combing smooth the green hair-like weed that had attached itself like limpets to the rocks. It was a wonderful feeling to know that I had time to reflect a little on our good fortune to be in this magical place. But at last, conscious that I must not let the day slip by without tackling at least some of the jobs I intended to do, I filled the buckets and struggled home with the water, pouring what was left into the copper urn.

My second task was to clear a strip of land in the garden so that I could sow broad beans. After an hour of digging and bending and pulling out weeds, roots and stones, I had cleared an area of about five feet by three, and felt very dispirited to have achieved so little. After lunch progress was even slower as my back ached and I had lost my initial enthusiasm. Less than an hour later I gave in and returned my tools to the shed. I longed for a hot bath but had to make do with a quick wash in water heated in the kettle. I spent the rest of the day making Christmas puddings in the pressure cooker on the primus stove.

Adrian arrived home after lunch on the Wednesday and, although tired after two sea journeys in less than forty-eight hours, he was eager to start work in the garden. He dug up the potatoes while I dumped the weeds and stones I had dug the day before along the eastern boundary. The potato patch was cleared by late afternoon and we were pleasantly surprised to find that we had about fifty-six pounds of sound potatoes. I sowed four rows of Aquadulcia Claudia – a broad bean seed suitable for autumn sowing – on the vacated land. Supper that evening consisted of tiny spuds swimming in butter and a glass of mulled blackberry wine.

Chapter Eight
Settling in with the neighbours

Meanus is a 'Townland' in the Barony of Dunkerran South, just over a mile east of Killorglin on the Beaufort road. In our time there it was a district of wide, flat, grasslands, some ploughed, most not, some rather wet and some poor quality bogland. The River Laune flowed serpentine wide and swift through the grass lands north of the road sometimes close sometimes further away. The road had a few scattered single-storey cottages, and even a couple of two-storey dwellings, the latter set well back off the road, homes of small farmers. Coming from Killorglin, on the right was one tiny cottage close to the roadside where a little old man lived and next to that, but set well back from the road, was Anne O'Neill's house. She was a widow with four daughters. Behind them, a mile or so to the south, rising quite suddenly out of the rough fields and bogland was - and of course still is - a majestic range of high mountains: MacGillicuddy's Reeks. The highest has a peak sharp and rocky like a truncated pyramid. This I soon discovered was Ireland's highest mountain, Carrauntoohil (3,406 feet). It was roughly due south of our cottage although the overgrown hedge across the road hid the view from our garden. Grand views of 'The Reeks' could be enjoyed from the lichen-covered limestone bridge 200 yards east along the road from the cottage. Coming back along the road from Killorglin, given the right sky and lighting, the view was unobstructed and superb. I revelled in the wonderful lighting effects created by the varying of the sunlight from its rising to midday to its setting in the west, always modified by the infinite variety of clouds sailing majestically in off the Atlantic Ocean just a few miles away.

Our cottage was old and built by poverty-stricken people. It answered fairly well to the 'typical west-of-Ireland cabin' described by Maurice O'Sullivan in his fine book *Twenty Years a-Growing*. It lay east-west in its length and about forty feet back from the road. It was fifty feet long and ten feet wide inside. The ridge of the rickety roof was fourteen feet above the worn-out, uneven cement floor, which was no more than a thin skin on earth.

The west end room, lit by one window, eventually became our bedroom. Its three slim concrete walls allowed a room about twelve feet square. The fourth wall was formed by the back of the ancient, stone-built chimney. The bottom part of the chimney was almost the width of the room, just leaving space for a doorway. The chimney hearth faced a room about fifteen feet long, lit by one window, ending at a lath-and-plaster wall. Beyond that was a space, maybe ten feet long, lit by a single window. The east wall of this room was concrete, with a chimney at the centre. On the other side of that was the east end room, about twelve feet square. It had a fireplace and was the best-lit space in the cottage with windows in the east- and south-facing walls. This eventually became our sitting room. The old lath-and-plaster wall was easy to knock down, giving us a central kitchen/living area twenty-five by ten feet, and lit by *two* windows!

The walls of the original cabin, the central length between the two chimneys, were two feet thick. They had been raised from the bare earth without foundations, using large stones held in place with earth. The walls were plastered with a soft, sandy stuff, lime-washed pale green, the dampest parts of which we had already knocked off during one of our stays in the cottage. The rest also needed to be stripped back to the stones and the stones re-plastered. Throughout the building there was a ceiling made of thin tongue-and-groove boards nailed to the cross-ties of the rafters. Ancient whitewash hung in flakes from the boards, exposing woodworm holes, and it was obvious that the entire ceiling and roof of rusting corrugated iron/slate would have to be replaced. An extension would be needed along the back of the cottage to accommodate a bathroom. Before that could be done we would need piped water and a septic tank for the sewage. In the absence of all that we bought an 'Elsan' chemical toilet. I dug a hole two and a half feet square and about five feet deep at the east edge of our plot of land near the roofless, concrete shed by the road. Into this I emptied the contents of the Elsan.

Our next-door neighbours, Pat and Agnes Clifford, lived in a neat yellow-painted, single-storey cottage. The front and side of the cottage had a gravelled area with a formal garden of grass and flowering shrubs to the road. Pat's farmyard came along the full length of the rear of our cottage, separated by a bank of earth and stones. Pat said his ancestors had lived in this cottage and farmed the land as tenants, then as freeholders, for at least 200 years.

Agnes was a slim, petite, bustling dark-haired woman of around 60 years of age. She had been born into a farming family living at 'Launemount', a largish, single-storey house set in the fields well away from the Meanus road. She had gone to a London hospital as a young woman, before Hitler's war, where she had trained to be a nurse. She had retained a nurse's bustling way and her care for others. She had stayed in London, nursing in that hospital, for the whole of the war alongside many other Irish women.

She had come back from London after the war, married Pat and volunteered her caring expertise to Killorglin 'social services', which were run under the auspices of the 'Legion of Mary' and the 'St Vincent de Paul Society'. She took on a caring role for several poor, single men who lived in hovels along the lanes, or *bohreens*, around the district. She cooked meals for them and delivered them in her old Ford Escort.

Agnes went, every day, to Mass. I happened to be passing the Catholic church one morning just as Agnes and her friends were holding what looked like a committee meeting on the pavement outside; they had just come out of Mass. Agnes stopped me and introduced me to the Committee. 'We're just going inside to say a decade of the rosary – come in and join us.'

I certainly didn't want to go with them but, surrounded by smiles, a refusal seemed undiplomatic given that I was a stranger in their midst and they were kind people. Surrounded by my pious captors I was hurried into the Victorian Gothic pile and was led to a varnished pine pew. We all knelt. There were maybe twenty women scattered around the vast, echoing space. As the crashing echoes of our footfalls died away, one of the twenty – the Forewoman of the Rosary – in some distant part of the church announced 'The First Mystery'. My heart sank. This was no decade, not ten 'Hail Marys' and a 'Glory Be' – this was the first of *five* decades – the five 'Mysteries' – comprising fifty 'Hail Marys' and ten 'Glory Be's'. I had been lured in by a lie! They rattled through the ritual, no full stops, or stops for breath – a whole prayer in one machine-gun delivery. They had a word blurring technique. Were they short-changing God, I wondered? But then, it was all over in half the time a respectful delivery would have taken.

Pat was as good-hearted, cheerful and bright as Agnes – but he only went to Mass on Sundays! He farmed maybe fifteen acres using a donkey and a two-wheeled, flat-bed cart for haulage. He had a cat, a cow, and two collie dogs. The youngest dog, called Kerry, was a black and white animal with one brown and one blue eye. He must have weighed half a hundredweight. When he was not out in the fields with Pat he lay around at the back of the house. If he heard the front gate open when he was at the rear he came around to the front at a surprisingly rapid gallop, skidding sideways on the bends at the corner of the house. His huge paws always hit exactly the same spot and over the years convenient indentations, footholds in the ground, had formed.

At the rear of their house was a space of grassy gravel, then the fence of the kitchen garden. To the left, on bare, hard-packed earth, was Pat's home-made, three-walled shelter for turf, its corrugated-iron roof supported with ash wood poles. In his kitchen garden Pat grew enough vegetables to feed several families, and some of this produce he sold to the hotels around the place, including the Hotel Europe, just outside Killarney. He grew crops of very large bulbs of garlic, which we thought was unusual in Kerry, but, with several smart hotels around, garlic was a clever thing to produce.

Immediately beyond the kitchen garden there was a field of

72

maybe two acres, which he ploughed with a horse borrowed from John Foley, who farmed on the other side of the road. One half of the field was used for potatoes, with oats in the other – rotating the crop annually. He sowed the oats by hand. The seed he would roughly incorporate into the soil using a piece of brushy, hawthorn tied to his donkey's tail. His nephew volunteered to bring his tractor, but Pat told me he would never allow a tractor on his land because, he said, its weight would compact the soil.

Some of the fields Pat reserved for growing hay-grass, others were meadow grass on which his cow grazed. Before our time he had three cows and he took the milk into the creamery each day on the donkey cart, but in our time he had one cow to provide milk for himself and Agnes and enough also for a pint a day for Susan and me.

The River Laune formed the northern boundary of his land, and from that he took salmon and trout with a rod and fly. Pat sold the salmon to the Hotel Europe and to Henry Dodd's smokery beside the Laune, at Killorglin. A beautiful *bohreen* led from his farmyard, between his fields, to the river. It was enclosed by stone walls, and the stones were bedded on earth, just like those in our cottage. Being open to the skies and to the rains, they had become a wild flower, moss and lichen garden. The floor of the track was paved with cobbles, overgrown with grass; tiny flowering plants grew between the stones among the grass.

Growing out of the top of the walls were fine ash trees. Pat coppiced these, taking off a large-diameter branch here and there, cutting them into convenient lengths, and stacking them for seasoning in a high-roofed, open-sided shelter at the edge of his yard. Ash wood is white, straight-grained and hard, which splits perfectly. It makes the finest fire logs, but Pat burned turf and from his store of seasoned ash he made *súgán* chairs to sell. In the evenings he sat in a chair by the turf fire making chairs. He had sawn appropriate lengths outside, and indoors used a hammer and chisel, a spokeshave and a small, sharp hatchet. The shavings made great fuel.

73

So Pat was a happy man. He had a wonderful wife. He owned his land, freehold. Every penny in his pocket he had earned with his own hands. He 'cut his coat according to his cloth' and owed no money. He had never in his life been further away from home than Tralee, sixteen miles away. He played the *Uilleann* pipes and the small accordion superbly well, and often when we went in the evenings to fetch our milk we were treated to a spontaneous concert of traditional Irish music.

Pat had never learned to drive a car. One day Susan and I were in Agnes's Ford Escort going to Killorglin via the back *bohreen*. This was because Agnes had to attend to her sister Eileen's holiday bungalow – Eileen lived in the USA. Going on our way after Eileen's we came to a T-junction. I noticed that Agnes was approaching this rather fast and she took the easier turn to the left rather than the sharp right over a river bridge.

'Tis *right* we want to go Agnes,' said Pat.

'I know Pat, but the brake has failed.'

'Since when have the brakes had anything to do with the steering?' said Pat, in a caustic kind of way.

On another occasion we were all together in the Ford, driving into Killorglin. We had come to a stand at the crossroads at the bottom of the hill, the Bianconi Inn to the left, Jimmy the Monk's grocery store and petrol pump to the right and the Allied Irish bank on the other side of the cross. Agnes waited as traffic from left and right and from the other side of the cross took their turn to pass by or draw forward and turn right in front of us, then we moved off.

'Why do we have to wait there for all those people? Why do you give way to them all?' asks Pat.

'Because they have right of way, Pat,' says Agnes in a kindly, tutorial voice.

'Ha!' says Pat, indignantly, 'Tis second-class citizens we are – living above in Meanus.'

We had been living in our cottage for a month or so when it was Pat and Agnes's turn to have Mass said in their house. This was known as 'The Stations'. There was a rota of houses for miles around and the priest went to each one in turn to say Mass. Agnes kindly invited us to attend. The house was packed, both main rooms, the congregation made up of farmers and their wives and single men – the children were at school – from along the Beaufort road out of Killorglin. When Mass was over, the priest, Father Moran, called for us. Agnes must have told him about the 'blow-ins' from England. He brought us into the hallway between the two rooms and introduced us to the assembly and said he was *sure* that all present welcomed us to the place.

That was the most effective 'ice-breaker' possible and indeed, no ice had been, or was ever, encountered. Not even after a *very* bad-mannered action on my part, which could have been an occasion for bad temper and a long-lasting enmity towards me on the part of the offended party.

To the east of our plot was a rough field leading to the little river where we got our water. We had only been in the cottage a day or two. I had spotted a handy-looking supply of firewood in the form of a fine young ash tree, the trunk four inches in diameter, growing out of the embankment carrying the road over the low-lying field. This tree had started life growing out horizontally and had then turned itself upwards – it had a great beauty – and I went in through the gate and sawed it down!

Just as it fell, a tall, thin man appeared silently, suddenly. He actually looked starved. His bony, unshaven face was topped by a sugar-loaf-shaped felt hat. He had a piece of sacking, like a shawl, around his shoulders and held across his chest by a twist of copper wire. Beneath that was a ragged jacket with the cuffs well above his wrists and his lower half covered by the baggiest pair of worn-out trousers, the legs of which, to keep in fashion with his jacket, ended well above his ankles. But the lack of socks – which must surely have been a fact – was hidden by ankle-length hobnailed boots.

The garb, however, held no clue as to the man. He was as straight as a ram-rod. He was very calmly self-possessed. His face was haughty in spite of its starved look and three days of stubble. His cheeks were hollow below high cheekbones, he had a hooked,

Duke of Wellington-type nose. His blue eyes were set deep in his bony face. His gaze was direct and piercing. I realised my sin before he spoke – quietly. ''Tis my field, and that,' gesturing to the fallen tree, 'is my tree. Don't be taking liberties.'

With that he stalked off, leaving me, saw in hand, consumed with embarrassment and wondering how to put matters right with this remarkable old man. Clearly he was a man of few words and apologetic words would not be as productive as actions. I set to work to saw the trunk, and those branches that warranted it, into fireplace-sized logs. Having made a tidy pile – several large wheelbarrows full – I stacked the first load and wheeled the barrow the 300 yards to my neighbour's farmhouse.

There was a wide, grassy gateway between two stone barns bordering the road. The wide, grassy, gravelly farmyard was below the level of the road. I pushed down the slope towards the farmhouse, a two-storey dwelling coated in pebbledash concrete. The whole place looked as derelict as the owner. I wheeled across to the front door. It was three steps up from the yard. I walked up, knocked and stepped back down again. A chair grated on a stone floor within, boot steps across the floor, and the door opened. He looked down at me without speaking, surprised perhaps. I said, 'I'm bringing you the logs. There's more.'

'Yerra, I don't want them. Take them away.'

'Thank you,' I replied, and without another word I tipped the logs onto the grass and wheeled away with the barrow. I barrowed the rest into my place.

The old man was Eddie Moriarty. He was from the outset our good friend, but always with the fewest words spoken.

I was still in English mode and was hurrying everywhere. One morning, carrying two water buckets, I was hurrying across Eddie's bumpy meadow to the little river at the field's eastern boundary. Eddie, as was his peculiar way, appeared beside me out of nowhere and said, 'What's 'oor rush? Slow doo-un. The river will be there in a thousand years.' And with that he disappeared.

Stopped in my tracks, I gazed around at the wide acres of very rough grazing spreading to the Laune. Behind me, to the south, the high, remarkably dramatic MacGillicuddy's Reeks. There was silence over the beauty of the place. I took his advice to heart and tried to adopt a more relaxed, Kerry way of living.

'What haram?' they would say. 'Take 'oor 'ase.'

Eddie Moriarty's field, down to the Laune, was a delight as Eddie left it to nature and to his coloured cattle. Alongside the rough track leading down to the river were yellow irises and flame-coloured Montbretia according to season. Eddie's scattered cattle standing around between the yellow gorse added to the colours. A hundred yards down the track from the road gate, Pat Clifford's field came alongside, lined by a wide, thick hedge of hazelnut trees. In the distance, across the river, was a line of low, misty blue hills. If one stood on the Beaufort road looking to Killorglin, the Slieve Mish Mountains, far across Dingle Bay, made the western horizon.

Our Baby Cat, the great hunter, revelled in the wide acres. She became dog-like in that she accompanied us when we walked 'down Eddie's'. Walking down to the river, she liked me to carry her along the cart track. Being carried gave her sharp eyes much more opportunity for hunting. She would spot something, thrust off like a rocket onto the grass and adopt *tiger* mode: sinking down low, prowling and menacing, having seen something in a bramble bush.

Once, when she prowled along the tall hedge of hazelnut trees, a blackbird close by set up his rapid 'tip-tip-tip-tip' alarm call. In a few seconds a squadron of fighters came whizzing across from the trees lining the brook and settled into the bushes around us. There were robins, goldfinches and wrens scolding with great energy. The chorus was so intense that the cat ceased to prowl and ran to me, mewing to be picked up!

Cycling into Killorglin early one morning in November, I entered the avenue of great beech trees and came up behind twenty bullocks herded by a dog belonging to a mountainy man pushing his old, black bike behind the throng. The road was blocked from wall to wall so there wasn't anywhere for the cattle to go but straight on, with the half-asleep dog at their heels. I drew up beside the drover and got off my bike, saying, 'Hello, fine day,' in the approved manner. He cheerfully agreed and we strolled along together exchanging polite conversation about the weather. This was the natural thing to do in Kerry. Drivers of cars passing me on the road would give a wave, cyclists passing the cottage would call out, 'Fine day.' This friendly politeness from total strangers was a delightful revelation, and we fell in with it at once.

The dog heard our relaxed pleasantries, relaxed altogether, and came in behind us. The head of the column of bullocks was then approaching a wide driveway, curving round to the left and rising steeply. Up this the leading bullocks turned. At first we two did not see this, but as the animals climbed higher we saw them. The drover shouted to his dog with a staccato of gruff commands, perhaps in Irish, but the dog didn't respond. I threw my bike against the right-hand wall, ran past the bullocks and up the drive with the dog now behind me, barking. We got to the front together, stopped the bullocks and tried to turn them, but the others were crowding in behind. Hooves churned lawn as the cattle tried to dodge out sideways. Anyhow, 'in the heel o' th' hunt' (as I later learned to say) the drover, his dog and myself got them turned and back on the road, leaving a fine mess on the driveway behind us.

Not long after we'd moved in, Agnes showed us a notice in *The Kerryman* newspaper, proclaiming a 'Group Water Scheme' for the Beaufort-Killorglin road. 'Anyone interested in taking part should attend a meeting in Beaufort village hall.' Susan and I were, of course, delighted and went along. Kerry County Council wanted to bring piped water along the Beaufort-Killorglin road; each household had to pay £10 to be registered, and later £450 as a contribution to the full cost, the rest coming from the County Council. Eighteen houses per mile were needed. We were more in need than anyone, so I volunteered to drum up interest. I visited seventeen householders from Tom O'Sullivan and Michael Doyle, above Meanus Cross, down to the Ulsterman by the river at Annadale, bringing the glad tidings. 'Mossy' Joy, a retired builder, in his spick-and-span cottage, turned his cold water tap on full.

Sparkling water roared forth. 'I have plinty water – why would I be paying to have it piped in?'

All I could say, feeling rather lame, was, 'Piped water is more reliable than well water. The well might go dry in a drought – and you won't have to worry about maintaining the electric pump.'

At each house I asked the householder to come to a meeting in our cottage to have the scheme explained and to sign up for it. On the appointed day a group of middle-aged and elderly Kerry men came to the cottage. They were in a tight group, caps in their hands, in a nervous uncomfortable huddle. My heart sank. They had been their usual open, friendly selves when I'd called on them the week before. This was a very bad idea, a 'blow-in' Englishman summoning the Irish to a meeting where I would ask them all to agree to pay £450 each so I could have running water. I felt truly embarrassed and the gathering looked mournful. But then, like the *deus ex machina* of an adventure novel, in came those most respected persons, Pat and his brisk, businesslike wife Agnes. We all lightened up at once. She also read the faces of the assembly and suggested it might be more spacious and comfortable if everyone came next door to her house and have the meeting there. Everyone was relieved and we all trooped purposefully next door. John Joy was elected Chairman with Agnes as Secretary. All present, not then enough to make up eighteen members, pledged their support. They also said they would get the rest of the road into the Group and told us that being cottagers and not farmers we would not be required to pay the £450 contribution: ''Tis out o' th' question!' Agnes and I jointly opened an account with the Allied Irish Bank in which to place any money – and I would go about as the distributor of signing-on forms and the collector of deposits.

Chapter Nine
The black range

A few days after we had arrived, I was outside the cottage when a man on a little grey Ferguson tractor stopped on the road and came in through the gate. He came up to me, his hand extended.

'Hallo-a,' he said in his wonderful Kerry accent. 'My name is Michael Dial (Doyle). I live up at the Crass (crossroads). Welcome. If ye need any help with anything, any time, just give me a call.'

It wasn't long before we took him up on his kind offer. As winter approached we had to give some serious consideration to heating the cottage more effectively than a turf fire on the floor of the open fireplace, the heat from which went straight up the capacious chimney. What was needed was a solid fuel range. For some reason we wanted a cast-iron range – the sort of thing one would have seen in an 1880s catalogue of the latest kitchen equipment. Perhaps because they looked more like steam engines! I asked the retired builder 'Mossy' Joy down the road where I could find one. Mossy was quite indignant.

'Ye're mad to be wanting one. Everyone's thrown out those old things long ago. Ye need a modern 'Stanley' range.'

We were not to be deterred and decided to pay a visit to Susan's grandmother who lived in Cahirciveen to see if she could help us.

My grandmother, now well into her seventies and a widow for several years, was a shortish, portly woman, dressed as always in a flowered cross-over apron that covered her everyday clothes. I can't ever remember seeing her dressed in anything else. She was very pleased to see us and, after exchanging family news, bade us sit down at the table and produced from nowhere a tasty, boiled bacon and cabbage dinner. But she refused to eat with us, preferring instead to stand a little to one side of our chairs, so that she could wait on us and yet still join in the conversation – a tradition she had always followed. She didn't know of anyone who had a black range, but suggested we speak to Pauline McGuire who kept 'The Anchor' in Main Street almost opposite where I had lived as a child, above the betting shop. Pauline was a blowsy ample-chested woman, who threw up her plump hands in horror when she heard that we were looking for an old black range.

'What would ye be doin' with the likes o' that?' she asked, truly offended that anyone would want to install one when everyone else was throwing them out. But seeing our determination she suggested that the owner of a garage nearby might be able to help us. The man at the garage was very helpful. The parents of a young lad who worked for him had recently thrown out a black range in favour of an oil-fired variety – he directed us to their house up the hill from Main Street. The house was attached to a decrepit-looking corrugated-iron hut – a bicycle repair shop – and the only way in seemed to be through this building. We knocked on the bashed metal door and an elderly stooped man emerged from the dirty dim interior. Yes, he had a range for sale.

'How much would ye be givin' me for it?' he asked quickly.

We asked to see the range first before agreeing a price. The old man disappeared into the depths of his workshop and came out a moment later with a burnished cast-iron oven door. It was beautiful, almost silver. He had polished it with pride and stroked it lovingly while we admired it. We wanted to see the rest of the range and, laying the oven door gently onto a workbench, he led us into the adjoining yard where the range, rusted and in pieces, lay in a huge heap against a brick wall. My heart sank – clearly the range had to be rebuilt in situ. We were not expecting this complication, and as for the rust...! But somehow he managed to persuade us that it would be easy to rebuild it and the rust would just disappear with a bit of emery cloth and some black leading. So, against his better judgement Adrian offered him ten pounds but the old man shook his head and said, 'Sure fifteen would be more like it!'

Just then a young woman, whom I took to be his daughter, came out of the house. She said that we could take the range away for nothing as it was only scrap to her. The old man looked so disappointed that we *gave him the ten pounds. He was well pleased with the deal.*

The proprietor of the garage agreed to make arrangements to have the range taken by lorry to Meanus. He would send a postcard confirming the date and time of delivery. The postcard duly arrived the following Tuesday, promising delivery around about noon the next day. We roped in Michael Doyle to help unload the range using his tractor and hydraulically operated manure bucket. We stood in the garden chatting and drinking tea, waiting for the lorry to arrive, but by two o'clock there was still no sign of it. Conscious that we were wasting the farmer's time, I cycled into Killorglin to telephone the garage. The lorry had broken down but would be with us by four o'clock. Michael did not seem to mind the delay, which was just as well as the lorry didn't turn up until four thirty. We unloaded all the separate pieces of the range and the fire bricks from the lorry, then Michael moved in with his tractor. Skilfully he manoeuvred the massive cast-iron hotplate – which was still bolted to the oven box and front panel and must have weighed more than a hundredweight – onto his manure bucket, lowered it over the garden wall and gently eased it off onto the grass. Job done. We paid the lorry driver and thanked Michael Doyle, who wouldn't accept payment, and went indoors wondering how ever we would get the great heavy thing into the cottage.

Somehow, between us, we managed to tip the huge unwieldy thing into the wheelbarrow. Susan steadied the load, and I pushed it across the garden, up the wooden ramp we had made across the doorstep and into the house. That was the easiest part. Only then, still out of breath from heaving our load about, looking at the existing fireplace, did I realise the problem I had set myself. The fireplace was too small. Within it above the floor there was no grate, but there was an iron bar across with hooks on which to hang pots over a fire. That was how we boiled water, in a cast-iron GWR signal box kettle, until we got a little Calor gas cooker. I was going to have to make a very large 'hole' in the stone chimney – and without tons of stone falling on me.

The other great problem was that this range was just a hotplate top and a front wall, on the inside of which was the box forming the oven. The fire grate was to the right. I would have to build the inside flues and firebox with brick, and all that internal brickwork had to be erected before the front and top was installed – so it all had to be done with great accuracy to match up with the cast iron. I had never laid any bricks but I had watched craftsmen doing it. I believed that if I thought carefully about what was required, measured accurately, I could, step by step, carry out the project.

To raise the height of the opening I needed a beam at the necessary higher level. Once I had inserted that, I could knock out the stones between it and the lower, wooden, lintel. I made a casting box about eight feet long and eight inches square and into this I energetically threw the cement. I'd used four of sand to one of cement so it was a powerful mix with steel reinforcing rods bent around like large hairpins for good measure. I tapped rapidly with a hammer on the sides of the casting box – I needed the cement packed in tight. While the cement was 'curing', becoming really hard, I took a cold chisel and 4lb hammer to the chimney breast to cut out a slot into which to insert the new beam. The breast was a thin skim of smooth, very hard, cement painted to look like bricks. Once through that I found that the chimney was made of the same rough stone as the walls – and no better secured. This made it easy to dig them out, but on the other hand it made it very easy for them to fall out! I was aware of a few tons of stone above and tried to prise the stones out delicately to make the slot to take the beam. Just once, a landslide started. I caught the stone with the heel of my hand and yelled to Susan to go and get the car jack. I stabilised the chimney with the screw jack under the errant stone and continued with the work.

I gave the new beam a week to set hard and between us we hoisted it up into position. I levelled it with the spirit level and some small stones and cemented it into position. Now I could knock out everything else and start on building the innards of the range.

While Adrian was doing all that I tackled the rust on all the outer surfaces of the range with emery paper and water – a filthy, soul-destroying task. At last, about three weeks before Christmas, the range was in place, black-leaded and shining, ready to be lit. Ceremoniously, Adrian set a match to the pile of newspaper and kindling in the grate. Immediately smoke poured from every conceivable crevice and refused to go up the chimney. In minutes the room was filled with smoke. We opened doors and windows but the filthy stuff refused to go away; it circled and hovered about us increasing in density as more poured out of the great black monster. We didn't know whether to put the fire out or leave it, in the hope that the smoke would diminish as the fire became hotter. Then, to our relief the smoke gradually diminished to a mere wisp and disappeared altogether after about an hour. The place stank but we felt the benefit of the beast quite quickly as it warmed the cottage and I was able to cook soup on it for supper. But it was never an easy thing to manage. We discovered that the range liked to be lit regularly first thing in the morning. If we lit it later the cast iron became too cold and condensation would build up, causing water to drip onto the embryo fire resulting in a smoky start. The range always seemed like a stubborn animal who had to be cajoled, seduced and pampered with tasty bits of fuel before it would condescend to work for us.

It is extraordinary to think that when the range was still in pieces on the kitchen floor, and with no modern facilities in the cottage, our friends Paul and Susie Dye, having been warned about the state of the place, came from Bristol to stay with us for a long weekend towards the end of November. We gave them our double bed in the east room and we slept on some old double bed springs, inherited with the cottage, and padded with blankets, in the kitchen. At least basic needs were catered for as we had the chemical loo, discreetly installed in the west end room amongst the packing cases. We also had the luxury of a 'Baby Belling'-sized Calor gas cooker placed upon an upturned tea chest, cleverly disguised with a red and white cloth, so we could cook proper meals for our visitors. That was the best we could do, but they were great friends, game for anything.

In their most recent letter to us they had said that they planned to catch the last train from Rosslare to Mallow and asked if we could pick them up from there on the Friday evening. Adrian replied, 'Yes, come, come, come.'

We also asked them to bring £2 worth of second class stamps for SAEs for Adrian to use in his enquiry letters for research, and 7lb of short-grain brown rice, unobtainable in Kerry.

We set out in good time to meet the train, arrived at Mallow after an uncomfortable car journey along badly made roads, and found the railway station deserted with no sign of a train. Adrian went to speak to the signalman in the box at the end of the station and came back with the news that the train had been cut from the winter timetable. Just to be sure, he checked the passenger timetable – there was no such train. What should we do? Should we go home or wait indefinitely in case a message was sent? Then a door in the station building suddenly opened and a dishevelled-looking porter came out onto the platform. He had clearly just woken from a nap. He had a message for someone by the name of Horn (that must be us – people were always mistaking Vaughan for Horn or Baughn). It was difficult to make out his words as he spoke in a thick Cork accent, but he seemed to be saying that an English couple were waiting to be picked up at Care. Care? Where was Care? The porter repeated his message and with the help of a woman who had just walked onto the platform we worked out that he was saying Cahir. Cahir? That was about forty miles away!

We needed petrol and had to knock up the local garage. The proprietor took pity on us and kindly allowed us to fill up in return for a cheque as we had no cash. We arrived at Cahir station at about midnight, having taken only two wrong turnings – the signposting was awful and we didn't have a map. The station was a beautiful, dark grey stone building with Gothick diamond-paned windows, illuminated by a conveniently placed modern street lamp. But there appeared to be no sign of life and when we got out of the car there was only an ominous silence. We looked at one another in disbelief. Was this a wild goose chase? Then a side door opened in the darkness of the building, revealing a brightly lit room. Two people shuffled out, weighed down with packages and bags. There was a murmuring of goodnights and thank-yous, the door closed behind them and a voice called out, 'Thank *goodness – we thought you'd never find us!'*

Paul and Susie squeezed themselves with weary thankfulness into the back of the Beetle, having put their luggage into the front boot, and we began the long journey back to Kerry. They explained what had happened. British Railways had given Paul an Irish timetable that was 'in use until further notice', giving the time of the last train from Rosslare to Mallow. On arrival at Rosslare he discovered that a new timetable had recently been issued and the times of the Mallow train altered. The nearest they could get to us, waiting at Mallow, was Cahir. They left a message with a porter at Rosslare and caught the train to Cahir. On arrival they found that the station was about to close. The station master allowed them to wait in the waiting room with the gas fire full on, so at least they would not be cold – and he sat with them and engaged them in happy conversation too. They had a long, anxious wait, making tired conversation while sitting on hard wooden benches, not knowing when they would be rescued. We arrived home at about three thirty in the morning, having driven about 170 miles for the round trip.

In spite of the ignominious start, the rest of the visit was successful. Paul and Susie generously treated us to meals out and as Sunday was warm and bright we drove them across the mountains to Valentia Island. Our guests saw little of the wild mountain scenery though, as they were overcome by the soft Kerry air and spent most of the journey fast asleep in the back of the car, gently snoring the miles away. On Monday morning, before they were due to catch their train home, we all walked down to the River Laune to fetch water for the cottage. In contrast to the day before, the morning was cold, sharp and bright. A layer of frost covered everything and crunched beneath our feet as we walked. In the gaps between the hedgerows we glimpsed the Reeks in the distance covered in a light blanket of snow. We knew then that winter had begun. A winter that for us would be without electricity, running water or a proper loo.

The conditions in the cottage would probably have been classified as 'unfit for human habitation' in England, and we might well have been prevented from living in it while we restored it. In Kerry we were left alone by the authorities to work out our own salvation. We viewed a medieval winter with equanimity – we had each other – we were a team – we would have the range for cooking and heating and there was plenty of dead wood lying around to supplement the turf we had bought. Outside of our partnership we had one great morale-lifter – a sense of total freedom to be ourselves. I had been very sad to leave the railway, but that feeling had been replaced by the new-found exhilaration of freedom and of an adventure starting. We drove Paul and Susie to Killarney station, hugged them and thanked them for their support. Then we turned for home – and in spite of all it *was* home. Neither of us felt any desire to go back to England. We had escaped and we were perfectly contented.

Christmas 1975 came and went very quietly in Limerick with Susan's family. My brother Gerard, and his girlfriend Cathy, descended on us as the Old Year drew to a stormy close. They came from England, via Cork, on a motor bike, which did not seem to me to be the most sensible mode of transport in mid-winter. Gerard enlivened the last evening of the Old Year by telling us that our move to Kerry was wrong, that our plans were impossible and that we were on a hiding to nothing. He was a highly qualified electrical engineer and I would have liked him to draw me a circuit to show how an electric ring-main worked. But he was too busy telling us how wrong we were. Leading up to midnight Susan got out her last bottle of rose-petal wine from Midford Castle, and we stood and drank to all our good fortune for 1976. Gerard and Cathy remained seated. Under those circumstances, to sing 'Auld Lang Syne' was inappropriate. Next day the gale of the Atlantic deepened and the rain came down 'whole water'. The fury of the storm was too much for our thoughtful visitors. They decided to go home. They mounted their motor bike and seconds after letting in the clutch they had vanished into the torrential rain and the mingling spray from their wheels.

Chapter Ten
Goats

In Kerry ordinary events often turned into adventures. On 8th January 1976 we went to an auction sale at a house in Boolansheera, near Ballyheigue in north-west Kerry, in the hope of finding a cupboard or a bookcase for the cottage so that we could empty another tea chest. The advertisement in 'The Kerryman' had sounded promising: 'High quality furniture, some antiques', in comparison to the usual 'Modern furniture and effects', which in our experience meant mostly rubbish. We asked directions of the proprietor of a tiny shop in Boolansheera. A tall gaunt man wearing large black boots, shapeless grey trousers and a dirty, torn jacket, he ushered us inside and insisted that we sit in the greasy, grubby armchairs by the fire. He plied us with tea, crisps and biscuits and regaled us with stories about Irish and ballroom dancing – he had been quite a dancer in his time. Soon we were anxious to get away, not wishing to be late for the auction, but every time we made to leave he said, 'Sit down, sit, you're here, there's plinty time, take 'oor 'ase.'

Somehow we made our escape and arrived at the sale five minutes before the advertised start of two o'clock, but no one else had arrived – the Irish dancer had been right after all. The venue for the auction was a large, two-storey, modern nondescript house situated on a bleak hilltop overlooking the sea. It was bitterly cold. The owners of the house were American and we could see why they were selling up and going home, their dreams shattered in this forbidding landscape. They invited us to come inside and look around while we waited for the auction to begin. We didn't think much of the furniture, but as we had come such a long way we thought it worth waiting to bid for an Edwardian mahogany bookcase, not exactly beautiful but practical, and we were also interested in a box of bits and pieces labelled Lot number 102, containing four brass doorknobs that would do for internal doors.

The house filled up with prospective buyers but the auctioneer and his assistant did not arrive until three o'clock. By then there was no room for them in the packed house.

'All outside!' the auctioneer commanded from the front doorstep and the vendors ushered people out into the cold – we were grateful to go with them for the atmosphere inside had become suffocating. But then he stopped the exodus, crying 'Enough! The rest of ye can wait inside and I will conduct the sale from here.'

He was a man full of his own importance, confident that no one would question his decisions. He took up a position on the front doorstep surrounded by people on the outside, more on the inside who were jumping up and down trying to peer over his shoulder, and others who leaned precariously out of the ground floor windows hoping to catch the action. The sale began.

'Lot number 1!' cried the auctioneer. 'Where is Lot number1?'

'In the house, sir,' called the vendor from halfway up the stairs.

'Bring it out then, man, bring it out so we can all see it!' cried the voice of authority.

But the poor man could not move without creating mayhem on the stairs, so two able-bodied men offered to do it for him. There were cries of 'Move aside, move aside' as the men struggled towards the sitting room for Lot number 1 – a three-piece suite. As the men came outside with the sofa the crowd on the inside had to move outside to let them pass and the auctioneer was pushed aside in the crush. Regaining his balance and grabbing his hat, which had fallen off, he went to reprimand those who had pushed him. But the guilty ones had disappeared into the crowd, which presented an innocent façade, so the red-faced auctioneer had to content himself with quietly swearing beneath his breath.

At last, Lot number 1 was in full view of almost everyone. The bidding started and had reached ten pounds when the rain began. The auctioneer looked up at the sky with a worried frown and continued the bidding uncertainly until twenty pounds was reached, when he declared that we should all go inside again because of the rain. The three-piece suite went first, the auctioneer and his frustrated assistant followed, *then the crowd squeezed inside once again. Mesmerised by the antics of the auctioneer, we followed the people in, looking forward to his next trick. The bidding for Lot number 1 was re-started because everyone had forgotten the position and in the end the three-piece suite was sold for thirty pounds.*

Lot numbers 2, 3 and 4 were sold without incident, but the atmosphere inside the house had become decidedly unhealthy with so many bodies jammed together. The auctioneer started the bidding for Lot number 5 accompanied by a terrible sigh and an exaggerated wiping of the brow. He whispered something to his colleague, who abandoned his post and made for the front door. The young man stuck his hand outside and cried, "Tis spitting, sir.'

'Right. Everyone out!' shouted the auctioneer.

The crowd groaned in unison and began to shuffle outside where the rain had turned to an icy drizzle. The auctioneer took up his former position on the doorstep and instructed the people who stood behind him in the hall to leave a gangway for the lot numbers to be brought out. The sale proceeded smoothly then, each lot being brought out so that everyone could see what they were buying, and taken in again when the sale was completed so that the items would not get too wet. Twenty lots came and went before the Edwardian bookcase came into view. The bidding began at two pounds and Adrian nodded – he was in the running against one other bidder. The bids went up to ten pounds when Adrian pulled out and the auctioneer said, 'Sold to the man on the right.'

Heads turned towards the buyer, who looked completely astonished. 'But,' he protested, 'my bid ended at eight pounds.'

There was a murmur from the crowd and the auctioneer whispered urgently to his assistant, who appeared to know nothing about the state of the bidding.

'Who was bidding besides this man?' asked the auctioneer.

Adrian indicated that he was. The auctioneer scratched his head in bewilderment and decided to end the confusion by asking Adrian if he would buy the bookcase in question for nine pounds.

'No, no!' shouted the vendor from his usual position on the stairs.

'It's a good piece of furniture – it must fetch at least ten.'

'Oh,' sighed the auctioneer, then to Adrian, 'Will ye give me ten for it then?'

Adrian said he would and the auctioneer cried 'Sold!' and moved triumphantly on to the next lot.

We rescued the bookcase before it was snatched back into the house and, having paid the auctioneer's assistant, lifted it onto the roof rack of the car and covered it in a polythene sheet. The rain had turned to sleet, it was icily cold and already very dark at half past four. We calculated it would be eight o'clock before Lot number 102 made an appearance, so we decided to forgo the brass doorknobs and make our way home.

The day after the auction the sun came out and the weather remained kind to us for two weeks. Susan and I worked outside every day it was possible, clearing grass and brambles, roots and all, ready for planting come the spring. Working on the top garden I used the spade to hack out the rank grass and create bare ground, then dug that and carefully weeded it to make space for the potatoes – the 'earlies' and the 'main' crop.

In the middle of January Pat's cow calved. We were invited round to look. Pat had the calf and the mother in the open-sided barn, behind a shelter of straw bales. Agnes was there and Pat's dogs too. Kerry was standing on his hind legs, front legs on the bales, ears cocked, eyes bright and his head moving to follow the dancing, frisking movements of the calf. Susan and I stroked the little creature; its hair was soft and curly.

In the evenings we continued to plan our future: restore, re-roof and extend the cottage. As well as growing our own food we wanted to keep goats and poultry and to build the various shelters they would need. All that work! I had never, except at school, which didn't seem to count, sawed a plank of wood, but the challenge was exciting – why shouldn't I be able to do all that? My confidence grew out of the splendid prospect of what could be achieved. I took measurements, made drawings, wrote on them building instructions to myself and, while doing this, realised that George Puttock's carpentry lessons at Garston Lane School, Wantage, had been helpful. I had, in fact, done some sawing – and some joinery – aged thirteen and fourteen. When I began to work out the amounts of wood and other materials the new roof needed I found that, without effort, I was using arithmetic at which I had always been such a tearful dunce, because now I had a real and exciting reason for needing the knowledge. One of my first accomplishments was building a sturdy work table for carpentry in the garden.

In the corner of our lower plot, in the right-angle formed by the north-south line of trees on the dyke and the east-west wall bordering the road, we had a ten foot by fourteen foot hut. The walls of this had been made of very pebbly concrete shovelled into a shuttering of planks. It had no door and was roofed quite effectively by large branches cut from a vast Leylandii tree that grew out of our roadside hedge – and which I later cut down. I properly roofed the little building, put in a door frame and made a door. Now we could store turf in there *and* have a stable for goats!

The whole last week of January 1976 was freezing cold. The Atlantic gale roared unceasingly through the trees. The days were like twilight in the pouring rain. The climax was reached on the 31st. The gale was actually frightening as its force threatened to tear off our corrugated-iron roof, which rattled as if in terror. The tall ash trees a few feet to the rear of the cottage howled as if they were in agony. Cars passed the cottage throwing up a bow wave that arched over the low wall and fell onto the front garden.

The rain and subsequent flooding showed me that to grow food successfully in front of the cottage – and if we were to keep the inside of the cottage dry, for it was four inches below the level of the road – some defensive measures were required. I dug a trench two feet wide and a foot deep across the gateway. In that I placed concrete blocks on edge and filled in with large gravel. Watching how the water moved in the garden I saw that I could help the water to keep away from the front door. I made a doorstep and dug the garden 'beds' with curved edges, making the edge of the grass form guiding channels following the natural inclination of the water.

92

Doing this I discovered that the water was flowing to a centrally placed drain. It was an excavation lined with thin, flat stones placed on edge and bridged across the top with more such stones. It was dug on a falling gradient to encounter the ditch in Eddie's field. I brought my channels round to make use of this excellent solution, provided possibly centuries before.

Susan and I were often a little bit 'under the weather' during these winter months. Maybe that was because we had to drink the river water, although it was always boiled first. Maybe we didn't boil it for long enough. Some days I woke up feeling dizzy and sick, but if the weather was clear and with a cup of tea and some soda bread and marmalade inside me I would totter outside to dig and gradually I felt better. One morning, while hacking away at the tussocky grass, I started to get a toothache. I fought against the pain for three days and on the fourth day it could no longer be borne.

There was no dentist in Killorglin, and the next nearest town was Killarney, thirteen miles away. I had earlier noticed a tarnished brass plate advertising a dentist on the wall of a house in New Street. The tarnish did not awaken suspicion. I pedalled to Killarney, leaned my bike against the wall under the deeply tarnished professional plate and knocked on the door. The door was opened by the dentist himself. He said he wasn't busy and could attend to me at once. I pointed out the painful tooth as we stood in the hallway.

He said, 'Hmmm – 'twill need a filling.'

He led me into a room devoid of any furniture and told me to wait. I was about to find out why he was at a loose end. He came back with a hypodermic syringe in his hand and gave me a pain-killing injection where I stood, saying, 'That'll take a few minutes.'

He went out, shutting the door and leaving me standing there.

My mouth started to fill with spittle and there was nowhere to spit it. My cheeks began to bulge and even then I couldn't bring myself to gush onto his floor. Ah! There was a sash window looking out onto a derelict back yard. The bottom sash lifted easily enough – was this a regular practice here, I wondered, as I discharged the contents of my ballooning mouth onto the weeds outside. A minute later the dentist reappeared and asked me to follow him. He led me into his surgery. The place was a museum. Standing beside the chair in which I was to sit was a tall metal post with a horizontal bar at the top and an armoured hose hanging from it. He was going to clean out and fill my rotten tooth with a treadle-operated drill!

I had been 'numbed', but even so the battering of the rough clearing drill turning at relatively slow speed was very uncomfortable. My head was vibrating and I was shaking as I wrote out my cheque in payment. And then there was the long cycle ride home.

I passed Eddie Moriarty's place on the bend and as I approached the humpy bridge over the swift-flowing 'little river' I saw a cormorant shuffling along in the middle of the road towards me. It was a miserable sight. On the ocean and in the air I had admired their grace and skill. This fellow was waddling slowly as if he wanted to be run over. When I was closer I saw he was trailing a shotgun-blasted wing along the road. He must have been in such pain. I was extra sorry for him since my pain had been cured. His could only be cured by death. Poor bird, victim of some cruel man.

Susan had been looking in *The Kerryman* for goats for sale and we looked at 'For Sale' postcards in the windows of shops in Killorglin, but it seemed that goats were not to be found in the ordinary way in Kerry. But, like so much in our life together, even our own first meeting, we found what we wanted by chance. We had accumulated an inconvenient amount of household debris, and the fact dawned on us that we had not yet seen a council rubbish collection lorry. There was an informal and disgusting rubbish dump in the avenue of trees along our road just outside the town, but we could not add to that, so we asked Agnes.

'Where do you take your household rubbish?'

'Well, you can – er – take it to the 'Dump' at Milltown.'

Her voice conveyed an embarrassment – the idea that this was not an advisable course of action. Agnes gave us directions. We followed her instructions, and turned right just before Milltown. As we went along we remarked on the wonderful display of seagulls ahead, swarming and wheeling chaotically in the bright, sunny, sky. Then the 'Dump' came into view. A chain-link fence was plastered with paper and packaging, in crazy patchwork. A little further on and the actual refuse rose into view. Access was through a muddy gap in the fence. There were pigs everywhere, young and old pigs, tunnelling the carelessly piled, acres and acres of rotting food, clothing, paper, boxes, mattresses, electrical goods – anything that had to be thrown away. The seagulls foraging – being displaced by the tunnelling pigs – rose in screaming clouds of white and grey, settled back down and screamed at each other, fighting over rotting tit-bits.

We were spellbound, fascinated and horrified all at the same time. It was unique and ought to have been part of the itinerary of every tour bus full of US citizens looking for their roots through the rose-tinted windows of hermetically sealed motor coaches: 'Dublin – Bunratty – Killarney – Milltown Dump – the Ring of Kerry'. The 'Dump' was perfectly medieval and the pigs and the seagulls were having a banquet.

In the middle of February, driving home after a trip to Milltown Dump, we spotted a pair of very hungry-looking goats – a piebald mother with long, curved-back horns, and her tan kid, tethered on a muddy lawn in front of a bungalow. They were thin and the kid was nibbling her mother's hair. I stopped the car at the gate.

The two scrawny goats were tethered to a barked tree stump on the edge of the spacious garden surrounding the bungalow. They were not the only occupants of what had once been a lawn – there were ducks and drakes, guinea fowl, a cheeky cock bantam and his dull wives, several geese and a gander – the lawn had been grazed down to muddy earth nearly everywhere and there was fowl shit all over the place. We walked up the curving drive to the bungalow, trying not to slither on the shit and warding off the geese, who hissed as we approached. Dogs barked from somewhere behind the bungalow and a plump man appeared at the front door in response to the furore. We asked if he would sell us the goats. He said he would, but first of all would we like to see his aviary? We shrugged, not really interested as we wanted to inspect the goats, but the man insisted and ushered us around the back of the property. He put his finger to his lips to quieten us and opened the door to the aviary with a proud flourish. Birds of various sizes and colours flitted about the enclosure, or perched on branches to watch us with beady eyes, their little heads cocked to one side. The bird lover introduced his feathered friends to us one by one, giving their names and most detailed histories.

After what seemed an age we were taken outside again, where several hungry dogs lurked by the back door. They were the strays of the neighbourhood who came looking for scraps put down for the birds. The man kicked at them impatiently and shooed them out of our way as he led us around the bungalow and across the 'lawn' towards the goats. He talked all the while about his poultry, until suddenly he spotted a large white goose egg lying in the middle of the muddy garden, whereupon he shrieked with delight – apparently it was the first of the season.

The goats were bleating piteously in one corner of the garden. There was nothing for them to eat – they were half-starved.

'Sure, 'tis a pity about the poor cratures,' he said, and explained that he had run out of grazing and was therefore reluctantly prepared to sell them. He wanted ten pounds as they were both in kid. Taken aback by the poor condition they were in, we immediately agreed to his price. Surely we could provide them with a better home than this! We handed over our ten pounds. The bird man untied the goats and led them, bleating, to our car. Assuring us that they were well-travelled, he ushered them onto the back seat of the Beetle, where they stopped bleating and settled down remarkably well.

The kid goat lay down on the back seat of the car like a dog, but the big, old mother sat like a human, upright, on her bottom, perfectly composed, waiting to see what her fate would be. Looking in my rear-view mirror she made a really novel sight. I realised that anyone driving up behind us would see a goat's horns, head and neck in silhouette, and I imagined the driver telling the tale in the bar that evening: "'Twas an English car and didn't they have the Divil himself sitting on the back seat.'

Back at Meanus, we put them on a running tether along the hedge on the top garden and they set to, ripping off leaves and crunching up the thinner, tenderer branches with the desperation of famine. From pity our feelings towards them quickly turned to affection. They had shaggy, hairy trousers on their legs with leather patches at the knees. The mother looked at me directly, questioningly, with her yellow eyes and rectangular pupils. There was no subservience. Her little daughter just stayed close beside her mother and bleated. They were put into the concrete shed at night, which was immediately reclassified as the 'Goat Shed' and turned out to eat each morning, early. From the first morning we found great satisfaction in 'going to get the goats'. Very quickly we discovered that the mother goat was named 'Magsie' and her daughter was 'Nelly'. It also became obvious after about a week, that we had just about run out of hedges on which they could feed; goats do not willingly eat grass – they like leaves and tender twigs.

Susan and I discussed the practicality of a running tether along the very unfrequented back *bohreen,* but, still being in an English frame of mind, we thought it a risk to leave goats unattended at the side of even such an unfrequented lane as that, and the idea of asking any landowner for the use of hedges within his fields simply did not occur to us. The problem was solved by Eddie Moriarty. Although we rarely saw him he had been keeping a knowledgeable eye on the goats' diminishing rations because, a day or two after we had started to wonder how we could improve matters, he appeared at our gate.

'What are ye doing keeping those goats in your garden?' he asked.

'Well, they were starving over at Milltown, so we bought them…'

Eddie interrupted, for clearly they were soon to be starving with us. 'Yerra, haven't I hundred an' tin acres acraass the ditch?' he said impatiently, pointing to his field adjoining our plot. 'Put them in there – they won't be ateing anything my coos would want. Let them worrk away-a in there.'

He mooched away, with our thanks following and him unconcerned.

Susan and I went into Pat and Agnes's that evening for our usual conversational, musical suppertime. Pat, a truly natural musician, encouraged me to bring my descant recorder and thanks to his kindness I got a bit better on the instrument and eventually learned to play *The Rakes of Mallow, Saddle the Pony, The Irish Washerwoman,* and *The Wearing of the Green* a song that had interested me greatly for many years. It went like this:

O Paddy dear an' did ye hear the news that's going round?
The Shamrock is by law forbid to grow on Irish ground.
No more Saint Patrick's Day we'll keep, his colour can't be seen,
For there's a cruel law against the wearing of the Green.

O I met with Napper Tandy and he shook me by the hand,
And he said How's poor old Ireland and how does she stand?
She's the most distressful country that ever yet was seen,
For they're hanging men and women there for the wearing of the Green.

So if the colour we must wear is England's cruel red,
Then let it remind us of the blood old Ireland's shed.......

'Always play that in good marching time,' said Pat, enjoying the craic.

So we sat around the turf fire and told Pat and Agnes that Eddie had volunteered his field for our goats. Maybe Pat was disappointed that we had not asked him, but at any rate it disturbed him and brought up memories of the Irish War of Independence against the British and the Civil War that followed. He said, 'During the War there was ammunition stored up at Eddie's – they were IRA then.'

'Well,' I replied, 'that was a long time ago and Eddie has been very kind.'

Agnes broke in and passed around her home-made scones and jam, so the subject was passed over.

Chapter Eleven
Ducks

We had come to Ireland well kitted out for the interminable rain. Adrian had his long, black, gabardine railway mac and I had something similar in PVC. We had 'sou'westers' and wellies to keep us dry from head to toe outside, but it was a challenge to dry the dripping garments once we had come indoors. Hanging from nails in the porch, they dripped wetly into puddles on the floor and at night time we spread the macs around the banked-up range, the steaming moisture gently dissipating as we slept. Fortunately we did not have to put up with wet washing hanging all over the place. About once a fortnight I took our dirty clothes and linen to the Starlite Dry Cleaners and Laundrette in Killorglin. We went back to fetch it next day, all washed, dried and folded. This I considered to be a necessity rather than a luxury. Keeping our bodies clean was more difficult to manage. One day, looking in the car mirror, I saw that my neck was absolutely filthy. It was easy to become lackadaisical about washing oneself when there was no cold – let alone hot – water on tap!

Our capital was steadily dwindling away on everyday living and there was nothing coming in to replace it. To preserve as much as we could for rebuilding the cottage, we made cuts to our weekly expenditure. We stopped eating meat – our meals consisted mainly of soups and stews made from pulses and root vegetables, which were reasonably priced. Pat had given us a pile of turnips (called swedes in England) and we had a plentiful supply of kale from the garden.

We made do with just half a dozen eggs each week, two of which were used poached or hard-boiled as part of a main meal, three went into a quiche and the final egg was used in a cake. One or the other of us made soda bread nearly every day, which did not require yeast to leaven it but buttermilk and bicarbonate of soda. The result was a soft-

textured cross between cake and bread and it was quite delicious, especially straight from the oven with a little butter melted into the warm moist slices. That was our treat.

We made other economies too – not using the car unless absolutely necessary, and biking everywhere even in the coldest and wettest weather. We also rationed our postage to four stamps a week – Adrian's mother, hearing about this, sent an SAE in a letter to us. He had to write back with thanks, but 'It's no use putting English stamps on SAEs. The Queen's head won't carry a letter out of Ireland!'

Every penny was counted and nothing went to waste. One week the groceries came to £2.70, postage was 36p and paraffin 12p. It was a challenge to manage on so little, but we didn't find it depressing. We felt proud of ourselves and in control of our situation.

Adrian made a substantial cold frame using breeze blocks and constructed two timber and glass lids that could be raised and propped up to allow access and varying degrees of ventilation for the growing plants. The weather was fair at the beginning of March and we set early potatoes and planted shallots and onion sets into the rich, dark peaty soil of the top garden. In pots in the cold frame I sowed tomato, pepper and celery seed and for a few weeks we kept an oil lamp burning to assist germination and get the little plants off to a good start. I sowed peas in two trenches that had already been dug and lined with our kitchen waste from the previous month. Following the advice of organic vegetable growing expert Lawrence D. Hills in his book 'Growing your own Fruit and Vegetables', I scattered a layer of soil over the composting waste followed by a layer of lime, more soil, then the pea seeds, scattered randomly in each trench before filling it in and placing twiggy branches along the edges for support. I also prepared a seed bed for brassicas and by the middle of March had sown summer broccoli, cauliflower, winter cabbage, purple sprouting and Brussels sprouts. We were now picking spring greens as well as kale from the garden.

With the garden growing well and the goats in kid, in our wisdom we decided that what we needed now was a few ducks to provide us with fresh eggs. We decided on ducks rather than chickens because the self-sufficiency guru, John Seymour, wrote that ducks will patrol the garden and eat slugs. We needed something to keep the bally things down and as he also said that ducks laid eggs from February until mid-summer, we needed no further convincing. We decided that Muscovy ducks would suit our requirements and were not deterred when the local agricultural department said they were not a popular breed in Kerry. We were given the names and addresses of two breeders. One lived miles away in remotest mid-Kerry. We eventually found the village and, unable to find the house, asked directions from a passer-by. 'Follow the telegraph poles and ye can't go wrong.' Seeing our bewilderment, the man explained that the telegraph poles would lead us straight to the house in question as it was the only one in the neighbourhood with 'the telephone'.

We followed the telegraph poles. They went on for miles, along narrow and narrower lanes eventually bringing us to a large, modern two-storey house high in the hills and utterly remote. The house was set in the midst of a large ornamental garden where peacocks displayed their brilliant plumage and a beautiful swan with a damaged wing preened herself beneath the canopy of a lush rhododendron already heavy with scarlet blooms. We stopped the car on the gravel drive and were immediately surrounded by a score of birds of all descriptions: farmyard poultry, water fowl, peahens, and numerous pretty pink-cheeked children. The boys and girls, all between the ages of about three and ten, shooed the birds away and shyly accompanied us to the door of the house where they called for 'Mammy'.

A tall, regal-looking woman of about forty-five came out to greet us and the children skipped away. We were shown into the drawing room where we were served with tea and scones spread with gooseberry jam by a pretty girl of about sixteen and became engaged in an interesting conversation with the mother. She told us about herself and her family. She had thirteen children but seventeen people lived in the house altogether: ninety-year-old gran, a dear old woman dressed all in black who tottered about the kitchen laying the enormous table for tea, the mother, father and the mother's brother, two children under school age, ten at school and one at university. I asked her how she coped with so many and she replied that it was God's will and He gave her the

*strength to do it. She also looked after the poultry and ornamental birds
– about fifty in total – while her husband and brother ran a large dairy
farm.*

*It wasn't long before it was time for the family to have their tea and
we took our leave. Two beautiful blue and green/black Muscovy ducks
were handed to us, nestling comfortably in the bottom of a sack. We
paid the miraculous mother, waved goodbye to the spotless children
who clamoured around the car, and set off in the direction of
Castleisland to call on the second breeder whose address we had been
given.*

This place was as difficult to find as the first. We stopped to ask the
way at a farm. Over the front door of the farmhouse was a stone
into which was carved: 'This house was burnt down by Crown
Forces. Rebuilt Oct 1921'. I knocked on the door, the man of the
house opened it and I asked for directions. These were given
willingly and politely and when I had them I asked about the
dreadful inscription above our heads. 'That's not all about it,' said
the man. 'The 'Tans' were looking for members of a Flying Column
and when they found none they shot my grandfather and came back
the following day and set fire to his house.'

There was no animosity towards me. I said I was sorry for that,
thanked him and walked to the car in a very sombre mood.

Still we couldn't find this second address and stopped at another
farm. It was a large house and as I walked towards it I saw how very
dingy it was, the front like a scrapyard. The front door did not look
as if it had been opened for years. I went to the side, into the yard,
to find the back door. It was wide open. It was dark within, great
flagstones, shiny with damp. Someone was standing at a sink. I
knocked.

The person turned towards me. It was an old woman, filthy and
emaciated. Her clothes were rags of cloth, coloured a deep shade of
filth, seemingly smothered in grease, evenly, all over. It was as if she
had put on a man's woollen vest at the rear of a garage, thrown
away after being used for weeks as an oily hand wiper. Her face

seemed smeared with black oil. She turned to come towards me. She did not take steps, but flung herself forwards. Grabbing hold of the draining board for support, dragging her legs till they were again underneath the rest of her body, she came closer to daylight and I could see that her face was not marked with oil but with bruises. Her fingers, clutching now at the door post for support, were fixed bent like talons with nails just like a dog's claws. Behind her, curtains at a window were like heavy-duty cobwebs. She was rigid with arthritis and must have fallen many times. I told her I needed directions and she said there was 'a young fella out in the yard'. I turned to look and found him standing directly behind me. He was strong, smooth-skinned, handsome. He gave me the directions concisely in an educated voice. How was this old woman so uncared for?

We eventually arrived at a long, low, pink-washed farmhouse, very simple and old-fashioned in comparison to the almost ostentatious farmhouse of the previous poultry breeder. We interrupted the owners at their evening meal, but they insisted that we come in and join them. The four children of the family left their places at the table so that we could sit down, there being no other chairs, but we politely declined their kind offer of food. The family helped themselves to potatoes bursting out of their skins from a steaming saucepan in the middle of the table. The farmer stabbed them with a knife and peeled them deftly with his dirty thumb until there was a big pile on his plate alongside a huge chunk of boiled bacon.

As the family ate we talked until halfway through the meal when the Angelus sounded on the television. Eating and conversation stopped. The mother, father and children all crossed themselves and remained silent, quite at ease until the bell stopped ringing, when they resumed their meal and the talking began again. I was impressed by their devotion, unfazed in the presence of English strangers. When the meal was over the woman quickly bustled about making tea for us.

After we drank it, I asked her if I might use the lavatory. She looked aghast at the request, and for a moment I thought she did not approve of such things being mentioned in the company of men, but it transpired that she was embarrassed because there was no inside loo. She took me outside and explained that it would be a waste of time and money to have 'conveniences' installed because they were soon to build a new house, which would have a bathroom and all mod cons. I agreed wholeheartedly, wondering all the while where she was taking me because I expected the outside loo to be somewhere convenient to the house. Eventually we halted by a large barn where she opened a sliding wooden door, ushered me inside and closed it again behind me. I was confronted by a huge brown bull, calmly munching hay, and several new-born brown and white calves curled up on beds of straw. Obviously this was where I was meant to go! I squatted down, keeping my eye on the bull, only to come face-to-face with a little girl who was peeping at me through a gap in the door. There was an urgent murmur of voices. The girl disappeared and I was left in the company of the bull and the calves to wee in peace.

Outside, the mother was waiting for me together with the little girl, who clung to her mother's skirts and looked at me with huge brown eyes. They showed me the Muscovy ducks. There were two drakes for sale and several ducks, although few of them looked like the two we had just bought. They were mostly either grey and white or black and white, but all shared the same red-wrinkled skinned faces characteristic of Muscovy ducks. We wanted to buy a drake and a third duck. The woman asked me to choose those I liked best and I pointed to a large blue and black drake and a smaller white and grey female, both seven months old apparently.

Two of the children, a boy and a girl aged about eight and ten, shooed them all into a barn and there followed a great deal of frightened quacking, accompanied by squawking from the chickens who were also in the barn, as the children tried to corner the selected birds. At last the little boy caught the drake. The mother produced a sack and the struggling creature was put into it followed by the white and grey duck, which the little girl had managed to secure by one wing. The sack was tied before I thought to ask how much she wanted for the birds, and I was taken aback when she said eight pounds for the pair. This was clearly a rip-off as we had only paid two pounds each for the pretty little ducks from the other breeder, but I felt it was too late to object and handed over my cash with a forced smile.

We left the barn to find Adrian engaged in deep conversation with the farmer in the milking shed. Who was soft-soaping whom? It was dark when I eventually dragged Adrian away and as we drove off the mother and her children waved goodbye to us from the cottage door, and the farmer held open the farmyard gate, cocking his hat as we passed through. 'Ha, he can well afford to do that,' I said grimly, and explained that we had been ripped off.

On that first night we put the two pretty black and blue ducks into one overturned tea chest in the porch and the white duck and the drake in another and secured the openings with netting. In the morning we discovered − oh, we were so naive! − the floor of the porch completely covered in foul-smelling shit into which the netting had been trampled, with the ducks sitting snugly and innocently in their respective boxes. Never again, I thought − they would have to make-do with sleeping in the shed with the goats until Adrian could build them a house of their own.

At first the ducks behaved themselves well, and I was glad I had followed John Seymour's advice. They seemed to confine themselves to the top garden where we had provided them with a sunken bath full of water, keeping clear of the front garden where we grew most of the vegetables. At night we confined them in the goat shed, securing the netting more firmly to the tea chests so they could not get out.

On the third night we put the goats and ducks away as usual. There was a tremendous storm that night, which we slept through, only to discover in the morning that in spite of the ancient and modern drainage channels, the garden was waterlogged and the goat shed was inches deep in water. The goats were standing on the turf pile looking decidedly fed up. The ducks were floating on the water inside the tea chests, their heads bobbing up and down close to the tops. They looked decidedly comical but thoroughly at home. After breakfast we bailed out the water in the shed while the ducks paddled happily in the garden and the goats stood miserably on the field track, the only dry ground in

106

Eddie's field. Only when we had finished bailing out did I notice to my intense dismay that every single daffodil head in the garden had been destroyed by the ducks. For a week or so we had enjoyed a marvellous display of daffodils and now there was nothing but wet, crumpled yellow petals scattered all over the garden. That was the beginning of the nightmare.

The first job for me after the flood was to draw up a plan of a lean-to duck house against the goat shed. It was finished on St Patrick's Day and from then on the ducks were properly housed at night-time.

During the long dark evenings we had a couple of ordinary, non-pressurised 'hurricane' paraffin lamps hanging from the ceiling, one over the kitchen gas stove and one at the centre of the ceiling. I sat at the table and worked on my book, *The History of Uffington Station and the Faringdon Branch*, typing on foolscap paper on the 1942 'Imperial' office typewriter garishly illuminated by the table-top Tilley lamp. Around us, ancient stone walls, stripped of all plaster, were waiting to be restored. During the day the kitchen was my workshop, where I made door frames and doors and whatever else was required in wood.

We needed electricity. The Irish Electricity Board (ESB) had agreed to connect a supply to the house if there was something in the house to use electricity. I went to see Murphy, the electrical goods shop and contractor in Killorglin, and asked them to come and install a fuse box and a single light bulb to begin with. They promised to send an apprentice to do the job.

'He can do it on his way home from work one evening – he passes by your door,' said Mrs Murphy smilingly in a 'there'd be nothing to it – you can give the lad a fiver' sort of way. I fitted a rectangle of wood to the wall over the inner door to the kitchen for the lad to attach a fuse box.

The apprentice called in one March evening and fixed a fully equipped fuse box and ran a wire to a fitting in the ceiling over the centre of the room. From a junction box he dangled a wire with an empty bulb holder. It took him half an hour. He charged me £25! I was disappointed. It was a lot of money for us and we didn't have it in the house. However, I didn't argue, he'd done the work I'd asked for – we hadn't agreed a price beforehand – and I'd had a lesson in electric wiring.

I told the beardless youth I would draw the cash from the bank in the morning and leave it at Murphy's shop. The look on his face showed that he had not considered this eventuality and that it was not a pleasant one for him. Next day I went to the Allied Irish bank and drew £25 – in £1 notes. These went into a small envelope addressed to him, a pleasantly bulky package, and I took it into the shop. Mrs Murphy was indeed surprised and a bit embarrassed. Maybe she had a word with the young lad, but nothing further, to my advantage, followed.

Sometime later in the month, when the weather was cold, a gale blowing and Susan ill in bed with a very painful stomach – or appendix, as we later found out, something she had suffered with, on and off, for many years – the ESB erected a pole opposite the cottage, brought a wire into the house and connected it to the fuse box. We paid £180 for the connection. I fitted a double three-pin wall socket and ran a wire to the fuse box so I could use my electric drill. In time I would completely wire the cottage. Electricity – what a blessing!

Building a new roof would now be a lot easier. I could also use my 'Gnome Alpha' enlarger and set up a photo printing business, printing photographs from my collection of railway negatives. That would require an outlay in paper, fixer and developer. It wouldn't bring in much, but 'half a loaf is better than no bread' so I'd have to invest! The problem was the lack of piped water to a tap to direct a stream of water to wash the chemicals out of newly developed films and prints. The water in the little river was clean enough to be our drinking water, boiled first, so film could be washed while still in the spiral holder in the developing tank using ten changes of river water over ten minutes. The fibre-based photographic paper needed to be washed free of chemicals by being turned frequently for an hour under running water. The new 'resin coated' paper only needed two minutes – but also in running water. If prints are not properly washed they fade over a few years.

I thought of my father's 1920s print washer. This was a galvanised metal cylinder, fully perforated, with water-wheel-type pockets at one end. It revolved in a galvanised box and was placed in the family's bath. Water, running through a hose, filled and overflowed the tank while rotating the cylinder: the prints tumbled over in constantly changing water, carrying away the chemicals in the paper. Taking this idea, I made a drum having wooden ends with plastic netting wrapped around. It revolved on wooden legs, forming an 'A'. The netting had a door. I loaded in some resin-coated prints and placed this ingenious contraption in the little river across the field.

The drum revolved and the prints tumbled encouragingly. I left them for half an hour and returned to retrieve them for drying. Lifting the washer out onto the bank I saw a night's work was useless. The resin coating had been scratched and white backing paper was showing. The damage would not have been caused if I had used conventional photo paper, but that took five times longer to develop, an hour to wash, and dried curled, so there would be more time spent flattening the prints.

With fibre-based paper my river washing system worked well. I put the washer back in the river. Eddie Moriarty, on his morning patrol, saw it and was, of course, puzzled. He realised it must be something to do with me and came round to ask, 'Is that your *yoke* in the river?'

'It is, Eddie.'

'What's it doin'?'

'Washing photographs. You don't mind do you?'

Eddie was puzzled at the idea of washing photos, but I was English after all, so he just shrugged and said, 'Worrk away-a,' and wandered off.

One morning when I went to retrieve the prints I found the drum empty. The fastening had come undone. I looked about, frantically, and there, downstream, where the river took a sharp bend, was a night's work piled up against the bank. Well, they certainly had been well washed. I waded in and was waist deep when I reached them. None were missing. I took them home, dried and flattened them and posted them away. Later on I got an order for fifty postcards. As that would be a very time-consuming job, I did not feel like risking them to the river. If only I had tap water.

Visiting Agnes one day, I told her and her sister Eileen, who was visiting from California, about my print washing problem. She and Eileen were bird-like, small in stature and bright-eyed, and gave close attention. I finished my tale of woe: 'I wish I had a proper dark room with a sink and running water.'

Eileen immediately solved the problem. 'You can use the garage and utility room at my bungalow in Ownagarry. I never stay there so it would be good to put it to some use.'

Eileen's bungalow was maybe two miles from us, past John Foley's and along the pot-holed back *bohreen*. I took enlarger, developer, fixer and paper there. I cycled there with an empty bucket hanging on the handlebars and the books of negatives in a plastic bag. I could now use quick-acting resin-coated paper and I'd wash the fifty postcards under running tap water in a deep sink, stirring them around until I felt they'd all had a good wash. The finished prints went into the now water-filled bucket and I cycled home – at two or even three o'clock in the morning. Susan said she could hear me coming home by the rattling of the bucket handle on the bike's handlebars in the stillness of the Kerry night.

Chapter Twelve
Bees

Our next purchase was a hive full of bees. In February we had attended a talk on beekeeping given by beekeeper Tom Prendergast. We were very enthused and after the talk we asked if he would sell us a hive of bees. He said he would – for £40 – and brought them to us in March with various pieces of essential equipment: a smoker, a 'super', which is like a second storey, and crates to hold the frames of foundation wax on which the bees would build cells and laboriously fill with honey. We positioned the hive at the back of the top garden in the point of the triangle, facing south but shaded by the trees lining the road.

The nightmare of the Muscovy ducks was going from bad to worse. Since the daffodil episode I constantly kept an eye on them, restricting them to the top garden, but once when my back was turned they completely demolished the lettuces, not eating but attacking them, leaving torn and broken leaves strewn about just like the daffodil heads. Their action seemed to have no other purpose than complete and wanton destruction. We bought some garden netting and secured it around the vegetable beds until the place looked like a battlefield, but it didn't deter the ducks! Clearly they needed much more space than we could provide. Also they hadn't started laying yet and we were paying for feed with no return. We were learning a hard lesson, and decided we had learned enough. We put an advertisement in 'The Kerryman' to sell them and waited anxiously for a reply. Meanwhile a poultry advisor from the Local Agricultural Department suggested that Indian Runner ducks might be more suitable for the confines of a garden. They were good layers and ate less than the heavier Muscovy ducks. We were given the address of a poultry breeder in North Kerry.

In early April we drew £20 from the Allied Irish Bank in Killorglin and drove over the hills to Tralee to buy two Indian Runner ducks from a Mrs Goodwin. The drive was sixteen miles each way so we were going to make a day of it. We planned to take our dirty clothes to the laundrette on the way, buy groceries in Dunnes Stores and get some small items for carpentry. Having done all that we went to Mrs Goodwin's house, but she wasn't in. The day was bright and sunny with great white clouds, so we drove out to Camp, then Castlegregory, to see what remained of the Tralee & Dingle Railway. For a very rare treat we bought Guinness and sandwiches at a pub and sat by a lagoon from the sea, and with the Slieve Mish Mountains behind us, ate while we enjoyed the wondrous views.

At five o'clock we went back to Mrs Goodwin's. She was very apologetic for delaying us all day and this may have had a bearing on the fact that she let us have the two beautiful fawn and white Indian Runner ducks for three pounds. Describing our horrors with the Muscovy ducks, Mrs Goodwin told us that they were too young to lay. Driving home out of Tralee and breasting the crest of the climb, the wondrous sight of Dingle Bay greeted us, miles ahead and hundreds of feet below, reaching westwards and silvery out to the Atlantic with the astonishingly theatrical, purple silhouette of the Reeks filling the horizon away to the left.

The Indian Runner ducks were as prettily comical as the others were ugly and useless. We called the pair Cora and Clarice after the twin sisters in Mervyn Peake's *Titus Groan*, because like the sisters they were completely dependent upon one another and did everything almost in unison, walking about upright a bit like penguins. They looked as if they should each wear a cloche hat with a long string of pearls dangling from around their necks. Next day each duck laid an egg. To be on the safe side we kept them in a pen in the top triangle of the garden, and although they often escaped and caused a nuisance in that way, they were nowhere near as destructive in the garden as the Muscovy ducks, being only slightly partial to a bit of lettuce. Three days later we sold the Muscovy ducks for twelve pounds, so got our original outlay back.

Good Friday was a remarkably silent day. No cars, no tractors, not even a bicycle passed by. Even the rooks in the great, tall trees all around were silent. On Easter Saturday, after a bit of lunch, Susan suggested we get some fresh air and exercise and we cycled to Beaufort to look at the Ogham stones, the derelict water mill and generally enjoy the place. On the way home we went into McGillicuddy's woods and collected fir cones for the fire. We had an Easter Day dinner with Agnes and Pat, and after pudding Anne O'Neil arrived with her beautiful daughters, Pat played his accordion and the girls danced for us.

Easter Monday was a very beautiful day. We went into Pat's home field to plant our main crop potatoes. Pat had volunteered a 'drill' – a furrow, a hundred yards long, for our main potato crop. It was seven rows in from the edge of the field, a good position. The soil was rich and dark from decades of manure. Pat had never allowed a tractor on it; the heaviest weight on that loam was a horse and plough and harrow or his donkey and two-wheeled trolley. The field was bordered by great ash trees on three sides, rising tall and serene, the sun lighting through their young, light green, spring-time leaves.

It was a peaceful pleasure to dig out the furrow, kneel on the soft, dark soil and place the seed potatoes at their correct distances, then to spade up the soil into ridges, burying the seed. Pat was working away at the same job, his dogs sitting at the field gate watching the proceedings. As we were coming to the end of the job, and beginning to feel exhausted, Agnes came out with tea, bread and cheese and Easter cake. We sat propped up against the grassy west wall and ate with the contentment of a hard job well done. The next day I set out on my own for England. It was a wrench to be leaving Susan and this fairy place, but there was work to be done, and a list of railway history questions to answer in the record offices and libraries of Reading, Swindon and London.

While Adrian was away I worked contentedly in the garden, enjoying the calmness of repetitive tasks: sowing, hoeing, weeding and watering.

I constantly fetched water for the growing crops as for once rain was in short supply. One afternoon I decided to pick some dandelions to make wine. I walked down the bohreen, towards Ownaggary townland, picking dandelions as I went. The air was heady with the sweet, almost musky scent of gorse and the hedgerows were full of tiny violets and huge crowds of pale yellow primroses. Buds were bursting everywhere. I met Eddie along the way. He was cycling with two pails of milk hanging from each handlebar and clanking gently together as he went. He had been to milk his cows in one of the fields above. He greeted me civilly and stopped briefly while I stroked his dog, before setting off again. I gazed after him as he cycled away on his rusty old bike and thought about his extraordinary character and the life he had led. I wondered did he ever travel, or had he always lived at Meanus? He wasn't a man you could ask.

My sister Karen and two friends, Noreen and Sinéad, came on Friday evening to stay the weekend. It was lovely to have company. Next day they were happy to muck in with the animals and do whatever needed doing. We gathered mint leaves from the riverside, where it grew in abundance, filling the air with its powerful minty aroma. Foraging was great fun and over the months I had experimented with various gathered ingredients to supplement our diet. I used young nettle tops for cooking and eating like spinach – not too keen on the texture – and tiny green hawthorn buds added a subtle flavour to a bacon and onion suet pudding. Dandelions not only gave us flower heads for wine and leaves for salad, but the roots made a very good substitute for coffee. We dug some up and dried them in the oven until they were brittle, before grinding and percolating.

Sunday was so fine that we had lunch in the garden, much to the amusement of passers-by. I was proud to present a completely home-produced meal: herb omelette, lettuce, dandelion leaf, spring onion and radish salad, followed by mint 'sorbet' and delicious smoky-flavoured dandelion root coffee. I was halfway through making the 'sorbet' when I realised I had no means of freezing it, so we ate it in its 'whizzed-up' unfrozen state. Needs must – it was OK! Karen and her friends left that evening and suddenly I felt very lost and lonely, but there were still five days to go until Adrian's return.

Later in the week, while shopping in Killorglin, I noticed an interesting-looking man languidly smoking a cigarette on the doorstep of the antique shop in the triangular 'square'. I thought he must be Henry Dodd, the owner of that establishment and of the salmon smokehouse down by the bridge. I went up to him on spec to ask for a job. Henry was unlike any other Irishman I had ever met. Aged about 40, maybe six feet tall and comfortably built, he spoke with a soft, educated, Anglo-Irish accent and exuded sophistication and charm. He offered me a job working Wednesday afternoons in the Killorglin shop and all day Thursday in his shop in Killarney. The arrangement suited me perfectly and the weekly wage of four pounds with commission of five per cent on anything sold seemed like riches! It was agreed that I would start work the following week.

I came back on the Swansea-Cork ferry, arriving early on Friday morning, 30th April. From Cork I set out on foot, thumbing a lift; I hadn't enough money for a long-distance bus. By car and Shanks's pony I finally got to Killarney, where I was in time to catch the bus for Killorglin. I left a telephone message for Susan, thanks to a kindly shopkeeper, to tell her that I would be arriving on the six o'clock bus. I was weary and weak after ten days of travel and the heavy concentration of research at the Record Offices. In my wallet the vital cheque for £330, my royalties from *A Pictorial Record of Great Western Signalling*, would help to defray my costs of ten days travelling. As the bus rolled into the triangular 'square' of Killorglin I saw my wonderful Susan waiting on the far side of the space. She came tearing across. Just being home revived me.

We treated ourselves to a wonderfully relaxing weekend, but on Monday life went back to normal. We took the goats to their browsing area in Eddie's field. In the evening Adrian went to bring them home while I prepared supper. He came back five minutes later, arriving breathless at the door, and gasped, 'It's Nelly, she's had her kid.'

We rushed down to the field and there sitting beside Nelly on the grass was a dear little dark brown kid with a white star on its forehead. It was perfectly dry and must have been some hours old.

As we approached, the little creature staggered to its feet and Nelly bleated to us, half in greeting and half in warning. I picked the little thing up and settled it into my arms much to Nelly's alarm, as she didn't seem to realise where her kid had gone. Eventually she understood that her kid was safe and slowly we made our way back home with Nelly following closely and Magsie impatiently in the lead, straining the rope that Adrian held. In the goat shed we made a cosy nest of straw for the new-born female kid, whom we called Kitty.

She did not settle at first and tottered precariously up the turf stack and tried to balance on the topmost sod but quickly tumbled down again. After suckling from her mother for a few seconds, she fell exhausted into her little nest. Nelly positioned herself carefully beside the sleepy bundle of soft brown fur and Magsie heaved herself into a comfortable position as far away as possible from mother and kid.

The next day we decided to tether Nelly in the garden so that we could keep an eye on her and her kid. Magsie was led away to her usual field, protesting loudly at the separation. Nelly chorused in agreement, but thankfully they both settled down to eat. Nelly was ravenous and quickly demolished the few brambles in the hedgerow that bordered the top garden before attacking the ivy, which had entwined itself around the stump of an old elder tree. As she was busy eating, her kid, now much more stable on her feet, began to jump and frolic, at first not wandering far from her mum but gradually becoming more daring until she landed all four feet in the (luckily) open cold frame. She pranced about, destroying several small plants before we could get her out and lower the lid. Then she tried to play with Cora and Clarice, who were completely unresponsive and walked sniffily by with their beaks in the air.

The kid turned away and came face to face with Baby Cat. They sniffed one another curiously but the little goat felt suddenly threatened and ran quickly back to her mother. At the end of the week we began to milk Nelly, tentatively at first, never having milked a goat before. Her udder and teats were very small so we could only milk with a finger and thumb, which was incredibly difficult and time-consuming. The milk came out in thin broken streams, taking fifteen minutes to fill a teacup. But as time went by our milking technique improved and soon Nelly's milk was squirting out and we had half to three-quarters of a pint of milk a day. But milking time was bedlam as Kitty frolicked all over the place and jumped from the turf stack onto the back of whoever was kneeling down milking, often upsetting the milk. If we took her outside she would bleat loudly and Nelly would refuse to be milked. In the end we built a pen in one corner of the shed into which Kitty was placed during milking time and we enjoyed some peace and calm. Later the kid spent the whole night in the pen so that we would benefit from the night milk – eventually one and a half pints – and Kitty suckled all day long.

Susan spent her first afternoon at Henry Dodd's antique shop on Wednesday 5th May and came home from Killorglin looking flushed and gorgeous after her cycle ride and bursting with an account of her experience. Her mentor at the shop was Mrs Lucy, a plump, florid lady of great charm and eccentric stories. Like the one about a man who had bought a ram while 'under the influence' at the monthly sheep and cattle fair. He then returned to the bar and forgot about the ram. The ram wandered the town and became very friendly. He approached people as a dog might, but if, on seeing him approach, the person shooed him away he would lower his formidable horns and charge. The man who had bought him never claimed him. Mrs Lucy said the ram was tolerated about the town for many years.

Animals on the loose figured largely in her reminiscences. There was the sheep who, taking advantage of the shop's open door on a hot day, came in, said a loud '*Baaaaa*', and went out again. On another occasion a wandering bullock half entered but was stopped by Mrs Lucy, with his rear end still on the doorstep. He couldn't turn and wouldn't reverse, but was dragged out by three strong men, hauling on his tail. She didn't say, but I imagine he made a china-vibrating *'Mooooo'* during that operation.

Henry Dodd's antique shop stood next to a public bar and was rented from the bar owner. There was no lavatory attached to the shop and a weird condition of the renting was that the lavatory in the bar was forbidden to the antique shop minder. Mrs Lucy had an agreement with Mrs Moriarty of Moriarty's ironmongery shop on the other side of the triangular 'square' to use the toilet there, so Susan could use it too.

The owner of the pub next door died on 2nd May. The bar was closed at once and a notice was pinned on the door announcing the date and place of his funeral. The notice was wreathed in Dickensian fashion by black cloth. People made the sign of the cross as they walked past. The funeral of such a well-known publican was the largest Killorglin has seen for some time. All the shops in the marketplace were closed and the funeral procession brought the town traffic to a standstill. At least one hundred cars followed the hearse and as many again following on foot – all except Eddie Moriarty, who walked in front of the hearse.

I needed the rest of the week to recuperate from the English trip, but in that time I did the planning and the sketching to familiarise myself as to what would be needed to renew the cottage roof and to build a bathroom extension. I became a 'Quantity Surveyor', calculating the quantities I needed: eighteen-inch concrete blocks, sand, cement, timber – four by two inches, and other sizes – hardboard sheet, corrugated roofing panels made of a cement-like material, nails, polythene collars through which the roofing nails would pass, then getting estimates from the two builders' yards, Chub Connor's and Richard Boyle's. I made drawings for two ladders and constructed them as soon as I got the materials. Each had three-by-two-inch main beams, but one I made fifteen feet long and the other seven feet three inches long. I cut slots in the beams to take, at a tight fit, two-by-one-inch rungs.

Susan was constantly thinking of ways to increase food production from our small plot of land. She was thinking 'tomato plants' this week, as those she had sown from seed had either succumbed to the cold or been ruined by Kitty jumping into the cold frame. After a lot of fruitless 'asking around' she was told she could buy some plants from a woman living at 'The Herons' at Caragh Lake. After lunch on Sunday, having bought petrol with Susan's first wage packet, we set off in the Beetle.

The day could well be described as 'the fairest that ever was seen', so we had a glorious drive into the hilly lanes to Caragh Lake. The Herons was a large, newish, two-storey house, the front of it swathed in a great froth of pale pink blossom that delighted Susan; she found out later that the plant was called Clematis montana. We knocked on the front door, standing under the twisting, arching cloud of blossom. The door was opened by a woman as pretty as the flowers. She was pleased to see us and with only half an explanation from us as to what we wanted, she swept us into the large and luxurious interior.

This was the first time we had seen why the scattered settlement of Caragh Lake was famous. She led us through to a conservatory as large as our cottage at the rear of the house. From the huge windows there was a superb view across and around the eponymous lake caught in the vast bowl below the Reeks. She left us to settle, somewhat astonished, into large wicker chairs filled with soft cushions and went off to bring us tea and cake. Susan and I looked at each other, and I whispered, 'She's genuinely pleased to see us as if we were long-lost relations.'

Susan said, 'It doesn't seem the sort of place to buy tomato plants – I was expecting more of a garden nursery place.'

The woman, whose name neither of us can remember, told us her husband was away on the lake most of every day, or over at Dooks for golf. She had been an actress and had worked for ENSA (Entertainments National Service Association) during the Second World War, travelling to the various countries to entertain the troops. She had worked with John Gielgud and Arthur Askey and Ernie Wise and generally had a 'very interesting war' – but she had no tomato plants. She said she did grow tomatoes but bought her plants from Latchfords in Tralee.

We drove home discussing her and our first experience of Caragh Lake: beautiful homes of wealthy men and lonely wives. When we got back to the Meanus cottage, we sat in the car and stared at our little place with its rusty roof and tiny windows, and burst out laughing – at ourselves!

The weather at the start of May was utterly magical. After lunch one Sunday we went down through Eddie's field to the Laune, sat on the bank and looked across the river to the hills way off to the north. The goats wandered over to be with us. We didn't always tether them if we knew we were going to be at home to keep an eye on them because the tethers tangled in the gorse bushes, shortening the space on which they could browse. The goats viewed us as part of their herd – and not necessarily the superior part. Sitting on the banks of the Laune, listening to the ripples of the river over rocks, having the goats nearby, we felt very contented.

Magsie goat was at this time heavily in kid. On 20th May I dug out more of the rank grass to make another vegetable plot for Susan, then fetched my Rolleiflex and went down the field to see how Magsie was getting on. I saw a group of animals standing in a circle, looking down – Nelly goat and her kid, bullocks, cows and their calves. I got closer and saw Magsie standing on the grass, at the centre of the circle, facing a big gorse bush in bloom. She had just given birth to a black and white kid, just like her, its umbilical cord still attached, hanging down, clear, like an empty sausage skin to the kid, which was flopped and limp on the grass. Magsie was making a hoarse coughing noise, as if trying to bark. Then I saw our skinny Baby Cat in the bush, looking predatory as a hyena. I shooed her away, then picked some tender hazel tree shoots for Magsie. She gobbled them hungrily and I left her to clean up.

At five o'clock it was time for them all to come home. I picked up Kitty, took her to the shed and went back for the others. Magsie had got her kid onto its feet and was walking up the field path with Nelly alongside, the kid tottering behind. Magsie was looking back for her kid, stopping for it catch up. I picked up the newborn – it gave a little screech – thinking Magsie would follow, but Magsie stood, bleating and looking all around for her kid. I bent down to show her the kid and she came on. I walked backwards, bent double so she could see the kid. It was slow but not as slow as waiting for the little creature to make a walk of three hundred yards on its own legs. I got them into the shed, set the kid down with its nose against Magsie's pink and distended udder, and walked out to leave them in peace.

As I did so Eddie Moriarty stepped over the garden wall from the road. He was an amazing person for materialising when interesting things were happening. The surprise was always enhanced by his wonderfully individualistic clothing. He went into the shed for half a minute, then legged it back over the wall, saying, 'The little cratur's feeding, he's wagging his tail.' Then he was gone. That was how we discovered that we had a male goat. Next morning I went into the shed to milk Nelly and saw the baby billy goat standing on the highest point of the six-foot pile of turf sods in the corner. He was strong and lively. I knew then what a 'pang in the heart' meant: he was destined for the butcher. Billy goats give no milk.

Chapter Thirteen
The new roof

Mangan's lorry delivered all the roof materials on Saturday 23rd May. The tin roof we had over us, while rusty, did keep the rain out and now the idea of taking it all off, then undertaking the large task of putting on a new one, scared me. I thought I had prepared myself, but now, stacked outside, were timbers nine feet by four by two inches, the embryonic rafters, and the fifteen-footers that would be the wall plates – expensive material in front of me, and I was scared of cutting it incorrectly, of making a mistake in measurements. Would I ruin £250-plus worth of materials and end up with a roof that looked like something out of a book of fairy tales?

This fearful lack of confidence bred procrastination, which went on for days. The weather was unsettled. I started to catalogue my photographic negatives. When I went into town to fetch or order something I would stand on the Bianconi Inn corner, opposite Jimmy the Monk's grocery store, usually joining two or three mountainy men in their cloth caps, collarless shirts and their ancient two- or even three-piece suits.

I was there on the day of the May cattle fair. The cattle were all over the triangular 'square', the pavements slippery and the gutters running with their green ordure. O'Shea from the cycle shop saw the huge bus coming over the many-arched Laune Bridge and called out. It was 'The Yanks' looking for their roots. From the bus, cameras were pointed. Our group was immortalised as the 'Real Ireland', myself included. I was very happy to be an assumed Kerry man. The doors opened with a sophisticated *puuf* as if on a spaceship, and the Americans descended, rotund and wobbly, cameras slung around large necks. The lean, horny-handed mountain farmers stared. A few minutes later an American gentleman approached us, having walked down from the triangular 'square'. In a voice of total amazement, he said, 'There are cattle in the streets and there is *filth* all over the shop windows and pavements.'

'Yerra – 'tis Fair Day,' said a mountainy man respectfully.

A few of the more venturesome returned down the hill with the *filth* on many a pair of shoes. The tourists heaved themselves into their air-conditioned conveyance. I wondered if, by the time they'd got to Glenbeigh, the smell would be such that they would wish they could open the windows.

Around eleven o'clock next day, working in the garden, I heard the crunch of tyres on the gravel outside Pat and Agnes's cottage, the iron gate squeal open and footsteps on the gravel to the front door. I heard Agnes cry out with astonishment. A short while later, Anna, Agnes's niece, came hurrying round, bursting with the news that the previous day she had married her big, incredibly cheerful, Galway man, Vincent, and would we please come round to help them celebrate. A quick change of clothes and we rushed off after her. The small front room was very noisy, crowded with the occupants all talking loudly together.

Agnes was there with her sister Eileen and another sister, Nora, Anna's Irish-American mother. We were introduced to her and to Anna's Polish-American stepfather, whose name was also Vincent. The excited shouting was because the family were astonished at Anna's shock announcement that she had married Vincent the day before. Her mother was very cross and was demanding to see the marriage certificate. In the subsequent rather heated exchanges, confusion arose over which 'Vincent' was being referred to. Anna said her stepfather should be 'Richard' for the duration and Nora didn't see why the other Vincent shouldn't have his name changed. Pat, who was still in overalls, having been working the vegetable garden when the visitors arrived, was ordered to get himself into a suit and Agnes and Eileen went off to the kitchen to make some tea and sandwiches, leaving Susan and me to talk to the new arrivals.

123

Nora was taller and larger than her diminutive sisters and louder too, but in a friendly American way. She told us that since being in Ireland she had had to *walk twice*. While she was talking, 'Richard' was telling me how much larger were the refrigerators of the US of A and recommended the sort of refrigerator I should buy for the cottage. He was a refrigeration engineer. After the refreshments it was time for photographs. I dashed home to get my Rolleiflex, and came back to find that they had already marshalled themselves on the front grass. The photo shoot over, Nora hurried away in a huff and *walked* the whole mile and a half back to her hotel in Killorglin, followed minutes later by 'Richard'.

Anna and Vincent stayed a couple of nights with Agnes. Before they left they sold us a 'Dansette' record player. To have music to listen to was a great blessing. We dug out from a tea chest my collection of long-playing records and went to bed listening to John Williams playing Albéniz's 'Granada' suite, and indeed we made love to the accompaniment of the gorgeous melodies.

The next day Susan drove away to Henry Dodd's antique shop in Killarney. I tidied the house, collected whatever eggs the ducks had donated, milked and fed the goats and tethered them down in Eddie's field. The two cats stood outside the goat shed each morning waiting for their ration of milk. They trotted, circling, around me into the cottage and I gave them their share. Then there was only the matter of 'The Roof'. I went outside with a ladder, climbed to the west end roof and began to take off the slates. By one o'clock only the flimsy ceiling lay between our bedroom and the open sky, and by five o'clock, just as Susan arrived back from Killarney, I'd removed the corrugated iron to the east-end chimney. Together we managed, in spite of a stiff breeze, to arrange an acre of polythene sheeting over the rafters front and back of the cottage, and over the west-end chimney all the way to the east chimney. That done, we walked down Eddie's field to fetch the goats and Susan told me about her day. It had not been entirely pleasant. She had sold an antique for £13, earning a five per cent bonus, but had

had to fend off an idiot male customer who had suggested they have a weekend together in a Limerick hotel.

That night we were both woken by horrible nightmares. A gale was blowing the polythene sheet, which was making a noise like thunderclaps – snapping upwards then slamming down under the drive of the westerly gale. Even a gentle breeze at night caused the sheeting to heave and fall, making rattling, cracking, crackling noises. Each morning we had to take off the polythene in order to work on the roof, then replace it at night to protect us from the weather. After a while the polythene began to tear, so we took it off permanently. Luckily for us, the summer of 1976 was one of serious drought: the grass of the Emerald Isle eventually turned brown. So we were only woken by a rain shower twice in the six weeks that the roof was uncovered.

In a day I had taken down all the rafters, some of which were made from two lengths of tree branches nailed together. By the end of the day, under a clear blue sky and a blazing sun, three quarters of the cottage walls were clear of rafters. Next morning I tore down the flimsy tongue-and-groove ceilings over the bedroom and kitchen. With the top of the walls clear from the west-end gable to the east-end chimney, I could create a level top on them using cement, ensuring that the front and back walls were the same height. On that I laid the eighteen-inch concrete blocks. The blocks had to be level along the wall top, easy enough, but also level and perfectly parallel with those on the opposite wall. I made a levelling and distance gauge, a three-by-two-inch timber, fifteen feet long with two vertical pegs set twelve feet apart. I could put this across from block to block and rest my spirit level on it. At intervals in the line of blocks I set upright a three-quarter-inch-diameter steel bolt with a broad washer and a nut so that when the timber wall plates were laid they would be drilled to fit over the bolts as a push fit, then nutted down.

I also made a doorway in the rear wall of the cottage in preparation for the bathroom extension. Because the cottage centre walls were just big stones bedded on earth, it was a simple matter to

125

take down enough to make the necessary gap. The result was very irregular, but with cement I plastered up both sides to make a smooth-walled opening three feet wide and six feet high. Water for cement-making had to be fetched from the little river. With the stones cemented I laid strong timbers across the gap to form a lintel. Shortly afterwards I put up the door posts and made a door.

At the back of the cottage I saw the need to keep the rains of Kerry off the foot of the old wall. I dug a trench along the foot of the wall and filled it with the stones I'd taken out of the wall to make the doorway. I covered the stones with several wheelbarrows of cement, smoothing it as a fall, away from the wall. I had some cement left over, so at the west end I plastered over an area about three feet by two feet, and in the wet cement, using a screwdriver, I drew the track plan of the biggest, busiest signal box I ever worked – Hinksey North.

The third of June was our fourth wedding anniversary. Only Susan remembered – I am sorry to say I had forgotten. Susan went into town to the antique shop and I worked in hot, sunny silence at the block-laying. She came home around five – with a bottle of Guinness! Anniversary bliss. She also brought the good news that Henry had asked if she would like to cook dinners for himself and other clients like the Caragh Lake set and Richard McGillicuddy, remnant of the Anglo-Irish aristocracy. Henry suggested she should charge £1.50 per diner. He also suggested swapping some smoked salmon from his salmon fishery for one of Susan's lemon meringue pies! Susan cooked our anniversary dinner and we shared the Guinness. Afterwards we walked in the warm evening gloaming across Eddie's rough meadow to the banks of the little river. We sat on the bank of close, rabbit-cropped grass, and watched as the river rippled endlessly past, the shadows grew longer, the red evening light gave way to starlight, and we kissed long and lovingly.

The next day Susan went to work in Killarney. I had to push the VW to get it to start. I milked the goats, getting nearly half a gallon, and took them down into Eddie's field. I cleaned out the goat and duck houses and weeded two beds of vegetables. The sun was scorching hot so I took a bucket for water and walked down to see how the goats were getting on. They'd got in under some gorse bushes for shade. I walked across to the little river and along its shady bank. It was cool where the trees leaned over from both banks, making light and shade on leaves and on the wonderfully rippling water. I stopped where the bank was broken down to make a path to the river. In the shallow, sun-sparkling water was a big fat trout. He was facing upstream, his tail moving from side to side to hold his position. Surely he was sunbathing! It was a great shame to disturb him, but I had to get water. In a silver flash he was gone.

I turned for home across the bumpy field. Not a cloud in the sky. Carrauntoohil and the Reeks sharp against the bright blue. The sun hot and the air still. Fifty yards from our garden I started to hear a great humming-buzzing. I hurried out onto the road to our gate. Over the top garden the air was densely packed with bees. I thought they were swarming, but they seemed rather to be shooting high and low past each other in a great mass – without hurting each other. I realised it was a frenzy rather than a swarm. In a few minutes the dance was over and the bees began to return to the Prendergast hive. In the next few days we saw male bees, the drones, lying around on the ground, and I realised that what I'd seen was the mating flight of the Queen.

Work on the roof was beginning to make me very stressed. I had to cut the top and bottom ends of each of the nine feet by four-by-two-inch timbers to make the new rafters. Accuracy of measurement and cut was crucial to producing a perfectly shaped roof. The *birdsmouth* at the bottom end of a rafter is a right-angled cut into what would become the underside of the rafter so that the cut would rest flat on the wall plate and a six-inch nail could be driven through it to the timber wall plate bolted down on the blocks. The top end had to be cut so that the rafter would, as it leaned inwards, have a perfectly upright face to fit against the ridge plank. The ridge plank had to fit tightly and perfectly level between the west gable and west chimney, then between the two chimneys.

I'd thought all this out on paper; I knew what I had to do but I was more than nervous of my ability to do it.

Prevarication prevailed again and I did anything rather than get on with the job. Susan became worried and cross about the lack of progress. I knew she didn't know the skill needed to saw by hand perfectly measured and *plane* cuts. I was panicky, making me feel angry, and I shouted at her loudly: 'I've never done anything like this before! If it isn't done right the roof will be a mess!'

I stormed outside, saw in hand. I laid my width gauge on the grass and put two four-by-two-inch rafters on top. I crossed the top ends of the beams exactly across each other and spread the bottom ends across the twelve-foot-apart pegs of the gauge. Where the beams crossed, I thought I could make a mark, giving me the line of cut. It was still, to me, a risk. Had I thought this out correctly? I was still wondering and worrying when the gate squeaked and Pat, who must have been in his yard and heard the shouting, came through carrying a carpenter's saw and wearing a big grin.

'What are ye doing?' says he.

'I'm trying to work out the angles to cut the rafters.'

He looked at the beams on the grass spread-eagled on the width gauge and asked, 'Where is the ridge of the roof to be?'

'Where it always was, Pat – you can see the mark on the chimney.'

'Right,' says he, and picked up a four-by-two, put it *across his knee* and sawed off a corner at the end of the beam. 'Cut all of them to that and ye'll be fine.'

Pat then saw that I was using my home-made ladders to get onto the walls. 'Ye'll need something more than a ladder to be getting a roof off and on,' he said. 'Ye must make some Kerry scaffolding to walk about on.'

The design was traditional, very simple and meant for a single-storey Kerry cabin. The wall of the house and the ground provided two sides of what, with the addition of a sturdy strut, became a triangular construction. He told me to screw two two-foot-long pieces of four-by-two together to make an 'L' shape, then to brace this diagonally with four strips of wood, two on each side. Two of these constructions were needed, one for each four-by-two-inch strut. Each was pushed up between the diagonal bracings and the assembly then placed against the wall. The vertical part of the 'L' pressed against the wall and the horizontal part supported a couple of scaffolding planks. The two supports could safely be placed fifteen feet apart and with the sturdy planks I had a secure platform to walk about on. I felt elated at the clever simplicity of it.

So a day later, with the scaffold in place, I used Pat's cut as my template at the ridge plank end and using the pegs of the width gauge I marked where I should make the uppermost cut of the *birdsmouth*. I did everything painstakingly so as to have one rafter cut exactly – to act as the template for all the others. Eventually I had a stack of nine foot by four-by-two-inch rafters sufficient to be erected over the room at the west end, and for thirteen feet from the west chimney along the kitchen wall to the east chimney. With Susan's help I got the ridge plank wedged and levelled between the west gable and the chimney. Eight rafters nailed into place, four on the front wall plate and four at the back. The *birdsmouth* and top cut had been done so well that the beams rested perfectly on the wall plates, while the top ends came flatly together – like two hands joined in supplication for a miracle. I grew happier as my confidence in myself grew until it was a real pleasure – putting a new roof on our house.

To take a break from work Susan and I often walked down Eddie's field to sit by the Laune to watch the goats. We were very fond of our goats – they were clearly fond of us. We liked to sit on the bank at the junction of the little river with the Laune, where there were sandy beaches and lines of sand 'cliffs', two feet high. While Magsie and Nelly grazed, the two kids played energetically, leaping off and jumping up the banks, bouncing on four stiff legs. I photographed them at play, but they moved too fast and were blurred on the negatives. A game they played was for Kitty, the older kid, to go down on her front legs and shove her head and neck under the billy kid, lift him up and carry him about until he fell off. When we left them untethered they would, at sundown, wander home in procession, mother Magsie, daughter Nelly and their kids. They'd announce their arrival by standing at the garden gate and bleating. They didn't like being out at nights.

Putting the new roof on was thirsty work, but luckily, much to our surprise, we had plenty of goats' milk to drink. Magsie gave us four pints a day and she was much easier to milk than Nelly as her udder was big and her teats bottle-shaped, although she did have an extra nipple that sometimes got in the way. The remainder of the milk went into tea, making yoghurt and cottage cheese. The kitchen area underneath the polythene sheeting was still usable after I had waged my daily battle against the filth and the dust and mopped up after a night of rain – so I could still cook. One day I made some lemon meringue pies, a couple for Henry in exchange for smoked salmon and one for a supper with friends who were coming to stay. As I was cooking this, our American acquaintance, Nora, drew up outside in the car they had hired and asked Adrian how work was progressing. He told her and added by way of making conversation that I was making lemon meringue pies.

'Gee whiz!' Nora exclaimed. 'I can't make a lemon meringue pie in a proper kitchen, let alone in that … that …' she pointed at the near roofless cottage and was lost for words.

I was up on the walls erecting rafters on the central section when Eddie called from the road. He had Houlihan the butcher standing with him. Houlihan had come to buy some cattle from Eddie but was also wondering if he could buy the two kids from us. Houlihan was no stranger to me. When, occasionally, we bought some meat, we bought it from him. He was a big bull of a man, with a square jaw, his face pock-marked as the moon. His voice was loud, his manner cheerfully carefree. While Eddie explained, Houlihan stood relaxed, in shirt-sleeve order, biceps bulging, hands in the pockets of his voluminous trousers, expertly rolling a chewed matchstick from one corner of his mouth to the other.

He looked rough, but in fact he was the most amiable man. I was in his shop one morning when he was serving a woman from behind his great beech chopping block. He was steadying on the block with his left hand a two-foot-long section of beef ribs. In his right hand he held a great cleaver, which he brought down between the ribs with great accuracy and nonchalant speed. His customer ventured to suggest that the price of his beef had gone up since the last time she had bought any. Houlihan, meat cleaver at the top of his upstroke, froze. Looking directly at the woman he remarked, 'There's nuthin' cooms doo-un but the ree-en, Ma'am!' And *crack*, the mighty cleaver flashed and sliced down between the beefy ribs.

Houlihan the butcher was keen to emphasise that he did not want the kids for slaughter. 'I'd rather kill a bull than a kid, any day,' he said.

I agreed heartily and went on to describe the games that the two little animals played together. Houlihan raised his huge fist, index finger solid as the barrel of a Colt 45, pointing heavenwards. 'That'd make £5 in *The Kerryman* if you could only find someone to take the picture.'

He spoke with considerable force and I noticed how the matchstick stayed in the corner of his mouth even when his mouth was open. Eddie was embarrassed by his friend's protestations and was looking away, head down. He turned his head, still looking down, and hissed, 'He is a photographer.'

Houlihan was not to be deterred and thundered on about getting a photo and how I might encourage the goats to play, until interrupted by Eddie telling him – loudly – that I was a photographer. Just then Susan came out to join us on the road and both men turned to greet her in the respectful way of Kerry men.

'We only want to sell the billy kid,' she told Houlihan, then to Eddie, 'We want to keep the female kid. Would you mind if we had one extra goat in your field, Eddie?'

Houlihan at once took our side and volunteered Eddie's field. 'Sure, you wouldn't miss a bit o' grass the goat'd take, Eddie!'

Eddie was certainly irritated by Houlihan's manner even though he was only being amiable. He shifted about with his head awkwardly inclined and moved his hand, as if brushing away his friend's words and ways, while mumbling something along the lines of, 'Worrk away-a.'

So Billy the kid was sold to butcher Houlihan for a pound. He took it away there and then and Susan and I went indoors in silence, feeling like a pair of Judases. We never had him long enough to find out what his real name was. Having livestock entailed killing as well as kindness – we suspected that the kid would be slaughtered in spite of Houlihan's protestations to the contrary.

Two days later the butcher came back at breakfast time. He had a grim face on him. I went outside and he silently beckoned me to follow. He opened the boot of his car. I expected either that the kid would leap out – a Lazarus-like tableau at the roadside – or that it would be all in chops and joints. Without a word Houlihan lifted out a bag of *beefsteak*, patted me on the back gently and with a grim, set face went to get back in his car. 'B-b-but what must I do with this?' I stammered.

'T'would be good for roasting,' he said in reply, got in his car and drove away.

We realised that he'd sold the billy kid – live – to a person who would rear him, and the beef was our pay (as well as the pound). The grim face was intended to make the surprise greater for us. Joy was unconfined. For supper that night we had a beef stew with our own carrots, potatoes and broad beans. Only the onions were bought.

Chapter Fourteen
The Listowel goods

The next job on the roof was to nail hardboard over the rafters. With both sides of the roof to cover there was a lot of hardboard to nail down and tarred roofing felt on top of that. As the weather had turned showery with heavy squalls at times, we wanted to get the hardboard and its waterproof covering on as soon as possible. Susan helped by handing the ten-by-four-foot sheets up to me and I nailed them into position. We got the rafters covered just before darkness fell. We were so tired that we left the polythene sheeting off and went to bed exhausted. Luckily there was no overnight rain.

The next day Susan went into Killarney with washing for the laundrette and a shopping list for Dunnes Stores. She was booked to cook for Henry Dodd and his friends that evening. I milked the goats and took them down the field. In spite of a strong wind and threatening rain I came back to start laying roofing felt on the hardboard. I stood the short ladder on the scaffolding planks so that it was lying on the hardboard. It was very difficult, single-handed, to get the cut length of felt up onto the roof and position it. When positioned I laid on it and proceeded, often with body and arms fully extended, to hammer in another felt nail. There was indeed much stretching and leaning over. Eventually, up near the top of the roof, I leaned over too far to the right, my feet pushed the ladder to the left, and the felt, with me on it, slid over the hardboard to the right. I whizzed down, bounced off the scaffolding planks and fell onto the grass, missing the various lumps and piles stacked around.

It was a big thump. I lay there, dazed, then heaved myself up and went indoors feeling very shaky. Too shaken to work, I started to tidy up inside – I couldn't just sit around. With shaky hands I dropped a Pyrex dish and a plate. My anger of frustration was intense. Oh blast! More trouble! And I couldn't find the dustpan and brush to clear up the debris – in a fury I went round to Agnes to borrow one. Agnes, always the nurse, said, 'Oh my! You are very white – what has happened?'

I told her. Hot sweet tea was produced followed by an invitation to stay for dinner, which was nearly ready, and as Susan was out for the evening I accepted the invitation gratefully. I went home feeling a lot better.

As we got further into June, the weather became drier and hotter and the construction of the new roof was progressing steadily as I learned my work. The ridge plank was positioned along the middle section of the cottage, rafters nailed, cross-ties put in place, hardboard attached front and back, roofing felt put on, and the two-inch-square purlins, to which would be nailed the corrugated sheets, were nailed across the rafters.

Pat, and later John, came to help with lifting the heavy sheets of corrugated cement onto the roof. Each one was secured with screw nails, their heads hammered down onto plastic collars, going through drilled holes at the crest of the corrugations. Susan helped when she wasn't otherwise busy, but mostly I worked on my own, carrying, lifting, drilling, nailing. Every day was hotter than the last.

Sunday 27th June dawned beautiful and we were going to have a restful day. Susan made some tea and we walked outside, each with a full cup, into a perfectly still, silent, sunny morning. The wind held its breath. The trees lining all sides of our bit of land stood tall and handsome with leaves still a lighter and more delicate green of the spring that had just passed. Not an infernal combustion engine, however distant, combusted. No alien sound waves to ripple through the silence. The perfect stillness was only enhanced by cheerful birdsong. Behind our cottage we could see into Pat's farmyard, overshadowed by massively tall ash trees. The bright sunlight dappled through to the mucky brown, straw-strewn ground. Occasionally a cow would give a *basso-profundo* 'mooo', suggestive of contentment. On the top garden the bees were dancing in front of the hives. The hedge on the other side of the lane was festooned with honeysuckle blossoming in cream and red trumpets. Foxgloves stood tall along the road side, purple and white. Susan picked some tendrils of honeysuckle, and cut some roses from by the porch. We ate our breakfast with a beautiful table decoration.

Later, Susan's family arrived from Limerick. John, a beekeeper himself, was interested in how the bees were faring, so we went to look. They were working *en masse* on the wax foundation, filling the cells and building more. John advised that we needed to add another 'super' with more crates of foundation wax, but he thought it unlikely that we would get much honey harvest as the bees needed one 'super' of honey for themselves. We took our visitors down to the Laune banks to see the goats, to sit on the grass and paddle in the river. Baby Cat met us on the path down to the river and ran ahead. When we settled down, legs dangling over the river bank, she sat near us, then out of boredom, or jealousy, attracted our attention with a variety of feline gymnastics and made us all laugh.

The next afternoon I met up with the social worker for the St Vincent de Paul Society. As much as my life was full and busy I wanted to do something that would make a difference to other people's lives. Sister Clavier introduced me to a small family who lived in a little single-storey cabin at the edge of bogland to the south of Killorglin. It was arranged that I should visit them weekly to help the two little girls, aged eight and nine, with their reading and general education. There was also an older boy in the family. Their mother Anne was a young, warm-hearted woman and we soon became firm friends. I don't know the circumstances that had led to Anne and her little family living in that utterly primitive place with no modern conveniences – a bit like our cabin when we bought it – but fortunately it didn't last for long as Anne met and married Timmy and her fortunes changed. And what goes around comes around – Anne and her family would help us out in myriad ways in the future.

A few days later, on a hot and hazy afternoon, Adrian and I helped Pat to turn his hay. The golden field stretched away before us, displaying its neat rows of newly mown hay filling the air with its fresh, sweet scent. We worked to the sound of a combine harvester throbbing dully in the distance, its monotony occasionally disturbed by an anxious bleat drifting across the fields from where Magsie was calling to her flock. We turned the rows of yellow hay, exposing the damp underneath to the kindly rays of the hot sun until at last the final forkful was worked and Agnes came out with tea and scones. Time to picnic in the dappled shade of an elegant ash tree.

At four o'clock I left to spend some time with Anne's two girls. We decided it was too hot to stay inside reading and went for a nature walk instead. We stopped at a field where row upon row of ripe golden hay sloped down to where a man was working, pitching huge forkfuls into his hay cart, while his horse stood patiently by in the shafts. We sat on a large flat rock and while the girls drew some wildflowers they had gathered, I sketched the scene below me. The hot afternoon atmosphere had a still, quiet, timeless quality about it, as if we were forever suspended in some forgotten land.

On 4th July I set the Kerry scaffolding against the wall of the east-end room. The weather was boiling hot with no sign of a change so I had to work in spite of the heat. By the end of the day I had the corrugated iron off, rafters down, old wall plates off. I worked faster because I now had confidence that I could do the job. I had a scaffolding plank resting across from the front to the back wall to walk on. Susan handed up the ridge plank that I'd cut to be a wedge fit between the chimney and the gable end. Then came the rafters, setting the *birdsmouths* on the wooden wall plate. We got them all up, and they remained where we'd placed them by their own weight against the plank and the wall plate.

Then I saw that the *birdsmouths* were not sitting perfectly flat on the wall plate, nor against the ridge plank. Why not? I panicked. I'd cut the rafters so carefully and now the bloody things weren't fitting properly! I was furiously disappointed. I got down, swearing horribly.

Susan said, 'Calm down. Let's have some lunch.'

We ate in silence with my black cloud of despondency hanging over us. After food I went into Pat's potato field and spent an hour weeding the long ridge of earth covering our potatoes, wondering what the *hell* I had done wrong. Pat's field was always beautiful, the soil was so good to the touch, the grassy, flowery walls and the tall ash trees. Gradually sanity returned and suddenly I realised that the lack of fitting must be because the ridge plank was not perfectly at right-angles to the end walls. Bloody fool, Adrian, I thought. Happiness blossomed as a rose bud and I hurried back to the cottage.

With the ridge planks, rafters and their cross-ties fixed into place I installed the seventy-gallon cold water tank on the cross-ties as close as possible to the wall plate. When full it would weigh 700 pounds on a base of 480 square inches, which I reckoned as 1½lb per square inch, but I didn't trust my arithmetic and fixed extra struts vertically from the rafters to the cross-ties to assist in bearing the weight.

Work on the roof became lighter as July progressed. I cut the projecting ends of the rafters, just out from the wall a little way, using a tightly stretched cord from end to end to create a guide for pencil marks. A set square guided the pencil down the side of the rafter, then a careful, vertical cut could be made. The whole roof had required patient discipline from me. I remembered a saying of my father, which in those far-off teenage years sounded like his usual grumpiness: 'If you want to do anything properly you have to *hurt* yourself.' Or, in conventional terms, *take pains*.

Raising and fixing the long fascia boards to the rafter ends was a two-man job, and Pat very kindly helped. John finished the job with me when he came to stay. We were doing this one sunny Sunday when we heard a quavering, high-pitched voice approaching, singing. We stopped and turned round. Eddie's gate clanked and grated as it was opened and the man himself came through, pushing his bike. He mounted and, still singing, pedalled off, in a wobbly manner, which might have been due to the rough surface of the track. Perhaps he was happy for us, knowing that we had more or less finished the roof. I have wondered, years later, if he had some special connection with the cottage; perhaps he had been close friends with the people who had once lived there, back in the 1920s, when he and they were young.

The VW Beetle was parked close into the side of the road by Eddie's field gate, only used occasionally, as mainly we cycled everywhere to save money. It was in any case no use for carrying bricks, large or lengthy building materials or scavenged firewood. For these things even a bike was better! Several times I came home from Chub Connor's yard pushing the bike with lengths of timber tied down, resting on the handlebars and saddle. Once I brought home forty-three feet of three-by-one-inch timber cut into shorter lengths, placed across the handlebars and saddle, and eight pounds of lead sheet tied and hanging below the handlebars and below the saddle. The front wheel suffered a couple of broken spokes, but it managed without them.

In the second week in July fate struck in the form of a very drunk driver coming out of town. He was weaving to and fro across the road and swerved from the wrong to the right side of the road as he approached Eddie's gate on the left. He failed to straighten up and was stopped by our Beetle. The driver was a man from Churchtown. He said he'd pay for the damage. I was told later that he owned a whisky distillery in Tullamore. The damage was estimated by Mr Kelliher, the Killorglin car repair man, at £55. I cycled to Churchtown along the Beaufort Road, presented the estimate to the driver who at once wrote me a cheque. The VW went off to be repaired and we decided to sell it once it was mended.

I needed to visit the Irish Customs office in Tralee to get custom clearance sorted in order to sell the car. That was a twenty-mile walk. I set off after breakfast, taking a camera with me to photograph the railway around Tralee station. I was very lucky, and got a lift soon after passing Chub's yard.

All the advice I got from Customs was 'write to Dublin'. So, fortified with that pearl of information and the address, I walked to the railway station to get some satisfaction for my great effort.

On the station I got into conversation with the driver of diesel No 002, which was the Station Pilot. The driver's name was John Power. He had had a wonderful career in steam days, firing the 3-foot-gauge 'Dingle line' from Tralee over the Slieve Mish Mountains to Dingle and on the standard gauge (5ft 3in) engines to Cork and Dublin. I listened enthralled, and John Power, being a friendly railwayman with the right instincts, invited me to ride with him next day hauling the 10.30 am goods to Listowel (the 5.45 am from Mallow). I told him that if I was able to get a drive I would be there. We shook hands and I set out for home. I walked the first six miles out of Tralee, the second mile being dead straight and level with the daunting bulk of the Slieve Mish rising at the far end. The road then began a steep, winding climb, at one point passing over a deep, narrow gorge on a narrow bridge set at right-angles to the general line of the road.

At the summit pass I sat down on the roadside verge to rest and to wonder at the superb view – the long range of the 3,000-foot mountains of MacGillicuddy's Reeks. Their silhouette against the midday sun was so extravagantly unlikely that it made me think of a theatrical painting at the rear of a stage. Carrauntoohil rose to a truncated pyramid of bare rock, 3,407 feet above sea level. From my vantage the bay seemed to be a drowned valley, miles wide where it merged with the Atlantic Ocean and narrowing between the Reeks and the Slieve Mish Mountains. There were two huge sandbanks, Inch Strand coming south, then Glenbeigh Strand going north, and a narrow channel between then. I saw how dangerous the banks would have been for a sailing ship running up the bay to Killorglin with the west wind behind it.

The bay came further and further into the land, tapering to a point at Killorglin, where the estuaries of the River Laune and the

River Maine fed into the sea. The vast panorama under a beautiful sky was a reward for the wearisome climb up and over the shoulder of the hills. I was enchanted entirely. I lay on my back on the grass looking up at the clouds and was nearly asleep when the sound of a car toiling up the gradient urged me to my feet. It came over the brow and I stuck my arm out. The good man stopped, and drove me to Killorglin.

The following day early, the call of the railway being that strong, I took the road for Tralee. A couple of miles beyond Killorglin I got a drive. The goods train was in the sidings, with engine 017 coupled to it. John Power got the signal to leave and drew into the platform, stopped, and I climbed aboard the diesel with John.

We had sixteen wagons with the guard's van and guard on the back. Leaving Tralee, with the Train Staff 'Tralee-Listowel' handed in by the Tralee signalman, we crossed Edward Street. To our left was the single line for Fenit; that branch was used only during the sugar beet season. Also on the left were the remains of the North Kerry line terminus and also some single-storey buildings, the remains of the Tralee & Dingle Railway – the 'Dingle line'.

Heading west towards the Rock Street level crossing we passed, without a care, a signal at 'Danger'. I guessed it was missing its 'Out of Use' white cross. The gates at Rock Street signal box were already opened for us by a man on the ground. The signal box was deserted. Clear of Rock Street crossing, John Power opened up for the rising track on a sweeping right-hand curve and, heading north up a steepish gradient, we reached 30 mph on half throttle, but with that setting unchanged the gradient wore us down to 10 mph at the summit.

Away to our left were miles of sand dunes and beyond that the glittering blue of the Atlantic Ocean. We rumbled under bright sunshine and pearly-grey and pure white cumulus, rolling, tumbling and rising in frothy columns. On along the tapering, shining metals of the single track we bumped and bounced at a sedate 25 mph between fields of shiny cattle. Scattered about the green meadows were the single-storey white-painted homes of the smallholders.

Miles away to our left the Slieve Mish Mountains were a great misty mass covered for half their height by a great, grey storm cloud, dropping rain thick as fog.

We stopped for several level crossings. At Abbeydorney level crossing the signal box was derelict, its windows replaced by sheets of corrugated iron. Our guard trudged and crunched over the ballast to open the barriers while we stood there. We crossed several brooks on bridges that looked none too strong for their purpose, but the much larger bridge over the River Feale looked sound enough.

At Lixnaw crossing there was a signal post with two semaphore arms side by side, one for each direction. They were at 'Danger'. I got down to take photos as the guard came trudging along to put the barriers across the road. A car arrived as he did so and quietly stopped. Without operating the signal the guard waved the train forward. John stopped with the van clear of the crossing, I climbed back up into the cab as the guard closed the barriers and climbed back into his van. John, who was leaning out of this cab, saw the guard wave 'All Right', gave a wave back, a hoot on the horn and eased open the throttle.

We rolled into Listowel station and a full hour of shunting ensued. Wagons of beer, cement, fertiliser and empty wagons required for loading were put off in different sidings and along the unloading platform. Then the train was re-marshalled with 'outwards' wagons. I went to the signal box for a look around. The signalman was outside taking the numbers and details of all the incoming wagons and those going out. He was pleased I was interested. There were twenty-two levers working in the frame. When he came back we had a conversation. He feared being made redundant, and having to drive forty-two miles each way to Tralee for his next job – if CIÉ (Córas Iompair Éireann) could find him one. If he left the service he'd lose his pension. With the shunting complete and the re-marshalled train standing at the platform, No 017 'ran-round' the train and came back onto the wagons facing

Tralee. John Power, his guard and myself went out of the station to the nearest pub to eat our sandwiches and drink a pint of Guinness.

Our Wedding, St John Vianney Church, Wantage. 3rd June 1972. From left to right: Best man Ken Fuller, Owen Vaughan, Keith Vaughan, Adrian's Granny Taylor in front of Keith, Edith Vaughan, Karen O'Sullivan, Gerard Vaughan, Adrian, Susan, Marilyn Beechey, Pamela O'Sullivan, John O'Sullivan, Susan's Grandmother 'Flo' and Grandfather 'Pop' Ashby. Bridesmaids Siobhán and Bernadette in front.

Susan gets water from the 'little river'. June 1973.
Our sole water supply until August 1977.

The cottage exterior in October 1975.

The fireplace in October 1975.

Makeshift kitchen, left side. October 1975. The zinc lined copper tea urn filled daily with river water. Used later for boiling towelling nappies.

Makeshift kitchen, right side. Adrian's first carpentry job was to make the dresser top with its railway inspired, serrated decorative edging.

Susan wielding the mattock to clear more ground for growing vegetables. December 1975.

Adrian working on the roof. June 1976.

Susan eating under the cobwebs in a roofless kitchen. June 1976.

Simple and effective. Kerry scaffolding to support planks.

Susan with Magsie and her kid beside the River Laune. July 1976.

Kitty goat stands on Magsie's back to reach a special leaf. August 1976.

Lixnaw level crossing. August 1976.

The black range in place supporting the centring
for the arch.

King Puck on his stand overlooking Puck Fair.
August 1976.

Collecting money for the Children's home. Puck
Fair. August 1976.

The Beverly Hillbillies. Puck Fair August 1976.

Susan with kid goat 'Shirley Temple'.
March 1977.

The May fair. Haggling the price seemed to be a form of theatre. May 1977.

Cattle stand in their muck in front of Starlite, the laundrette at the May fair.

'The regular cattle and sheep fairs were a sore trial to the shop keepers and their windows. May 1977.

Eileen Foley led her father's donkey in hauling gravel from the riverbank to the cottage. July 1977.

Adrian working on building the septic tank. August 1977.

The 'Imperial' typewriter. Rebecca showing early potential as a writer. December 1978.

Eddie Moriarty came for his photo and improved the event by scooping up Rebecca onto his horse. August 1980.

Pat Clifford and his Sleán. September 1980.

Adrian sawing wood with Rebecca. Shortly after this he made a 'sawing horse'. September 1980.

Rebecca helping Susan hang out the snowy nappies. March 1981.

The cottage exterior in May 1981.

The completed kitchen showing ladder to the sleeping loft. May 1981.

Susan and the children with her grandmother Mary (Molly) O'Sullivan. May 1981.

Henry Dodd in his opulent house with Susan and baby Constance. May 1981.

Timothy (Chub) O'Connor T.D. and his daughter Dolores. May 1981.

A bank of turf at Oolagh bog. June 1982.

John Foley carefully placing Connie on the horse. July 1982.

Going to the hay field. July 1982.

Rebecca helping the Foleys by inspecting the fastening of a bale. July 1982.

Pat Clifford plays for the dancing at a garden party. August 1982.

Agnes Clifford at the party with Connie on her lap and Rebecca trying to escape. August 1982.

McGillicuddy's Reeks seen from Meanus bridge over the 'little river'.

Camping out in the 'Hunter' estate during house hunting in Norfolk. September 1982.

Susan, Rebecca, Connie and new baby Beatrice in Drayton Maternity Home. September 1986.

Chapter Fifteen
Puck Fair

1976 was one of the hottest, driest summers ever recorded in Ireland and we constantly fetched water for ourselves, the animals, the building works and the vegetables as the drought went on. Work on the house continued, pleasantly interrupted by visitors. The roof capping was fitted with some modifications and, with the help of some friends over from England, we painted the grey corrugated roof a nice mid-green. The walls were Snowcemmed and gutters erected. Adrian made shelves in the duck house to take tins of paint, tools and much else to do with the rebuilding of the cottage. As a result the inside of the porch and indeed the main room, which was to be our kitchen, took on a more civilised look.

Friends and family came and went throughout those summer months, sometimes spending an uncomfortable night on the 'kitchen' floor, camping in the field next door or staying at a local guest house. They came for sightseeing or to climb Carrauntoohil. Adrian's sister Frances and her new husband, honeymooning on Valentia Island, called in to see us and took us out for a meal. Having friends and family around gave us an excuse to relax, especially in the evenings. We spent hours talking and reminiscing, lingering over home-grown suppers long after twilight had fallen.

Swimming was wonderful in the heat of that summer. We often took a quick dip to cool off and wash in the evenings when we went to fetch water. Once or twice I joined a group of young people who congregated on the banks of the River Laune at the bridge on the Meanus road near Killorglin. They swam and mucked about and made a great deal of happy noise. But the nicest place of all to swim was from a lovely sandy beach on the Cliffords' land, providing the cow pats could be avoided. Often on a Sunday afternoon Agnes would invite us to swim and we

143

enjoyed a few hours together while Pat fished upstream away from our chatter and noise. The Cliffords' dogs came too. Joey, an old boy, loved to swim, but Kerry was afraid of the water. He would bark furiously in an attempt to stop the old dog from getting in the water until Agnes would intervene, shooing Kerry away and escorting Joey in for a swim.

Not all our visitors were helpful. Gordon (the cousin of a friend) arrived early one morning when we were still in bed. He was the proverbial 'elephant in the room' and didn't lift a finger to help, not even fetching water. He always cleaned his plate though. A few days later he departed, saying he was off to Dingle. He left us a five-pound note.

My younger brother Gerard arrived a week later intending, he said, to stay 'for two or three months'. That was alarming – from past experience – but I thought we'd give it a try. He was mathematically and scientifically highly trained and perhaps he could be helpful. He pitched a tent in the garden. Next day he slept most of the time. The Kerry air does that to visitors.

On the second day he sat on the roadside wall as I strung a cord taut along the bottom ends of the rafters to mark off where to cut each one back to enable the fascia board to be screwed on. He didn't offer to hold the other end of the cord or use the pencil to make the cut marks, but he did tell me how much easier it would be to use a laser. That evening after dinner he volunteered to play some busking folk music on his violin. We'd never heard him play so we settled down for the concert while he fiddled with his fiddle, getting it in tune, playing a few notes and stopping to twist the pegs. This went on for some time, but eventually he set off into a nice tune really well played. He had inherited our father's virtuosity on strings: Dad had played cello and viola and also piano, all expertly. Gerard got to the end of the tune but then put the violin down.

He began to talk about his encounters with the Cheltenham BNP skinheads. They'd mugged him of his busking contributions and stamped on his first violin. We were truly dismayed, horrified, to hear this. To stamp on a violin! Clearly they would find the burning of books entertaining too. What a terror and trauma he must have suffered. We tried to get him to play some more, but he gave up after several false starts. He could play the fiddle really well and I thought the shock he'd suffered in Cheltenham might have had more than a passing effect. The evening was young, so I suggested we go to the Cromane bar, the ex-Coastguard station at the top of the Strand, to listen to the fiddle music of a great Irish music virtuoso, Johnny Cahillane. Gerard was not readily dazzled by anyone's talent, but I told him he would be sure to be impressed and inspired by Johnny's virtuosity. Gerard emerged from his tent carrying a tape recorder.

Over at the Cromane bar there was a crowd. Cahillane's music was superb; sometimes the tune was plaintive and emotional enough to turn the stones to tears, sometimes he played a reel with the speed of a fiercely bubbling cauldron of water. His fingering was unbelievable – but there before one's eyes. Gerard was captivated. 'I wish I could do that', he said. 'Wow!'

That was the first time I'd ever heard him say such a thing. He got his tape recording going. We got pints and stood to watch and marvel. Johnny was maybe fifty-five, thin, in shabby clothing, wearing an old trilby with the correct tear at the top front fold where his fingers pinched it in lifting it off. He wore glasses, one lens of which was smashed but still in its frame. His eyes were shut. He was somewhere other than the noisy, swarming bar room. In 1968 David Lean, the director of the film *Ryan's Daughter*, had come to the bar while he was exploring the area looking for a location for his film. He heard Johnny playing and signed him up to play the background music in the film.

After a couple of pints we had plucked up courage to approach Johnny and ask him to listen to Gerard play. Gerard played a whole tune through. Johnny was impressed and said, 'Carry on playing a while so,' and he went to get a whisky from the bar. Gerard did just that. The tunes weren't Irish but English folk song tunes and Morris dance music. Some heads were turned to see who was playing this strange music, but it was played well enough so that the talk and the drinking went on. Johnny came back after a couple of whiskies and took his place. We found somewhere to sit and listened as Johnny played some more tunes, with Gerard recording all the while. He was so amazed and delighted that next morning he announced he wouldn't be staying with us any longer but would go home to Cheltenham to listen to his tapes and practice. He left the following afternoon.

Susan and I did not know about Puck Fair when we moved to Ireland. It was the vocal forebodings of Agnes, during our first August at Meanus, that brought it to our attention. The three-day fair was the subject of clerical disapproval. As a devout and respectable Catholic, Agnes hardly needed the Canon's disapproval to object to the presence of the Travellers and the widespread drunkenness and fist and knife fights on the streets. I got the impression that the fair in the 1970s was an embarrassment to many Killorglin-ites and, indeed, the Gardaí too. It was they who would put themselves at risk of serious injury should they be obliged to attempt to break up the fights.

Puck Fair had pre-Christian origins, as did the Christian feasts of Easter and Christmas, but St Patrick had not been able to Christianise a billy goat on a tower. The Killorglin Puck Fair is the only survivor of this ancient tradition. King James I granted a Charter for a fair in Killorglin in 1613 to take place on the 1st and 2nd August, but when the Julian calendar was replaced by the Gregorian, the Fair was held on the 11th and 12th. The fair became very famous for the buying and selling of horses, pigs and cattle. Buyers and sellers came from ever further away and at some stage an extra day was added to the fair – 10th August – to give these people time to arrive and rest before the main event in the morning. Adding this extra day was apt because it was a 'pattern' day – the feast of St Lawrence, the patron saint of Killorglin.

Puck Fair means 'Fair of the He-Goat' (Aonach an Phoic). Traditionally each year members of the Houlihan family go up into the mountains and capture a billy goat. They bring him back down to Killorglin and

146

take responsibility for his welfare. They ensure that he is well fed and watered until his release back into the mountains when the fair is over. On the first day of the fair the goat is crowned 'King Puck' by a young girl, herself crowned the 'Queen of Puck' prior to the event itself. He is then hoisted aloft in a covered crib to the top of a three-tier stage in Killorglin 'square', where he will reign supreme for the duration of the fair.

On 10th August 1976 the first day of Puck dawned bright and clear with the promise of a sunny day ahead. After completing all our chores we cycled into Killorglin, passing dozens of cars and horseboxes parked under the trees in the avenue leading into the town, before arriving beside The Bianconi at the crossroads at about eleven o'clock.

Posters on lamp posts advertised pipe band recitals, variety concerts, street dancing, sky-diving, novelty sports, competitions in traditional Irish music, a children's fancy dress competition and numerous other entertainments as well as the livestock fairs. Killorglin was already jammed to bursting point with people and horses and the atmosphere buzzed. Brightly dressed, buxom Traveller women with plaid shawls wrapped around them to support rosy cheeked babies jostled alongside denim-clad tourists and local people, mountainy men and farmers. There were almost as many Traveller children as horses. They poured into the town from the outskirts where dozens of caravans had been parked. The little girls and the bigger ones too were unfailingly pretty with rosy cheeks and auburn, red or dark uncombed hair. Although their hands and faces were often grubby, their brightly coloured clothes were clean and new-looking – they had dressed up especially for the occasion. The young boys were cheeky and bright and threw a 'Can ye spare a penny?' in the direction of any obvious tourist, avoiding the locals, who swore at them to go away.

One little lad in particular caught my attention. He was squatting beside a grimy old woman and two unwashed, ragged old men who were sitting on the pavement outside a bar passing a whiskey bottle between them, wiping their lips with grubby hands in between swigs. The boy, about ten years old, had a closely cropped head and was dressed in something akin to skinhead gear. For the most part he kept a

147

silent vigil beside the three and did not join in with the other boys begging for money. Later we saw him messing around on the stage, untying the bunting and scattering ribbons about the road, encouraging other boys to join him. Eventually, a Garda approached, the other boys ran away but the little skinhead turned to face him. There were words of abuse, a slight scuffle and the Garda escorted the kicking youngster from the stage, presumably to deliver him into the hands of his parents or guardians – wherever they might be.

The air was full of the smell of sweat and beer, frying chips and onions and the sweet grassy smell of horse manure trampled underfoot. There were caravans selling hot dogs, chips and candy floss, and dozens of stalls with brightly striped awnings displaying tawdry trinkets and ornaments decorated with the ubiquitous shamrock. Salesmen with big voices proclaimed their wares. One stall boasted hundreds of colourful cowboy hats, each bearing the inscription 'Puck Fair 1976'. Second-hand clothing, much like bundles of rags, was laid out on cloths on the ground.

Horses were crammed along Market Street, just off Bridge Street, and I couldn't help but feel a little bit afraid as we walked by them. Huge chestnut mares lined the pavement, impatiently stamping their hooves and scraping the ground, raising clouds of dust into the faces of the people squeezing past. There were groups of frightened little ponies, corralled together in corners avoiding the men with sticks, and there were the inevitable donkeys waiting patiently by the side of a small child or an old woman put in charge of the sale. We worked our way along the street until we came to a number of people gathered around a beautiful silver mare and her dusky foal. We stopped to admire them too.

A stout elderly lady, clearly an English horsewoman, brisk and business-like, in tweeds and wellingtons, was in the process of examining the pair. She made her offer, the farmer started to protest with the ritual haggling, but it was a good offer and he knew it because the woman cut him short, snapping, 'That's my offer – take it or leave it.'

The farmer took it. The woman instructed a young man, presumably her groom, to lead the mare and foal away while the farmer, his pockets bulging with ten-pound notes, made for the nearest bar.

The coronation of 'King Puck' was scheduled for six o'clock according to the posters, but we felt that was too long for us to wait, so we cycled home to a late lunch. We came back on the last day so that Adrian could take some photographs. The atmosphere felt a little flat after the excitement of the first day and the crowds had thinned, but nevertheless people were still enjoying themselves. We watched a girls' pipe band playing a lively tune, leading a straggly procession of children in fancy dress up the hill towards the 'square'. There was a cowboy, Little Bo-peep, a couple of footballers and an excited gang of 'Beverly Hillbillies', among other fancy dress participants. A tall, stately nun dressed in white was collecting money for St Mary of the Angels children's home. She was accompanied by an enthusiastic young boy who was carrying a tray of flags given in exchange for payment. Eventually we made our way up to the centrepiece of the fair: the gaily adorned three-tier stage of scaffold-like construction, its poles chequered blue and white, which rose up like a tower above the swarming crowd. Three little girls were dancing a jig to the accompaniment of an accordionist seated behind them, and there, up above the performers on the third tier, was 'King Puck'. He certainly was a handsome fella, large, white and hairy with huge curled horns. We wondered how the Houlihans had ever managed to capture him. He certainly seemed none the worse for his enforced stay in his crib high above the stage. He seemed very calm and quiet, surveying the noisy crowd below from his lofty throne with an interested but slightly aloof and superior expression, as is the way with goats.

Cycling out of Killorglin one hot day in August, on the long straight after the Glencar turn, I saw a horse walking and trotting and swerving about in the road because cars were rushing past him, dangerously detouring around his uncertain movements without slowing very much. I pedalled hard and caught up with him and called out to him 'Whoa!' and other horse-soothing pleasantries. The horse stood. He was a sixteen-hand working horse, a grey. He seemed glad some human was taking notice of him rather than scaring him with their cars. I got off the bike and, catching hold of his long neglected mane with my right hand and pushing the bike with the other, I got him clip-clopping sedately along. He was used to being directed.

We had just got under way when a well-built young man walked past going into town. He turned and came back. I twisted my head around as best I could, said, 'Hello,' and again faced front. The stranger walked behind me without a word. When I got to the cottage, I put my bike against the wall and brought the horse to Eddie's gate, pushed it open and let it into the field. The animal at once went trotting off down the track towards the river, it was as if he knew where he wanted to go. So out of curiosity I followed. I'd gone a few paces when I heard this young chap coming along behind me. He said nothing. It was very strange and unsettling. The horse was going straight for the river at the trot. I hurried on and was just in time to see the grand old chap ford the river, the splashing spray shooting up like thousands of diamonds in the strong sun. When I turned back, the young chap had gone.

I was working in the garden next day when this unsettling stranger stopped, leaned his bike against the wall and came into the garden. He told me he had recovered from LSD addiction and said that he was looking for work or money. I told him I couldn't help him with either. He then asked if there might be work at St Mary of the Angels. 'Well, you can try,' I said. He went away. I gathered from his thick accent that he was Dutch. The day after that, I was away from home and this young Dutchman came to the cottage and knocked on the front door. Susan opened it and was very surprised when a well-built young man walked straight past her without a word, into the kitchen. He told her was looking for work or money. Susan was more indignant at his barging in than scared of him. She told him she couldn't help with work or money and asked him to leave. That he did. We never saw him again – and to this day Susan has no recollection of the incident although I recorded it in my diary.

150

We had a really good harvest from the garden that summer in spite of the drought. We had lettuce, tomatoes, onions, carrots, beetroot, potatoes, courgettes, peas and beans. I was particularly proud of a big crop of large unblemished cauliflowers, which I have never been able to grow successfully since. They made a delicious soup when cooked with potatoes and onions. We ate it with home-made soda bread spread with our own parsley and garlic cottage cheese. I gave a cauliflower to Agnes who repaid us with a box of Black Magic chocolates! We also gave spare lettuces and bunches of parsley to Pat, who took them to sell at Hotel Europe together with his own produce. I bottled peas, broad beans and fruit and made pounds of blackberry and apple jam. We were picking the blackberries from the middle of August and we got apples from a tree in Eddie's yard. I also made blackberry wine and used up all the demijohns we had brought from England. It wasn't going to be easy to find more. We also had an excellent harvest of potatoes from Pat's field, approximately seven hundredweight, most of which we stored in an earth clamp for the winter.

The goats were giving us a plentiful supply of milk and I tried my hand at making some hard cheese. We had located rennet at Michelstown Dairy, Paul and Susie had bought us a thermometer, and Adrian made me a small rectangular cheese press out of mahogany. John Seymour was my guide and I hoped his method would work as well for goats' milk as for cows' milk. He advised using the milk from two milkings only, morning and evening, to avoid over-acidity and off-flavours, and suggested five gallons as a decent amount. Unfortunately I only had about half that, but thought I could make do. I followed his instructions meticulously – which wasn't easy in a building undergoing renovation. We had to wait several weeks before the contents of the press was ready to sample. It was hard and whitish in colour, a bit rubbery in texture, but not bad and not too dissimilar from hard goats' milk cheeses I have tasted since. BUT it was mainly rind with no middle. All that milk had compressed into a cheese only about an inch or so thick, so clearly that's why five gallons were needed. It was an interesting experiment, but one that I never repeated.

151

An old bachelor came knocking at the door one fine September day. He was Jimmy Grinnane who lived along the back *bohreen* in a tumbledown cottage in which I would not have stored a lawnmower. He had a plot of land around this ancient stone hut and a fine old fruit tree. I knew his name because he was one of the poor old men for whom Agnes cooked meals and kept an eye on their health. He had brought us a two-gallon bucket brimming with beautiful damsons.

'Would ye be buying these from me?' he asked.

'Yes, of course. How much are they?' I replied.

'Give us 50p?' he said, uncertainly.

The damsons and a 50p coin changed hands. I stoned the fruit and Susan bottled some and made jam with the rest. When she'd done we took the bucket back to Jimmy. We found him sitting out in the sun on the grassy wall beside his gate.

'We've brought your bucket back, Jimmy, and we'd like to buy more damsons.'

He said that they were all too high up now to be reached. I suggested that I could climb up and pick them myself.

He was hesitant. 'Ye'd be falling and hurting yerself.'

'Not at all,' I said. 'I can climb up there easily.'

He shrugged his shoulders and said, 'Ah well, worrk away-a.'

I climbed into the tree, handed down damsons to Susan, filled the bucket and asked him if he'd take 50p.

'No, I won't,' he said emphatically. 'I've money enough for the winter.'

Chapter Sixteen
Eros

Early in September Colin Judge of Oxford Publishing Company promised that the proofs of my book *A Pictorial Record of Great Western Architecture* were nearly ready and he'd post them shortly. Later in the month he wrote to say that he wanted me to rearrange the layout of the book and I would have to come to Oxford to do it. He didn't offer to pay my fare, of course. I had been working since I came to Meanus on my *History of the Faringdon Branch and Uffington Station*. I had a long list of research questions and a lengthy visit to England was needed to get the answers, so I could go to OPC at Headington to see about the Architecture book. It was such a grand design and a unique book that I was sure it would be a good earner for us while we restored the cottage.

Susan would come with me and we planned to be away from Meanus from early October to mid-November. The cats could look after themselves while we were away. We had hardly fed them through the summer; they'd been eating young rabbits and massacring the rat population too, but hopefully not eating them. Pat and Agnes next door had noticed the lack of both pests and said they would give the cats some milk now and then. Knowing that we were going away we had sold the ducks in August to the same people who had bought the Muscovy ducks. But the three goats would need a temporary home. All were 'in season'.

The two young ones, Nelly and Kitty, advertised this on several mornings when, on being released from their shed, they went bounding about our garden, then jumped the hedge and ran off into Pat's land. They jumped onto his stacks of firewood and teetered precariously, they bounded up the hay bales in his Dutch barn, jumped down from several feet up and ran around his yard. During

153

these exhibitions old Magsie was very concerned and stood in our garden bleating. So it was to Gus and Les that a letter was written asking if we could bring three goats to them for board and lodging – and mating with their big, white Puck goat, the aptly named 'Eros'.

Susan had met Gus and Les in Killorglin market place earlier in the year. They'd come down from their house at Mealis, on the lower slopes of Carrauntoohil, with their young son Paul on their horse-drawn cart. They were an English couple who were obviously 'self-sufficiency' enthusiasts. Our mode of dress was untidy but they were interestingly dreadlocked and hippie-scruffy. They stood out a mile and Susan went across to speak to them. They were glad to meet approximately kindred spirits and invited her to visit their place. We went together, the last half-mile up a steep, stony track. Just before the cottage was a 'For Sale' sign.

Their cottage was an unusual shape for a single-storey Kerry cabin, especially one so high up the mountainside. It had a larger, rectangular floor space. Behind it was a solid stone barn in a poor state. The steepness of the Reeks rose sharply at the back of the building, but at the front, looking north, the land fell away for miles giving a grand view over the Vale of Killorglin, across Dingle Bay, which one could see as a blue sliver of water, to the misty grey-blue silhouette of the Slieve Mish Mountains.

They did not grow vegetables but kept goats and poultry and were very proud of their big cob horse and wanted to find land with a level field of soil so they could use him for ploughing. The running water for the cottage came by the simplest of means. There was a foot-wide brook that rippled and clattered, crisp and clean, overhung with the gorse and bracken. Above the cottage it fell into a natural pool in which was placed a one-inch-diameter plastic pipe, which went down to a tank in the roof of the house, many yards below. Gus and Les sold their cottage soon after our visit, but they had told us where they were going – a bungalow on a hillside above the Kenmare River, near Eyries, on Kilcatherine Point, almost in West Cork but just inside the Kerry border.

I filled the VW with eight and a half gallons of petrol at the BP garage – which cost £7.50 – and we fitted the back seat with a polythene sheet in the hope of protecting the upholstery from goat urine. We fitted planks of wood onto the floor, loaded the goats, and set off for Eyries via Killarney and Kenmare. The three animals were crammed in across the narrow seat and sat on their bottoms very still. Then Nelly goat succumbed to travel sickness, slid off the seat and stretched herself across the floor. The other two gratefully rearranged themselves. Goats are very intelligent, thinking, animals.

The narrow road, high above but parallel to the Kenmare River – a deep inlet from the ocean, in fact – was lined with fuchsia hedges, all in bloom. The hillsides rising above us were green and brown with long ribs of grey limestone exposed. We saw what must be our friends' home, an old and windswept bungalow, plastered with grey cement, up above the road with thousands of acres of rock-strewn hillside rising high above. We stopped in a field gateway and let the three goats out of the car. I opened a gate in the hedge and the goats walked cautiously through. Gus's herd of goats had seen the car stop and were standing, heads raised, looking to see what was happening. Gus had seen us and was walking through the field to greet us.

Gus told us that he had some land of his own and the use of maybe three thousand acres of rough pasture, over the hill and far away. He had a dozen nanny goats grazing the hill; his horse and donkey and the poultry also had the run of it.

'We've our own milk, meat, eggs and fish,' he said proudly, 'and Paul's down on the beach below fishing.'

He said he bought very little food but went by horse and four-wheeled cart into Eyries for supplies such as flour and paraffin.

By now the home herd had mustered and was advancing in line abreast down the hill, led by the Chief Nanny. The Puck was nowhere to be seen. 'Now watch them,' said Gus. 'They'll make a ritual challenge to yours before they accept them.'

Our three advanced a little way in an arrowhead formation with Magsie at the point. Gus's herd stopped and the senior nanny

155

advanced. There was some glaring eye contact, sniffing, standing, staring each other out, then, sharply, Gus's nanny snapped her head forward, Magsie met the blow and horns were locked. It was all very formal. There was some twisting of heads, left and right. Then, horns unlocked, the home nanny stepped back and turned around, walking back to her followers. Magsie and her two followed, merged with the herd, and they all went up the hill. We watched long enough to see Magsie jump up onto a ledge of rock, teetering with all four hooves close together. She stood motionless, her long beard blowing in the wind, as she looked out over the water-filled valley far below, to the Kerry mountains beyond. Goat heaven.

'Come on indoors,' said Gus, and over a cup of tea he asked, 'What would you like for dinner – chicken or duck?'

'Oh, er … duck?' said Susan hesitantly.

Gus went outside and returned ten minutes later with a dead duck. 'I had to chase it around a bit,' he said apologetically.

While Les prepared the duck for cooking we went outside on a tour of the estate. The milking parlour was an ancient byre with a raised floor along one half of the length where the goats stood to be milked. We still hadn't seen Eros. Milking time was now approaching and Gus went outside to call them in. Obediently the herd turned downhill, our three bringing up the rear. His goats filed into the byre in proper order, jumping up onto the raised part and walking into their respective milking stalls. Ours stayed outside clearly wondering what to do, turning their heads this way and that and bleating. Gus brought them in and put them in stalls near the entrance. Just as he did that Eros came sauntering in. Gus set about the milking while Eros walked along the rear-facing line of goats. He noted the condition of ours in a rather obvious way – his horizontally erect, bright red penis ejaculated onto the floor.

Les asked me to make some gravy for the meal using the duck fat as a base. I made a roux with some flour, but there was no stock available, the only seasoning being a jar of Marmite. I made the gravy with this against my best inclinations. I love Marmite on toast but not anywhere else! The duck and the potatoes would have been delicious but for the pervading Marmite flavour. But the peculiar taste was somehow in keeping with the dark, grungy kitchen. The old bungalow and the byre building were both shabby and neglected and there was no evidence of renovation or even painting to spruce things up a bit. An air of despondency hung over the place. I dare say the problem was down to a lack of finances.

We were invited to stay the night. It was obvious that the little family lived a very lonely existence in this isolated place, so they were pleased to have company and conversation for the evening and we were thankful for the offer. It was getting rather late for a long drive home.

Henry Dodd volunteered to drive us to Killarney station. We caught the Dublin train as far as Mallow, where we 'alighted' and caught the Dublin-Cork train. We sailed on the *Innisfallen* to Swansea and got the train from there to Didcot, where my father collected us. We stayed in 'Tudor Cottage' next door to my parents' cottage for a couple of days and I went to Oxford to rearrange the layout for the Architecture book. Then we went on to my sister Frances in Chelsea. Susan has vivid memories of the busy Chelsea street and the amazingly diverse people and different, multi-coloured shops. She had never before seen that intimate, domestic, side of London. I travelled the 'Tubes' and tramped the record offices in order to consult only official papers to get the most correct information; there was no central Public Record Office until mid-1977. GWR archives were in various locations: 66 Portchester Road, Paddington; the Record Office for the GWR; the Berkshire Record Office in Reading; and Swindon Reference Library. I also used the Board of Trade railway files kept at Ashridge Park near Tring.

The Record Office on the first floor of 66 Porchester Road was furnished like a gentleman's club. I sat in a sumptuous leather armchair at a priceless mahogany table. Ranged around the wall were early Victorian mahogany bookcases, the doors glazed with hand-made glass. Staff waited on me. I consulted their catalogues, filled in a duplicated paper ticket requesting a document and handed it over. It was very homely and friendly. Usually I was the only researcher there. While waiting for the man to return with the document I could read a GWR Staff Magazine or one of the hundreds of interesting books available from one of the bookcases.

The Portchester Road documents had to be copied out by pencil or photocopied, and I could only afford so many. I recorded everything I had listed and left London for Tring, then we went on to spend two days in Bristol with Paul and Susie. We got home on Sunday 14th November having spent £200 on travel, food, films and photo paper in six weeks. But now I had all I needed to complete the Faringdon branch book. A bill from Chub Connor for £272 was waiting for us. There was also a letter from Irish Customs giving me permission to sell the VW Beetle. We kept our collective nerve.

The following Friday we set off in the car to collect the goats from Gus and Les. They were very pleased to see us and wanted us to stay the night again, but we had to harden our hearts and say we had loads to do at home – which was true – and we'd have to get back straightaway. Young Paul wanted to come back to Meanus with us. We did feel a bit guilty, but self-preservation overrode a kindness. We paid them for having the goats mated and also gave them a hundredweight of potatoes. We drove away on the long, lonely road home. We had seen how our goats had enjoyed the wild, rocky hillside overlooking the deep *fiord* of the Kenmare River and the vast Atlantic Ocean, but it was also obvious that they too were glad to be home and went around looking at and sniffing at all their favourite places.

We sold the VW Beetle to a man I suspected could not read or write. With his money we paid off Chub's bill and had a bit left over, which we spent on the cottage. The weather was deteriorating as November days passed and Eddie, knowing from experience, that sometime soon his field beside our place would be flooded by the overflowing Laune, had moved his cattle onto his turf bog to the south of the back *bohreen*. He came to us and suggested we should move our goats onto this land, and took me over there to show me the way. The days when the wind rose stronger became more frequent, and the rain fell heavier and the evenings darker. I went out onto the road to bring in the goats one evening and saw them coming down the road towards me from the Meanus Cross direction. Magsie had clearly had enough of the wind and the growing darkness but, instead of coming home the way I'd always taken them, she had led them to avoid John Foley's dog, browsing their way all along the lane, then crossing hedges and ditches to get onto the Meanus road. Magsie was a clever old goat with a great sense of direction.

One evening I went to fetch the goats from Eddie's bog and, at the entrance to the grass track, snagged onto a bramble, was a large piece of a brown paper bag. On it was a message from Eddie, in large pencilled letters: 'Please take the bale which is above in the road to the cattle on the bog. And oblige, E. Moriarty.' I was very pleased to help and glad he'd felt able to ask. Seeing that I had done as he requested, the following evening he came down to the cottage and called for me. We were walking past John Foley's when he said in a worried voice, 'I've two bales of hay above in the road. They're the last two I have.'

I suggested that he buy some of John Foley's bales as he had a barn full of them. Eddie, who was taller than me, snapped his head round and looked down at me fiercely, then, as quickly, his face softened. 'Ah, ye wouldn't be knowing – there is nothing but the animosity between us.'

I was astonished not just by what he'd said but by his wonderful use of words. Eddie was a lover of the nature all around him. As we walked we passed a young holly tree. 'De burrds planted that,' he said, pointing.

He described to me how the mother swan – the pen – goes on the current, down the Laune, with her cygnets on her back and her wings folded up around them; he made the up-folded wings gesture with his hands and arms. Eddie treasured all the wild flora and fauna on his land. He never cut the gorse for himself, yet he said we could cut his furze bushes for firing.

He told me of all the stone cottages that existed on the bog when he was a boy, back before the First World War. He pointed up onto the slopes of Carrauntoohil, to the stone grotto halfway up. 'D' ye see that? De poor fella that carried those stones up there was heading for the top but couldn't make it. So he built it there. The poor cratur. He wasn't right in his head.'

Eddie sold cattle at the various marts in the town but he didn't always remember or care to cash the cheques he received. He was clearly another man who felt he had 'money enough for the winter'. His nephew Brendan told me: 'If you ever were to get into his kitchen you'd see the cheques he's been paid trodden into the floor. He goes to the mart for the craic. If he has cash he might spend a bit on some food, but cheques he'll take and never cash them.'

It seemed that not only did Eddie not spend money, he didn't really want it in the first place.

Walking back off the bog one windswept twilight, the goats trailing behind, Eddie told me one of his parables of a man who sold a heifer to Tom Houlihan for slaughter. 'Your man took the cash into Daly's Bar and drank most of what Tom had given him.'

Later Susan and I went round to Pat and Agnes's for a little supper and a musical evening. I told Pat that Eddie had invited us onto his bog.

''Tisn't his bog at all,' said Pat scornfully. ''Tis the common bog, but no one uses it because the turf is useless.'

My heart sank. 'Oh? Eddie said I could take as much as I liked.'

'Ah well, he would and you can. Your cottage probably has turbary rights on it, but the turf's no good there,' Pat replied.

Later, on a wild November afternoon, I was with Eddie going to the bog, each of us carrying a bale of hay for his cattle. We tramped along the track past a derelict cottage, and fifty yards on we saw a cow in a drain, the high banks level with its head, the icy water touching its belly. It was silent and in a poor way.

'Go and fetch the 'Bear' and tell him to bring a rope,' said Eddie.

'Who's the Bear, Eddie, and where will I find him?'

'Jer Connor – ye know where he lives.'

I did. I had never spoken to him but I'd seen him on the road. He struck me as a grim, even menacing sort of man. I knocked on his front door. He was taken aback to see me there and without any preliminaries I told him Eddie was on his bog with a cow in a drain and needed him and some rope to pull her out. With a grunt and a nod he shut the door. Soon he came around to the front with his dog and a rope. 'Come on,' he muttered as he walked away.

The light was failing as we got back to Eddie standing on the bank of the channel. He looped and tied the rope around the cow's horns and the three of us pulled. The cow was helpless with cold, legs useless. Jer got his dog to bark at the cow but to no effect. But somehow we dragged her up and out and towed her through the bracken and between the gorse bushes to the derelict cottage. She lay on the floor, legs out straight. The room grew darker as the sun went down. The dog was told to bark. Eddie fetched an ancient pitchfork and advanced towards the frozen but still breathing cow. Alarmed at what he might be intending I blurted out, 'Don't you think you ought to call a vet?'

'Don't be telling Eddie his business,' growled Jer.

Eddie prodded the cow with the prongs of the fork. There was no response. 'Well,' he said with a sigh of resignation, 'she's oot o' her troubles noo-ah.'

With that Jer shrugged and shambled off. Eddie and I left the cow in the darkness and went out to where we'd left the hay bales, broke them open and scattered the slices over the darkening bogland.

Heavy, icy rain began in late November. The constant downpour had the Laune flooding into Eddie's field, which became a large lake. Eddie's bog was a quagmire, putting the goats at risk of drowning, but we trusted to Magsie's sure-footed intelligence. The deluge petered out after ten days of torment.

The weekend was sunny and on the Monday morning we cycled into town for some urgent grocery shopping. A big cattle fair was in progress. The Travellers were there in force. Moving through the crowds, we staved off the begging children and the

161

whining, hands-outstretched women, jumping out of the way of cows being startled forwards as they were shooed away from shop windows by irate shopkeepers. The animals always seemed to be parked with their rear ends facing the glass with results that I've no need to describe. Cattle were shoulder to shoulder, rear ends of some within the wide entrance to the *Oisin,* the cinema, and all down Langford Street with their human minders standing around, their dogs lying on the road. People, cattle, dogs, shoppers, and the merely entertained observers, thronged the little triangular 'square' and the streets around. The Travellers and others had market stalls or even tarpaulins on the road for stalls, selling clothing and shoes. Men and women were trying on prospective purchases, hopping about on one foot, a partner supporting them, or even, if it was a single person, with no assistance from the stall-holder, who seemed to be watching as if it were an entertainment, waiting for the customer, wobbling dangerously, to dip a foot into the green mire. I have to admit that Susan and I found it a great craic too.

Christmas Day 1976 was a Saturday and New Year's Day was also a Saturday. Many working people of all classes started the holiday on two or even three days before the 24th and all those who possibly could did not go to work from 24th December until 3rd January 1977. The BBC news informed us that, 'Foreigners have expressed concern that millions of workers in the UK and Ireland have ceased work for so long.' Susan and I stayed in the cottage throughout the holiday. We couldn't go away, not only because of the goats but because we had no car to get us to Limerick. But it was OK. We now had a strong roof, an electric light and a three-pin wall socket. The Victorian range wasn't that good for cooking, but it kept us warm, and the Calor gas cooker was at our service.

Chapter Seventeen
Turf cutting

New Year's Day brought an inch or two of snow, bright sun – and cold. Susan boiled a kettle for tea, we drank up, dressed warmly and went outside to take the goats to Eddie's bog. The usual walk, past Foley's and along the lane past Jer Hartnett's dismal cabin, was as fairyland, transformed by the snow-draped trees. Walking up the track from the lane to the bog, we passed through the line of snow-laden trees and were stopped in our tracks by the awesome sight of Carrauntoohil and the whole range of the Reeks thickly covered in a blanket of snow, brilliantly white in the cloudless sky. The pyramid top of the greatest mountain was sharply etched against a bright blue sky. The goats were entirely oblivious to the view and were greedily eating bramble leaves. Susan and I stood there, our arms around each other's shoulders, absorbed in the amazing vista. What a place to be!

When we got back indoors, I was still exulting in the snowy landscape of the Reeks. I wrote in my diary:

'We have had a lovely time. Not because of the public holiday but owing to the weather, which has prevented all but essential outdoor work being done – mostly cutting gorse and scavenging for other firewood. The gorse is on Eddie's bog, which is a happy place to work, with the goats for company and the snowy Reeks to look at. I am sitting here beside the fire-crackling range, eating bread and marmalade at 11.00 am listening to the St Matthew (singularly inappropriate seasonally but very good to hear). Uncle Tolly cat is indoors sitting close, hoping to jump onto my lap so as to get closer to the fire. Baby Cat has gone out hunting, all eyes and ears and whiskers; snow and cold doesn't deter her even though she's full of food from us. So Susan and I float between heaven and earth, all projected work for 1976 accomplished, fuel is stacked, the garden can sleep till spring, the typewriter will shortly be in use for there are books to be written. We have no worries, no 'hours' to keep, free people as far as that is possible to be. The public holiday will soon be over but all those close to the land will continue to float until the earth returns to life, the sun grows strong above and draws us all out for another year's work.'

The next day I had to write: 'The gale has brought down electricity wires in many parts of Kerry – but not here.'

January passed with days of beautiful sunshine and more days of snow, enormously strong gales and torrential rain followed by utterly magnificent, glorious lighting, with great clouds, huge, towering, voluminous, white and all shades of grey. Through howling gales and winter sun I clattered and thudded away daily on my 'Imperial' typewriter hammering out the last of the Faringdon branch book as well as letters full of research questions to retired GWR engine drivers Charlie Turner and Jim Honey, to family, and to David Collins, who had recently become a co-founder of the Signalling Record Society. Years later he became Chief Signal & Telegraph Engineer of the Western Region. The Faringdon branch book was completed on 2nd February.

The winter nights were long but not tedious. We had a cosy time sitting on our hard little kitchen chairs cushioned for comfort in front of the friendly range. We didn't have television and didn't hanker for one either, but found Radio 4 to be very good company and enjoyed listening to the evening dramas. We read a lot, getting books from the library that had been newly opened in Killorglin. One of our best finds was Michael Ende's 'The Grey Gentlemen' (reprinted as 'Momo') which we both enjoyed. The heroine of the book is a young girl called Momo who comes from nowhere and takes up residence in an ancient amphitheatre in a crumbling city of long ago. The local poor people welcome her, giving her food and helping her make a little home for

164

herself in a dungeon at the base of the amphitheatre. Momo has nothing of her own of any material value but she has plenty of time and uses it to listen to help people sort out their problems. The story becomes sinister when the Grey Gentlemen arrive. They start to take over the city by stealing people's time. Momo, with the help of her friend the Professor and his tortoise, eventually defeat the men in grey. Ostensibly for children, this story spoke to us about an important concept: 'time' and the way people are urged to 'save it'. Begging the question in our minds, 'For what purpose?'

I also read my way through a stack of paperbacks that Anna had given me, and so discovered writers like Sartre and his sometime lover Simone de Beauvoir, an author who excited and exasperated me in equal measures. I rediscovered D. H. Lawrence. I had started reading 'Lady Chatterley's Lover' when I was about fourteen. I had left the paperback copy lying on a blanket in the garden after sunbathing, and had gone to visit a friend. When I came back I had found the book torn into tiny pieces and strewn all over the blanket. My father was furious with me and slapped me round the face for my licentiousness. I hadn't even got to the sexy bit!

When Adrian wasn't hammering away on his big old-fashioned typewriter, I was, and to this day I 'hammer' on the computer keys rather than lightly touching them, which is all that is required. During that second winter at Meanus I wrote a couple of stories and a few poems, but mainly I made a record of our life as we lived it, a memoir called 'The Simple Life'. I had the fanciful notion that one day I would turn it into a book. But perhaps not so fanciful after all, as some of the material for this book comes from that early draft written over forty years ago.

March 1977 came in like the proverbial lion. Gales and heavy rain. Eddie's field became a lake. Magsie developed a cloudy grey eye; maybe being out in the storms affected it. We bought ointment from the vet and applied it daily. After breakfast on 9th March I went out into a gale and teeming rain to the goat shed. Magsie was lying down with a new-born she-kid beside her. All-over white, just like her father, Eros. Magsie had licked it clean and eaten the afterbirth. Her eye was a lot better than the day before. The infection must have been very irritating for her because she showed me her thanks by *kissing my hands* when I moved them close to her head to put ointment on the infected eye. She acted towards me in a humanly affectionate way. Her little she-goat was so well formed and pretty that Susan named her 'Shirley Temple'.

So, leaving Magsie to feed her kid, I led Nelly and Kitty out into the storm and tethered them in the field. By midday the wind and rain had cleared, and the sun came out amidst those glorious Kerry cumulus clouds that reflect the sunlight to the ground, making all colours intense. At five o'clock on Sunday I went down to bring the goats in. Nelly had just given birth to a he-kid – a Puck goat. He was a poor little thing compared to Shirley Temple. He had no hairs on his ears, his legs were very thin and didn't look properly formed. Maybe he was a bit premature. I picked him up as he could only totter on his brand-new legs. He had a very loud voice and bleated for his mother. Nelly stood there looking around, mystified. I bent and showed her the kid. Calm descended, I stood up and walked on. Nelly stood and bleated and the kid called back. I had to walk backwards, bent double, showing the kid to his mother all the way to the gate. Inside the goat shed, Magsie was either angry or jealous on seeing the new kid: she butted her daughter all around the shed.

Later, Kitty gave birth to a Puck goat and we gave this kid to Honest Houlihan the butcher, who brought the little fellow back to us in joints. It never does to become too fond of animals.

On one very moonlit March night, when Susan and I were fast asleep, naked, in bed, she woke with a shout of 'Bloody sheep!'

I woke instantly. 'What's the matter?'

'There's sheep in the garden! They're eating the cabbages.'

I leaped out of bed, stark naked, and dashed outside. There they were, white, woolly and very Stanley Spencer in the moonlight. Frantically I chased them across the garden. They were leaping the bank into the field like steeplechasers, galloping on. I fell straight down into the 'Pit of Shit'. Two years' worth of the stuff. I was smothered in splatter turds. I'd thrust my arms outwards as I went in and now heaved myself out and, shouting 'Put the kettle on!' to Susan, I followed the sheep, jumping the bank and into Eddie's field, running for the little river. I jumped in off the bank and lay down in the swiftly flowing, unwarm water. I was washed clean as a lamb. Back indoors, teeth chattering as she helped to dry me, I asked Susan, 'Were you actually woken by the sound of sheep crunching cabbage *outside?*'

'Yes,' she said.

Her hearing has always been good. The shivering gradually subsided as I downed a large mug of hot sweet tea.

Later that month, after Susan had gone to bed, I cycled to my darkroom in Eileen's garage and printed thirty-seven postcards showing examples of Great Western architecture for the publisher Michael Joseph. They had asked for help in illustrating a book written for British Railways by O. S. Nock and Gordon Biddle. All the pictures were taken on 'the wrong side of the fence' and those detailing the special roof of Slough station were taken *on* the roof. They chose to use eleven for the book, no questions asked as to the obvious trespassing on railway property. That book was *The Railway Heritage of Britain*.

When I handed over the final draft of my Faringdon branch book, I reckoned on waiting a year to receive any royalties. In fact, I waited two years for it to be published, then another year before I received any payment. Between 1971 and 1977 OPC published four of my books but the income trickled in more slowly than the hole in the overdraft deepened. Orders for photographs came in from other railway authors and the OPC asked for prints on behalf of their other authors, but copyright fees were equally slow in arriving. I had worked hard and nothing much had been gained. I started worrying. Sometimes the stress was so great that it brought on asthma and I'd dress and walk along the road in the dark hoping the fresh air would help my breathing.

My tome *A Pictorial Record of Great Western Architecture* was published on 18th April 1977. The book has 442 12-by-10-inch pages with about 650 illustrations. I got my copy on the 27th. Christy Riordan, the postman, stopped outside our gate in pouring rain. I went out to meet him.

'I have a big fella for you today,' he said, opening the back door of *An Post*'s little green Renault 4.

I reached in to pick it up.

'Ah – there's £1.50 duty to pay for that,' he said.

I straightened up. 'It's a book I wrote – I haven't the money in the house. It's my free copy, years of labour.'

Christy, who was a good kind man, hesitated for a moment. The rain was teeming down. Then his sense of duty reasserted itself. 'Ah well, you'd best be coming to the Post Office with the money.' He closed the doors on the book and drove off in a cloud of spray.

I got the bike and cycled rapidly through the rain to the Allied Irish Bank, took out five pounds and retrieved the book. A slow, wet ride home ensued, cycling one handed with the book under the other arm. Excitedly ripping off the damp wrapping, the book emerged. This was my *magnum opus*. The glossy dust cover was exposed! Most prominent in the picture was the foreground, one-third of the picture, fifty yards of black tarmac rising to a view of the back of an arsenic-green Western National bus and rising beyond that, in the background, the Great Western & *Midland Railway's* Joint station at Bristol Temple Meads. It had strong Midland Railway overtones, and overall in bold, gold letters was *Great Western Architecture*!

I was shocked and generally disappointed. For the dust jacket of the book I had asked my artist friend Sean Bolan, a fellow signalman, admirer of the GWR and a fine jazz musician, to paint a picture suitable to the title. This he did with pen and coloured inks in his meticulous style, a display of authentic GWR architecture: Box station, showing many of the buildings featured in the book. OPC had discarded that without any consultation with me. The contents were, however, unique, and a national 'first'. I still hoped the book would be our support as we continued to rebuild the cottage. I wrote on the title page: 'For Susan, from Adrian. The light at the end of the tunnel!?'

Late March and early April was the start of the turf-cutting season. I could have bought a load but I wanted to cut my own. I had no idea what that would entail, I just liked to do things by my own efforts. I had had a look at 'Eddie's bog', but even I could see it was useless. We asked around and found that we could rent for the season a bank of best-quality turf for one pound per foot run. I paid £33 for a bank that was eight sods high. Timmy and Anne volunteered to come and help cut the bank because they knew that we wouldn't have a clue as to how to go about cutting turf. They also provided transport because we still didn't have a car.

Early on a lovely day at the beginning of April we travelled out from Anne's house along the Caherciveen road and eventually turned left onto a rocky 'bog road', rising up until it reached the rim of a 'bowl' in the hills. There before us, over hundreds of acres, lay Oolagh bog. It was to the west of the Caragh Lake and possibly within the district of that name. Timmy had brought his turf spade – the *sleán* – and a two-pronged pitchfork. The word is spelled *sleán*, but Pat Clifford pronounced the word to rhyme with 'ah' – slahn.

The *sleán* was an ancient tool, the design surely unchanged through centuries of hard labour. I'd like to describe it. The 'L'-shaped steel blade did the cutting, the metal rising to form a steel socket clinched around the squared end of the wooden handle. A wooden wedge was hammered in between the squared end of the handle and the steel socket. The wedge had a projection outwards from the handle for a boot to press the blade into the soggy turf. The wedge was always formed from a piece of elm that had a knot in it, so when the wood was cut to become a wedge, the knot wood rested on the top of the metal socket. If that was not done, the pressure of the boot on the projection would cause the wood to break off following the line of its grain. Standing in a shelter for eleven months of the year, the wood would dry and shrink, so well before the cutting season started the *sleán* was put in a bucket of water to make the wood swell and fit tightly.

169

Anne brought matches and kindling. While this seemed a practical thing to do, apparently it was actually necessary to light a fire on the bog to bring good luck to the turf-cutting. She also brought a kettle and some food. Susan also brought a basket of food for a long day.

Timmy stood on the turf bank eight feet high, at the foot of which was soil, small white stones, trickling water and me. Timmy cut away a broad swathe of heather that covered the bog and rolled it up like a carpet. Then he walked to the corner of the bank, where it turned a right-angle, placed the *sleán* on the top of the solid black mass of turf, a few inches away from the edge of the bank, and drove the blade down for the first of hundreds of cuts. The *sleán* was driven down at a slight outwards angle. I expected him to cut it vertically but the bank had to 'lean back', otherwise if might fall forwards owing to the weight of soggy turf behind it.

He levered out a long, rectangular chunk – a sod. It fell to me. I picked it up on the prongs of the pitchfork, and tossed it to his son, who tossed it to Anne, who was standing a distance away on the heather. This was called 'brinching'. Anne and Susan arranged the sods close together at a good distance from the edge of the bank, leaving that space to be filled with the sods that would be cut, without any one of them lying on top of another. Timmy was like a powerful little bull and cut away so fast that he had to stop now and then to allow me to clear the sods he'd cut. I never imagined it could be so tiring.

To give me a break from 'brinching', he occasionally gave me the *sleán* for a while. Even using that needed some practice. I got the hang of it in the end. We silently worked for hours up to one o'clock, when he asked Anne to make up the fire with bits and pieces of last year's turf lying about, and get the kettle boiling. The kettle boiled, the tea was brewed and we ate in the springy heather under a beautiful April sky. They sat and talked and kindly told us how well we were doing, while Susan and I were straightening our backs lying flat out on the heather. I was aware that this was only 'half time'.

Timmy got everyone going again before an hour had passed. We cut and 'brinched', cutting the edge of the bank back and back and down and down till we were several feet back from the original line of the bank. Timmy didn't call 'tea-time'. The shadows were lengthening. He was down the face of the bank close to the bottom. The *sleán* made sucking noises as it levered back and pulled the ever more waterlogged sods free. He was lifting them his arm's length above his head to reach me on top of the bank.

He drove in his *sleán* again and a horizontal column of brown water exploded noisily out of the bank, hitting Timmy amidships. He managed to jump sideways as the force of the water hit him. He was soaked just about all over.

'That's why we cut the bank down at an angle,' he called up with a big grin. 'That could have brought the bank down on me otherwise.'

The water was coming out of the bank in a stream now and Timmy started cutting again, soon cutting with his boots under water, sloshing and squelching in a soggy quagmire.

The light was definitely failing now and clouds of tiny, stinging midges were like a cloud around us. I swallowed clouds of them, coughed and hawked in my throat and spat them out. They preferred to sting the skin of sweaty arms and the half circle around the bottom of the eyes. Still we kept on. Timmy had exhibited leadership all day and I was wondering when he would cry 'Hold – enough!'

Across the twilight bowl of the bog I could see that work had slackened; some men were standing around, some digging and some seemed to be looking in our direction.

'What's the time, Timmy?' I asked.

'About eight o'clock.'

'When do we stop? It's getting dark.'

'Ye can stop whenever ye like,' said he. 'Everyone knows we've an Englishman cutting turf and no one's going to lave off until you do.'

'Well, for God's sake, man! Let's get out of here now,' says I with a grateful exasperation in my voice.

Timmy called time to his family and Susan up above, and in a few minutes we were walking to the car, tools shouldered – and drawing the entire workforce of the bog with us. Timmy, in the car, reckoned we had '…a good four cubic yards of turf – all ye've got to do now is get it dry. Ye'll need to be up here regularly to lift the sods up on end and lean half a dozen against each other and then one across the top.'

Timmy and Anne refused to accept any payment for all their hard work and we felt humbled by their kindness.

In May our solicitor, wrote to say that he had received the final Rulings on Title and that he had sent them to the vendor's solicitor for Registration. He enclosed his final bill: his fee of £58 plus costs of £35.57½p with the promise that he would send the title deed in due course.

On 18th June a cheque arrived from OPC for £515. Relief was great, with an afterthought of disappointment; I thought with two books earning there would have been more than that. Susan and I bought some much-needed clothes, paid the solicitor's fee, paid our latest debt to Chub Connor for building materials, and what was left went into the overdraft. I hoped the Allied Irish Bank would see I was a committed repayer and continue to lend to me. In by the right hand, out by the left.

Chapter Eighteen
The Sunbeam Vogue

With next winter's supply of turf cut and drying on the bog, I had several hard jobs ahead of me indoors, including plastering the walls, making tiled floors, providing ceilings of tongue-and-groove matchboarding for the bedroom and sitting room, internal doors to make and running an electric ring main.

The twenty-five-foot kitchen/living room now had a series of planed timber rafters and wall-top-height cross-ties making a set of business-like triangles rising to a peak fourteen feet above our heads. It seemed a pity to close in that space by fixing up a matchboarded ceiling. From that splendid book *Twenty Years a' Growing*, I had learned about sleeping lofts in the cottages of the Blasket Islands lying off the Kerry coast. I laid four-by-three-quarter-inch tongue-and-groove planks over the rafter cross-ties from the kitchen chimney ten feet forward above the room. Then I built a ladder from planed pine, with the rungs 'half-lapped' and screwed into the side beams. We thought of painting white the hardboard on the rafters above the sleeping loft, but then thought it would be cosier with the plain brown board. It was almost a 'minstrel's gallery' to the cottage interior.

The next job was running a ring main around the cottage with plenty of three-pin plug sockets and wiring for the electric lights. I had thought about the ring main in terms of water running through a pipe with branch pipes going down or up to the wall sockets, keeping the red and black wires separate and continuous in and out of junction boxes. It was a straightforward job to do – and indeed it was still working safely when I last saw the cottage in 2012.

Proper cement floors needed to be laid in the kitchen and bedroom at the west end of the cottage. The cement floor in the

173

east-end room was in good condition. All the interior walls of the cottage needed a coating of Portland cement. The kitchen walls were the original, ancient walls of large pillow-shaped stones, bedded on earth; there was no mortar between them, and they had originally been covered with a sandy kind of plaster that we had knocked off. A lot of cement would be needed to fill all the spaces between them and bring about an acceptable degree of verticality and adequate smoothness. They wouldn't ever be perfect but I reckoned that perfectly smooth, upright plastering wouldn't look right in this, originally poverty-stricken, cottage.

I would have to buy cubic yards of sand and cement powder, so it would still be wise to obtain some training. Timmy was working as a plasterer with other craftsmen renovating a saloon on New Street in Killarney. He good-humouredly agreed that I could come along with him to the bar and be his helper and watch him at the plastering. Joining in with a cheerful group of workmen, and being accepted as one of them, was a nice change from working alone and in silence, when Susan wasn't there. Going home in his van on the Friday evening I asked him if he would come to the cottage some time and give me a lesson, and stand by me while I tried my hand at plastering with cement in the small sitting room.

He turned up one evening the following week around seven o'clock. He'd had his dinner and now he was ready to set to work with the plastering. We were just finishing dinner.

'I'll give ye a start,' he said. 'Ye can watch me and then take over.'

I went out into the garden, mixed up cement in the big wheelbarrow and took it through to the east-end room. He loaded the mortar board, which I had earlier made, swiped a load onto the wall and swept his hand around in a quarter circle. And again, and again. Well, there was no stopping him in spite of his having been at work all day! He was 'on a roll'. He gave me no opportunity to practise under his guidance. I'd mixed the Portland cement at the right consistency and it went on beautifully. I stood and watched for a while, then slipped away until he came asking me to mix some more cement. I mixed some more and he carried on. Susan crept off to bed. I was exhausted, the room had no fire and the night chill was getting to me because I was just standing around. I felt I couldn't just walk away and leave him to it. It didn't seem possible to ask to have a go. He was a robot plasterer. I mixed the last barrow-load by the light of the window at half past midnight, and by one o'clock Timmy had completed two walls. He came for two more evenings after that and did about fifteen hours work in total. As he walked from the cottage after the three evenings' work he said to me in a very satisfied kind of way, 'Well now, ye'll know well enough how to do the plastering.'

And he was right! Somehow I managed to plaster the remaining wall. My work wasn't up to his standard, but it served well enough.

With the walls in the sitting room plastered, it seemed fairly straightforward to complete the renovation. Adrian made a little sketch of what the room should look like and we worked to that plan. We put up a pine matchboard ceiling and varnished it, bringing out the golden colour of the pine. We put in a Victorian cast-iron fireplace surround to hide the plain rectangular fireplace opening, then Adrian fitted a wooden mantelpiece on top and built a tiled hearth on the floor in front. We bought a brand-new shiny black fireplace grate with a solid front, which neatly fitted into the opening. Finally I painted the walls white and the floor with red floor paint, finishing it off with a circular hessian mat. Adrian built wooden shelves to one side of the fireplace and it felt very satisfying to have somewhere to put our books and the Dansette record player. I hung my William Morris 'Golden Lily' pattern curtains from The Old Chapel at the windows, using dowel for curtain poles, and put pictures on the walls. Finally we painted our mahogany GWR table a matt sage green – it was perfect to use as a writing table with plenty of room for the 'Imperial' typewriter. So now we had a white, green and gold sitting-room-cum-study. It seemed very fitting! All we needed now were some comfortable chairs.

We slept in the sleeping loft while work in the bedroom was going on. I had won first prize of £50 in the local lottery, so we were able to buy two single foam mattresses that fitted snugly into the loft. We dismantled our big heavy bed and between us staggered it to one end of the kitchen so Adrian could start work.

It took me two or three arm-aching and very tedious days in the bedroom, in scorching weather, to hack the old cement, damp in places, from the walls, with my eyes, nose and throat full of grit and dust. Then I broke up the thin cement skim of the bedroom floor and dug down into the earth, shovelling the debris out through the bedroom window into the wheelbarrow and took it onto Eddie's track, filling deep ruts. I was glad to do something useful for Eddie.

I intended to lay down a membrane of heavy-duty plastic sheet over the soils and undermine the walls a little so the concrete, when it was thrown in, would push the plastic in under the wall and provide some kind of a damp-proof layer. I needed some clean gravel. I asked Eddie if I could take some of the sandy gravel that lay in piles at the riverside end of his meadow beside the Laune. Ever obliging, he just said, 'Worrk away-a.'

Having experienced the effort of wheelbarrowing debris along his field track, I looked for some less energetic mode of haulage and thought of John Foley's donkey and flat-bed trolley. He said the donkey would only work for him or his daughter Eileen, but she would come round with the donkey and trailer after he'd been to the creamery with his milk churns on Saturday morning. And so it was, backwards and forwards over the rough track all day, loading the gravel onto the little cart. Progress was slow, as slow as the pace of life in Kerry, but we got there in the end. During the following week I mixed the concrete in the big, navvy-sized barrow and tipped surely more than a ton of it onto the plastic sheeting, levelling it approximately with our garden rake. When the concrete was hard, I set up a rectangular framework of three-by-two-inch timber, wedged tightly between the walls and perfectly level side to side. The enclosed space was then filled with a hard mix of 3:1 sand to cement, and levelled with the ten-foot-long 'screeding' timber.

I was in the garden, mixing cement, when an American couple walking by stopped on the road and opened a conversation. The obvious restoration of the cottage appealed to them.

'We're from Chicago', said the man.

He worked in a bank there, but felt he'd rather live in Kerry. 'If we came to live here, do you think I could get a job in a Kerry bank?' he asked.

They were genuinely interested in the work I was doing and were sure Susan and I had the right idea in wanting to live in Kerry, so I invited them in. I gave them tea, soda bread – which I had made myself – buttered and spread with Susan's home-made gooseberry jam. They went on their way most happily and I got back to finishing laying the bedroom floor.

Then I re-plastered the walls with cement, putting the lessons learned from Timmy to good use until I felt I was quite good at it. I still couldn't get a perfect 'Timmy' finish, so I'd wait until the cement was firm but not set, then go over it with a dead flat, rigid three-by-two-inch timber, after the manner of a wood plane. Any hollows I would fill with a handful of wet cement, worked in. It was a good technique to use except that the wet cement tended to burn my skin and leave bad sores. These slowly healed with the judicious application of butter or Ponds cold cream. Putting up the tongue-and-groove matchboarding ceiling was tedious, working with arms high and looking upwards all the time, but eventually I got it done. I finished off by making and hanging an ordinary plank door for the room.

To furnish the room we found, in a second-hand furniture store in Castlemaine called 'The Castlemaine Emporium', a handsome Edwardian mahogany wardrobe with a bottom drawer, a mirror the length of the ornate central door, and a three-drawer, mahogany dressing table with a nice oval mirror on top. The owner, Eugene, delivered the furniture and carried it into the bedroom. When that was done, in went our big bed. We had a bedroom! We planned to paper it later and Susan ordered some pretty wallpaper from Laura Ashley. But in the meantime we had to move back into the almost finished bedroom to make way for summer visitors to use the sleeping loft.

We had been without a car for seven months. We had to ask various good-natured people for help in getting heavy building materials out to our place from Chub's yard. Michael Doyle had brought us loads of cement in his tractor and trailer and we had borrowed a friend's light lorry to bring home large loads of building timber that the bike couldn't handle. The people around us looked out for us and if we asked for help they would give it, but I didn't like continuously having to impose on their good nature.

We needed a large 'estate'-bodied car for carrying cumbersome loads. All we could afford would be a rebuildable rust bucket. In *The Kerryman* I saw a 1970 Sunbeam 'Vogue' advertised by Kelliher of Tralee at £250. With the rear seats folded down it would become the equivalent of a van and just the thing for carrying building materials, firewood or turf. At the age and price of this one I knew that it would need some mechanical attention, but I had always carried out repairs and replacements ever since my first car in 1959.

Susan had seen an advert for a Morris Traveller at an auction sale at East Grove House, near Cobh. Nostalgia took over. I went to the Allied Irish bank in Killorglin to ask for a loan. Entering the bank I found a typically shabby Kerry farmer at the counter unloading bank notes from every pocket. He formed a large, loose pile on the counter. He must have sold some cattle. He turned away and walked to the door saying, 'Book that in for me.'

The bank official leaning against the wall at the far end of the open counter didn't move but called out he'd see to it, then said, 'What can I do for you, Adrian?'

The informality was pleasantly reassuring. There were no glass screens, just the counter. In response to the bank man's question, I said, 'I have to go to Cobh to buy a car. Can I have a loan for £300?'

The gentleman heaved off the wall, came along the counter and, with the back of his hand, pushed the pile of money towards me.

'Take it out of that, so,' he said.

I counted out £300 and, the delightfully carefree atmosphere being infectious, I put the wad of notes in my pocket and turned to leave.

'Ah – you'd better sign for that, Adrian,' says your man.

'Oh – of course, sorry,' said I, and signed the form and that was that.

On 14th July Susan and I got up early. Outside there was a summer fog that heralded a beautiful day. With Susan sitting on the parcel carrier over the back mudguard (her bike had been stolen a few months earlier), I cycled us into Killorglin to hitch a lift – get 'a drive', as they say in Ireland – to Killarney railway station and a train to Cork City. The town was silent. We stood on the magnificent, eight-arched stone bridge and hoped for a drive. The mist was blowing through the central arches like smoke through chimneys. A 'rigid' ten-tonner came down the hill, we stuck our thumbs out and he stopped. He was 'in the forestry' going to Killarney. We climbed into his cab. We were at Killarney station booking office at a quarter to eight. We bought tickets and were told, 'Take the 8.30 from here and change at Mallow.'

At 8.20 the train came rolling down the slope of the Tralee line, merged onto the Mallow line and went on till the end of the train was clear of the points. Then it reversed into the station. We were away at 8.30 am. Outside Cork station we walked towards Cobh along the Glanmire road, thumbs out, and again we got a drive all the way to East Grove House! The land around was very beautiful. We were dropped off at the entrance to the tree-lined driveway. The house was part very elegant, very early nineteenth century, and part red-brick Edwardian. Behind it stood a folly castle. With one's back to the house the land fell away in well-cared-for lawns to a pier, the river and some yachts. It reminded me of the Dart estuary at Kingswear.

We found the Morris Traveller that was up for auction. Only then did I realise that Morris Travellers were too small and too flimsy for the hard work I had in mind, and this one wasn't even in good condition. My heart sank, but we had made such an effort to

179

get there that we stayed for the sale. The day became sweltering. We were short of water and hadn't brought enough to eat. Five uncomfortable hours later, at four o'clock, the rusty little Morris Traveller was knocked down for £410!

The money in my pocket had to be saved to buy a car, so we would have to walk home and hope for a lift. We set off down the drive and in seconds a car stopped. The old lady driver asked us if we wanted a drive. She was going to Cobh town. That wasn't really on the road home but maybe it was a start, so we climbed in. She drove us through forests, over rutted tracks, but eventually we got to Cobh, a remarkably handsome town.

We were getting tired and we were *hungry*. We would have to get a train to Cork. At Cobh station there seemed nowhere to get a ticket. I asked a man in CIÉ uniform on the platform beside the three-coach train where we could buy a ticket. He said, 'I'll sell you one on the train.'

We climbed aboard. The train left at six o'clock and stopped at several tiny stations, overgrown with bushes and grass, and, by then quite crowded, arrived at Cork, a half-hour run. The CIÉ man hadn't taken our fares, nor from anyone else within my sight. I reckoned forty ticketless people walked off that train. Was it known as a free train? How did the CIÉ man expect to keep his job? Surely the profitless line would have to close. It looked as if the wayside stations already had.

Susan was feeling unwell, hot and hungry, so we went to the station buffet and bought 'two teas, two sausage rolls and two sweet buns' for ninety-six pence. That cleaned out the last bit of loose change. We spoke our gratitude to the memory of the guard of the ticketless train. After that snack and a sit down Susan felt better and we set off, walking for home, about sixty-seven miles away. We walked through Cork City, admiring the buildings and deploring the amount of paper rubbish blowing about the pavements. We walked and walked. At the start of the long straight, past the enormous Eglinton Asylum, we got a drive for a few miles, then began the walk uphill off the coastal plain. We walked through villages and on

180

and on, sometimes side by side, but as time went on more and more with Susan lagging behind. The next lonely car that approached I stood out into the road and waved my arms. The driver swerved around me and the car's rear lights disappeared around the bend.

Ten minutes later we got a drive to Macroom. It was 8.30 pm. We thought of finding a B&B but there was still midsummer's fading twilight and we walked on. We had covered quite five more miles. The sun was low, the sky looked bruised and threatening, red and purple. I was getting worried for Susan. Were we going to have to sleep in a wood? We walked uphill towards the rapidly setting sun. Around ten o'clock we approached the lighted windows of a solitary bungalow. We went over and knocked on the door to ask if we were anywhere near a B&B, thinking maybe the occupants would take pity on us and ask us in. The lady who answered the door said, 'Yes, my sister runs a B&B – she's just along the road a way. I'll take you there.'

We must have made a sorry sight and maybe that helped. The B&B lady was most solicitous. She made us a very welcome supper, crusts delicately removed from the white bread, and sent us to bed. She woke us at quarter to eight next day. She apologised for the early call but said her brother was 'in the forestry' and was driving his lorry to the Kenmare area and would take us with him. 'He'll be here at half-eight,' she smiled.

We had orange juice and cornflakes followed by poached egg on white bread toast, followed by more white bread toast and marmalade with lots of tea. The brother wasn't knocking on the door at 8.30 so we thanked the lady for her kindness, paid her bill of six pounds and went outside to wait for her brother.

We were still waiting at 8.40 and Susan was actually in tears. She had to be in Henry's Killarney shop at ten o'clock. Five minutes later the brother turned up and off we went. He took us through Kenmare, climbing higher until the road was running alongside a rushing river, then a lake, and clearly, without a word being said, beyond where his business would have taken him. He stopped at Ladies View, the summit of the climb, and turning to us with a smile said, "'Tis eleven or twelve miles to Killarney from here and I'm sorry I can't take you any further. May the road rise to up meet you.'

It did, as he had intended. We thanked him most gratefully and walked on. We walked until we came to a B&B. It was 9.30. We knocked on the door and asked if we could use their telephone. Susan wanted to warn Henry that she was going to be late for work. We thanked the lady of the house and offered to pay something for the call but she wouldn't hear of it and we went outside to walk on. We'd not gone a mile when a car driver took pity on us and brought us into Killarney, the road twisting and winding, past walls of rocks and forests of gnarled and ancient trees. We got to the shop at five minutes past ten!

I took a look around Killarney's second-hand car dealers. There were large estate cars, but nothing we could afford. As I walked out of Killarney, along the Killorglin road, without a thumbing arm out, I'd got as far as the cathedral when a perceptive and sympathetic car driver stopped and offered me a lift. He was bound for Killorglin and, as I wanted Meanus, he kindly turned off at the Beaufort turn, over the ancient, mossy stone bridge across the Laune, turned right by the Beaufort Bar and along the Killorglin road. The feeling of relief at seeing our little cottage was so great that I forgot our labours and recalled with a great warmth of feeling the kindnesses that had been showered upon us.

The following day I set out walking to Tralee hoping to buy the Sunbeam 'Vogue'. A mile out of Killorglin I got a drive. Michael Doyle's brother recognised me. He was driving a Sunbeam 'Vogue.' I bought Kelliher's £250 'Vogue' for £200 – I had learned that in Ireland one haggled. In England it would have been sent to the crusher. It was dark blue and its name was NIN, a Kerry registration. My diary records:

'The rear half of the silencer is missing. The driver's door is sagging on its hinges. The nearside chassis strut is rotted off. The engine is off-beat. Throttle pedal is almost u/s due to rusted floor and the handbrake *is* u/s. But it runs quietly enough, no gearbox noise. The oil pressure gauge shows 30 lbs per sq.in when the engine is hot, which is good. The alternator charges. Every accessory works, the heater, the indicators, all the front and rear lights, the reversing lights and the wipers. Should be a decent old car when I've tidied it up.'

It got over the long steep climb to the summit of the hills to the south of Tralee. I warmed to it.

I bought rear brake linings and fitted them, which put the handbrake into working order. An adjustment to the distributor and new sparking plugs brought the engine back to 'four-beats-to-the-bar'. Kelliher's garage in Killorglin did welding repairs to the floor, chassis and strut. Hey presto! Not such a bad old bus after all. It was insured third party with Susan as the other named driver. Six days after that the clutch release mechanism failed. I replaced the hydraulic cylinder and all was well.

Just about the time I was putting the Sunbeam into order, *The Kerryman* newspaper of 13th July 1977 reported a court case from Charleville, Co Cork, whereby Mr R., a resident of Charleville, had, in July 1974, bought a car from a garage in Mallow, with the promise from the salesman that it was in perfect condition and a loan from a Dublin finance company. Mr R. drove the car to carry out his work — driving around eighty miles a day. After two weeks all four forward gears failed. He could not afford to buy a new gearbox, lost his job and went on the dole with a wife and four children to provide for. He continued to use the car to take his family to Mass, driving four miles each way in reverse. Being unemployed he was unable to keep up his repayments to the finance company, but it was not until July 1977, when the latter was owed £510, that Mr R. was sued for repossession of the car. The judge gave the finance company possession and Mr R. drove the car, in reverse, to the showroom from which he had bought it.

Chapter Nineteen
The septic tank

It was such a relief to have a car again. I had been working full time in the antique shop in Killarney for the past two weeks as the woman who normally worked there was ill. Hitching lifts in and out of Killarney nearly every day was no fun and driving seemed a great luxury after that. I worked three weeks full time altogether and the money it brought in was welcome, but I was glad to get back to normal as there was so much to do at home. The garden had been very productive through the summer with broad beans, peas, lettuces, courgettes, delicious new potatoes and a long cylindrical variety of beetroot that was particularly good grated raw into salads. The French beans and runner beans were coming on and I urgently needed to bottle our second crop of broad beans and peas.

As I was harvesting these, a woman passing by stopped to talk. She seemed fascinated by what I was doing so I invited her in to have a look at the garden. It transpired that she had never seen peas growing in pods before, although she knew about peas in tins and had never heard of broad beans or runner beans. She was utterly amazed by the idea of bottling vegetables and making jam.

'Sure, why bother when you can buy them in the shops?' she said.

I didn't have an answer to that – it just felt too difficult to explain.

In July the bees from the hive we'd bought from Mr Prendergast last year swarmed. The swarm landed on the branch of a tree in the hedge on our side of the road. While they were busy clinging in a buzzing, humming, dark brown ball, Adrian got a large cardboard box and a large stick and, with me following in some trepidation behind, advanced on the swarm. Holding the box in his left hand and the stick in his right he gave the branch a good thwack and the swarm fell into the box. He took it over to the new beehive he had made and leaned it against the landing platform. It didn't take long for the bees to occupy their new home. We were of course thrilled that we had another hive of bees, but an old adage leapt warningly into my brain: 'A swarm in May is worth a load of hay; a swarm in June is worth a silver spoon; but a swarm in July is not worth a fly.'

One day Agnes brought us three fine trout that Pat had caught while fishing for salmon. We had them with fresh mushrooms picked from the field, new potatoes and peas from our garden, cooked on the range from a hot fire of wood cut the previous winter. The cats also made contributions towards our menu. Once Baby Cat caught a cock pheasant which had been wounded by shotgun pellets. I was working on a plank of wood in the garden and heard a terrible hissing and growling over the hedge of Eddie's field. Then the hedge started to quake and the cat came backwards through it into the garden with her little sharp teeth clamped tightly around the neck of the live and struggling pheasant. I took the plank out of the vice, ran across to the action, shoved the cat out of the way and whacked the pheasant over the head with the plank. That quickly put it out of its misery and gave us the chance of a meal. Susan plucked and gutted the bird. We had a roast pheasant dinner that evening and pheasant soup the next day, and Baby Cat had her share too.

Shortly after that I was walking down Eddie's field to check on the goats and Tolly cat was following, crying for me to find him a rabbit from my elevated position above the path. He was sniffing all the bramble bushes at the same time, then two baby rabbits shot across the track. I called Tolly, who came up at the double, all ears and whiskers, and I shoved him into the reeds in the direction of the rabbits. There was a scuffle, Tolly bounded high into the air over the reeds, disappeared and came up a few feet away with a struggling rabbit. I left him to it, but when I came back a few minutes later he had gone off and left it lying dead on the path. So I took it home and we had it in a stew that evening with carrots, onion and potato.

The rabbit stew was very tasty and I determined then to buy a gun, but father-in-law John loaned me his single-barrelled shotgun. There were lots of rabbits further down towards the river where there were grassy sand banks. I killed several but found it difficult to skin and gut them. I hadn't reckoned on my squeamishness. Shooting is easy, impersonal, but the hand-to-hand stuff is difficult. Susan did it, but had to hold her nose against the bad smell as she hooked out the guts. Shooting finished when I broke the gun. I had wounded a running rabbit; it was lying, kicking, on its side, and I used the butt of the gun to club it on the head. The butt killed the rabbit but broke away from the barrel. That was decidedly embarrassing to report to father-in-law, but it was also a relief as I could now stop shooting rabbits!

Late in July I had a look inside the old beehive – then went to fetch my protective clothing in order to take honey, subduing the bees first with a few whiffs from the smoker. Susan watched from the cottage door, well away from the frantic scene. The bees fought bravely for their hard-won honey, buzzing around me in their thousands. They did not seem to be much subdued. Bees stood on my gauntlets and worked their stings into the leather, just as I would try to force a bradawl through a leather belt. Only one bee managed to sting me, but their frantic efforts bore in on my conscience. Hardening my heart and quelling my conscience, I took 36lb of glorious comb honey. In August I was able to take some more, leaving enough to see the bees through the winter. We had 42½lb of honey in total. The second hive did not have any spare honey and in fact needed supplementing with a sugar solution.

While shopping in Killorglin, Susan met an English woman, Linda Scott. She and her husband Michael Clabburn had not long come back from South America where they had been living and working, and had bought Gus and Les's old place at Mealis. Linda introduced us to her family. Her father, John Scott, owned a tap and die factory 'Scott's Tools' in Killarney He told me he had been invited by the Irish Government to open the factory so as to train and employ local people in that branch of precision engineering. It

186

was a happy bunch of people there. John Scott was a good employer. He and Linda became our kind and helpful friends.

One evening in late July we went up to Mealis to have supper with Linda and Michael. She offered us her shower room in a diplomatically offhand way and we enjoyed a wonderful hot shower before sitting down to the meal. A man called Jack Chowne was also a guest. Jack was the estate manager for the absentee owner of the Churchtown estate near Beaufort, four miles along the road from our cottage. As the evening and conversation moved on, he told us he'd started his farming career as the manager of a farm on the Englefield estate of Sir Henry Benyon, Lord Lieutenant of Berkshire, in 1950. I was astonished and said, 'My older brother Keith started his apprenticeship to gardening in the walled gardens and greenhouses of the Englefield estate in 1950 under the Head Gardener, Mr Bath. Keith used to come home with peaches and nectarines, courtesy of Mr Bath.'

The coincidences multiplied as the wine bottles emptied. I learned that Jack also knew Childrey, the village our family had moved to in 1953. He was a friend of Major Dennistoun, a racehorse trainer in Childrey, for whom I had worked as a schoolboy stable lad looking after his daughter's two showjumping ponies. Dennistoun had supplied me with an Arab/Connemara pony and his daughters, Tory and Ginny, taught me to ride. Jack asked me if I remembered the horse called 'St David'. I did. It belonged to Colonel Flewellyn, who, in 1952, on his legendary horse 'Foxhunter', was Captain of the British Olympic Equestrian team. I'd gone with Dennistoun in his antique Albion horse box to Monmouthshire to collect 'St David' and bring him back to Childrey for Tory to ride.

Dinners at Linda's, which she cooked after a full day's work in her father's factory in Killarney, were evenings of good food, wine and conversation. They were a great relaxation from our Spartan existence – not that we were at all discontented, but they were always, for us, sparkling occasions.

There was other entertainment too. Susan finding work with Henry Dodd was a great blessing, not only for the wages she received, but also for Henry's real friendship. Occasionally we were invited to his home, which had once been a two-storey house but had been reduced to a spacious bungalow at some distant past time. It was furnished entirely with beautiful antique furniture: clocks, carpets, silver and porcelain. Opulent, as one would expect from an antique dealer.

Henry was a very urbane, sophisticated personality. He must have had a very different schooling from anyone else I'd met in Kerry. His voice was pleasant with an educated English accent laced with a soft, Irish one. It was ideal for a raconteur. Henry told stories of the eccentricities of the people of his circle and beyond. He spoke with affection and a smile. He remembered to us Lady Fitzmaurice, who was the last survivor of the family of the Earls of Kerry, a bunch of aristocratic 'ne'er-do-wells' apparently. Her ladyship was devoted to her flock of dozens of cats. She gave dinner parties for her friends but would leave in the middle to attend to a sick or dying cat. She earned a living as a farmer and drove about the Killorglin district in a battered old green van, delivering eggs, butter and home-made jams and pickles.

Only once did he say anything about his background, his family. After dinner with him one evening, when the room was softly lit and warm and the wine was fine, he broke into a family tale. After his father had died, when Henry was eleven, his father's cousin, well into his seventies, had taken Henry 'under his wing', as the saying goes. He was married and lived up at Caragh Lake. The couple always dressed in worn old clothes fifty years behind the fashion. Each winter his wife went to London and the old man went to Jamaica. He had to travel cheaply, so to Jamaica he went in a banana boat, but surely not *that* cheap – these banana boats had swimming pools!

The old man liked to swim in the ship's pool but his swimming costume was the one he had bought as a young man before the Great War. It had horizontal dark blue stripes ringing the legs, trunk and sleeves, but the moths had eaten out the crotch. The old man was nearly blind and was not aware of this and his appearance at the pool caused more than ripples. He refused to part with his costume, but he lost it in the end when bathing from a Jamaican beach. Leaving it on the sands, he went away for a cigar or something and came back to find that the tide had risen and taken his precious costume out to sea.

It was through Henry that we were made aware of the concerts held regularly in Killarney cathedral. I was in the Killarney shop with Susan one Saturday in early July when Henry walked in bringing a friend, a Welshman with the soft and musical accent of the South Wales valleys. Henry introduced us to Keith Jones, who was a tenor soloist with the Guinness choir, the other tenor soloist being Frank Patterson.

The choir was in Killarney to sing J. S. Bach's 'St John Passion', accompanied by the Killarney Bach Festival Orchestra. Living among the smallholders of the Beaufort road we enjoyed and respected their musical talents, but had no idea that there was also music of this polish to be heard locally: music I had grown up with as a child. Henry and Keith were going to a hotel for drinks and invited me to come too. Poor Susan had to stay to mind the shop. Over drinks the tenor soloist in the religious musical drama kept us laughing with a string of witty, blasphemous jokes. The following evening Susan and I went to St Mary's Cathedral, Killarney, to hear the great work of music and listen to Keith Jones sing the part of the Evangelist, St John.

During the summer the Group Water Scheme got under way and water pipes were laid along the Meanus Road. I set out to make the kitchen properly habitable and ready to receive the piped water. I cement plastered about five hundred square feet of rubble wall, dug out the mud floor, two hundred and fifty square feet and six inches deep. I laid down heavy plastic sheeting, bringing it up the side of the wall to floor level. John Foley again loaned me his donkey, flat-bed trolley and his daughter Eileen to bring up gravel from the banks of the river. The floor was laid after six full days of work.

With the prospect of piped water I started to think about building the bathroom extension, which should just fit between our back wall and the bank that formed a boundary with the Cliffords' farmyard. We were looking forward to replacing the dreadful Elsan chemical toilet, now located in the old duck shed, the contents of which had to be emptied into the Pit of Shit just outside the shed. But a flushing lavatory would require a septic tank – something I'd heard of but never seen.

In Killorglin Library I found a book on septic tanks. According to this book I needed to dig a two-foot-square manhole with a pipe connection into a tank seven feet deep and eight feet long. The neatly excavated hole would be lined with concrete blocks. I would dig out the soil and make casting boxes to construct the lids for the manhole and tank. The only place it could be dug was alongside the trackway in Eddie's field, nearly opposite the gable end of the cottage. Would he give us permission? How much would he want for his permission? I had to ask, and went along to his farmhouse, feeling somewhat nervous. He looked very puzzled and I had to explain why I needed this 'septic tank'. He made allowances for the odd ideas of a young English chap, overcame his puzzlement and replied with his usual brevity: 'Worrk away-a.'

I was 'blown away' by his off-hand generosity, thanked him profusely and hurried home.

I retrieved my pick-axe and spade from the shed and went into the field. A few yards from the east gable end of the cottage, at the side of the track, there was a grassy space between the jungles of flag iris and montbretia. I swung my pick-axe. Thud. Oooff. The point went in four inches and stuck. I pulled it out with difficulty. There was blue clay on the point. I would never be able to dig a pit there. My heart sank.

Going back to the road, I saw the JCB digging out the roadside trench for the mains water pipe. They were nearly at our gate. Salvation! I went to the driver. He switched off his engine, always ready for a chat.

'Now I'm getting the water, I'm wanting to build a bathroom and a septic tank. Eddie Moriarty says I can dig the pit in the field there but there's no way I can dig into that ground by hand. I'm wondering – would you be able to dig a pit for a septic tank in there?'

'I will o'course,' was the instant reply. 'I'll do it this evening after we've finished. We need somewhere to park the digger off the road. Can we be puttin' it through your gate there?'

'You can of course,' I said delightedly, glad to be able to do something in return.

I never told him the dimensions of the hole. I thought he would know, him being a water pipe layer. He set to work with his JCB and in minutes he had made all I needed. But he didn't stop and before I'd realised he made three more 'bites o' the bucket' and I now had a huge pit that would need to be filled after I built the tank.

'Whoa! Whoa!' I had to shout at him, over the noise of his tractor. 'The tank is to be eight feet long. That's more than enough!'

I built the septic tank to the correct dimensions, inside the gigantic hole, and shovelled the piles of earth back to fill the unwanted space. I dug a space for the manhole at the back of the cottage, then a trench, with pick and shovel, diagonally, on a gently falling gradient, across the track to the tank, according to the plans in the book. I then laid the sewage pipes down, before infilling the trench. Pat heard my labours and came round.

''Tis a grand job you're doin',' he said, 'but I'd not be bothering myself.'

I was astonished. 'Surely you have a tank yourself?'

'Ah, no, I have it piped away into the ditch above. There's a little stream there.'

And indeed, it worked perfectly – even Susan with her delicate sense of smell had no idea about this arrangement.

At last the cottage was connected to the mains water pipeline. I built a makeshift framework to support a pressed steel sink with a tap and connected the water pipe to that, and eventually used

191

matchboarding to clad the framework, making a rough and ready kitchen unit with a shelf inside.

In September our turf, stooked on the bog, was dried hard. For several days we drove to and fro, a wheelbarrow tied on the roof of NIN, along the Caherciveen road and left, climbing the stony bog road into the bog-land hills. We wheelbarrowed the sods of turf across the heather to where we'd left the car, and stacked the hard-won fuel in the boot. We brought the lovely stuff back to Meanus and stacked it neatly, in order to get as much in as possible, in the goat shed. A major operation of days. But the weather was glorious and driving through such scenery, under such great cloudy skies into the hills, was sheer delight.

Having got all our treasure home, we began to have second thoughts about the range. It looked magnificent with its burnished cast-iron and black backing, like something from a Sir Walter Scott novel. But the top plate never became really hot and the oven never got hot enough to bake potatoes. The 'draw' on the firebox wasn't strong enough and wasn't directed over the oven properly. I'd built the innards of the thing by thinking what was necessary, but without proper knowledge. I remembered Mossy Joy's words: 'Ye'll keep yourselves warm running in and out with the fuel.'

At the end of November I saw in *The Kerryman* an advert for a second-hand 'Stanley' range with a back boiler at Farranfore. Michael Clabburn had a two-wheeled, home-made-looking wooden trailer. I asked to borrow it and Michael agreed. We didn't know how much a Stanley range weighed, perhaps five hundredweight. Michael's trailer looked none too strong for the task ahead. Michael didn't ask questions but bravely said he'd use his car to tow it and be an extra pair of hands when it came to getting the massive thing out of the Farranfore house, down the path and up into the trailer.

So in moonlit dark – after he had finished work at Scott's Tools and had some dinner, we set off. The road from Farranfore was, of course, bumpy. Driving home at 25 mph with the range in the trailer, the bumps became awesome, tugging the car back and shoving it forwards, jerking up and down. When we got back to the cottage we could see even in the moonlight that the trailer was not as it had been at the start of our journey. Michael made no comment, which was generous of him, though I apologised profusely, and somehow we got the range out and onto the ground.

Next day I asked Michael Doyle to come with his tractor, fitted at the front with the usual hydraulic lifting bucket, to carry the range close to the porch. After that I had to get it through the porch and into the kitchen. Susan has a hazy memory that I used steel tubes beneath it on which, between us, we rolled it in. I suppose the hydraulic car jack I'd brought from England could also have been useful. Getting the cemented-in Sir-Walter-Scott-vintage range out of its alcove was traumatic. I hacked it out and knocked down the brick innards I had so carefully constructed. It was so awful getting it out of the alcove, then out into the garden and finding someone to take it away, that I have wiped the saga from my memory.

All through December I worked on the Stanley in between other jobs. We got the range up onto the plinth and, once in place, I was able to fix up the plumbing to a hot water storage tank and from there to the sink. I also fitted an immersion heater so that in the summer, when we didn't want to have the range going, we could still have hot water. On 31st December 1977 I lit the Stanley range for the first time. It burned the turf and got very hot and the water in the pipes began a frantic 'hammering'.

Being at a loss to know what to do, I swallowed my pride and went for advice to Timmy O'Shea, a builder, down the road, near Killorglin. He came and had a look at what I'd done. He was very diplomatic. Avoiding the mirth he must have felt at the sight before him, he said gently, 'Go to Boyles and buy a three-quarter-inch and a half-inch spring for bending pipes. Make curves – don't use any more of these right-angled connectors.'

I did as he said and, with the streamlined piping in place, I lit the range. The hot water system worked perfectly.

Chapter Twenty
A new life

In the autumn, between working on the kitchen, building the septic tank and installing the new range, we fitted in another trip to England, but before that we had a sad job to do. One early morning when the sun shone from a clear blue sky, lighting up the low-lying mist in the fields and the diamond dew-spangled cobwebs stretched across the hedgerows, we took another trip across the mountains to Eyries. But we didn't have the heart to enjoy the beauty that nature offered. We had reluctantly decided to part with our goats. They were such engaging, amusing, independent and lively creatures that we loved them dearly. We were keen on the milk too. But they were a terrible tie and to keep them in milk we had to keep them in kid, which often meant a horrible betrayal to the butcher. We didn't much enjoy the meat under those circumstances. We had already sold Nelly and her kid for £15 in the summer. Now we were taking Magsie, Shirley Temple and Kitty to join Gus and Les's large herd on the wild, rocky hillside of Kilcatherine Point.

The goats were subdued in the back of the car and so were we, but they didn't hesitate to scramble out when we got to the other end. Gus and Les were very welcoming. Shirley Temple was much admired for her snowy white coat and dangly toggles, inherited from Eros, and her playful, energetic nature. Magsie gave us a rather scornful look before leading her little herd away to join the other goats on the rocky mountainside. No money changed hands; we were only too pleased to know that our lovely nannies were going to a good home. We left them behind with a great sadness in our hearts.

We went to England in October. Adrian needed to do some more research and he had also planned a railway photography trip with his signalman friend John Morris. I tagged along and John drove us to photograph the signal boxes of the Hereford-Shrewsbury line, staying in

B&Bs along the way. The weather was awful – grey and misty – so the photographs were not much good, but they enjoyed each other's company taking their photos and talking about railways. I wasn't particularly bored as I had other things on my mind. I had purchased a pregnancy testing kit from a chemist and tested my wee in a B&B. The result was positive. We were delighted, of course, as we had been waiting for this. Adrian and I had been married for five years and the thought of having children hadn't entered our heads. That is, until the summer when Anna and her beautiful, smiling, gurgling baby Una came to stay next door. I was immediately captivated and nothing seemed more important to me then, than starting a family of our own. Adrian, slightly bemused, agreed and I came off the pill. I was lucky in that I had been prescribed the pill in the first place. Contraception was illegal in Ireland from 1935 until 1979, when it was legalised for 'bona fide' family planning purposes, i.e. for married women, under the 1979 Health (Family Planning) Act. That was the Prime Minister Charles Haughey's 'Irish solution to an Irish problem'. But enlightened doctors were already prescribing the pill to an estimated 48,000 Irish women, myself included, to help 'regulate' our menstrual cycles. I guarantee it did a lot more than that!

So there I was on the Welsh Borders quietly contemplating my newfound state of being and feeling ever so slightly sick while being trundled around the countryside. I can't remember much more of the trip except that we stayed with various good friends and purchased some wooden flat-pack Afghan chairs from a shop called Oasis in Oxford, just right for the sitting room.

We returned home on 2nd November to find that the weather had been so wet with almost constant rain that Eddie's field was flooded. Not only that, but the contractors who had laid the water pipes had not restored the drainage ditch properly, so the water had come off the road, into the garden and seeped through the front door of the cottage. The whole place felt damp and clammy and there was a white mould growing over the wooden furniture in the kitchen. Luckily the rain had stopped by then, so we mopped up and lit fires. The sitting room soon became cosy and comfortable with a roaring fire in the grate and our two new Afghan armchairs placed on either side of the fireplace.

A few days later, dear old Uncle Tolly was killed on the road. We felt bereft and so did Baby Cat, who went looking for him and came back puzzled and lonely.

Nineteen seventy-eight came roaring in off the Atlantic. The Stanley heaved heat, the cottage was warm and we had gallons of hot water on tap. The stack of turf in what had been the goat shed was buried under ash tree logs, furze and dry hedge cuttings courtesy of John Foley, who the previous autumn had done a major hedge-cutting and field furze clearance. He was glad of our offer to carry it all away. The raging winds of January across our solid new roof and through the tall trees behind the cottage emphasised the warmth and security of our little place. We worked away busily inside. Susan baked soda bread in the range and we ate it warm with butter and our own honey. We also had jam, bottled fruit and vegetables, stored potatoes, beetroot, onions and carrots, with leeks and kale still standing in the garden. We did not have to buy much, which was just as well as we were £500 overdrawn in the Allied Irish Bank.

We lived in good hope. OPC asked me to write two 32-page A5 size picture books for their 'Track Topics' series, one on Western Region signals and one on trackwork. They offered me £100 for each book. I set to work printing the pictures and writing the captions and posted the whole lot off before we both came down with the 'flu. I received at around the same time a letter from the publisher David & Charles asking if I would write for them a history of the life of staff and passengers on the broad gauge GWR drawn from GWR records and letters to newspapers. I turned down the invitation because I wanted to write the story of my association with the steam railway, 1945 to 1965. I had rehearsed and recalled studiously for years the memories of great times, great friends. I even had a notebook written at the time recording events. The working title of the book, *A Signalman's Life*, was coined from a book I had read as an eight-year-old, W. H. Hudson's *A Shepherd's*

Life. Signalmen were the shepherds of the railway, herding the trains safely along the tracks. I started to hammer away again on the iron typewriter, but the writing did not get off to a good start as I was still suffering from the after effects of a bad dose of 'flu – depression. It was clearly too soon to be embarking on heavy writing as I was also plagued with coughing and chestiness well into the spring of the year.

It was also depressing hearing and reading the news. We were, of course, very aware of the mayhem of civil war in the North. My diary for Sunday 5th February records that a man in Belfast was severely beaten, then shot eight times by members of the 'Republican Club'. The shots were aimed so as not to be immediately fatal. Women who went to his aid were also beaten.

Sometimes, when extra-terrible events like this took place in the North of Ireland, Kerry people were shocked. Some, driving along the road, would stop, come into the garden and apologise to us: "Tis a fright. "Tis terrible. I can't imagine what you must think of us.'

'We don't blame you!' I'd say. 'It's not your fault – you don't have to apologise to us.'

We'd walk back to the gate with him or her and with a friendly 'Goodbye' and 'Good luck' exchanged, the reassured person would drive away.

In the Republic there were different tensions: unseen difficulties and confusions that many Irish people experienced due to Catholicism. On 24th February 1978 the death was announced of a Mr Joseph B. Murray, aged 70. He had been watching *The Spike* on RTÉ television. This was a 'controversial soap opera' about daily life in an Irish Vocational school. Mr Murray was a regular viewer and, as a member of the 'Irish League of Decency', a regular complainer. In the episode that evening viewers were given a glimpse of a naked actress, Madelaine Erskine, posing in front of the sixth form art class. The excitement generated in Mr Murray brought on a heart attack, which proved fatal.

197

On the same day a letter was published in *The Kerryman* from a 'worried mother'. She wrote that she had been married for twelve years and had had six children. However, she had recently been enjoying sex so much, due to her husband's 'methods of stimulation which do not lead to full intercourse', that she had developed 'guilty feelings'. She had asked the advice of her celibate parish priest twice and on each occasion she was told to 'do your best'. The reply from the newspaper was reassuringly headed: 'Medically and Morally OK'.

That winter, whilst ill with the 'flu, we slept in the sleeping loft at night and dozed there during the day too, only staggering outside to fetch wood and turf to keep the Stanley going. It seemed to take a long time for me to recover – no doubt being pregnant didn't help, but Adrian was up and writing after a few days, though he was still feeling ill and chesty and we were both coughing and sleeping badly. I also had a fierce neuralgia on the left-hand side of my face, which lasted well into February. It was around this time that I began to feel the first fluttering of the baby's movements. This was exciting! I knitted baby clothes and we made plans for the baby's arrival. For various reasons we decided to go back to England for the birth. I felt that I would have more support to give birth 'naturally' in England and Adrian wanted to be present at the birth, which was not acceptable practice in Kerry at that time. Also being in England would give Adrian the opportunity to do some research and we could stay rent-free in Tudor Cottage, the other half of Adrian's parents' cottage in Childrey – completely self-contained and with a bathroom! Our bathroom was a long way off completion. We still had the extension to build and there was the kitchen to finish and myriad other jobs to do before the baby came.

In February a royalty cheque arrived from OPC – £575. The overdraft was paid off and we ordered £80 worth of red quarry tiles for the kitchen floor from Boyles in Killorglin. They were delivered at the beginning of March and next day, feeling ill with a head cold and dosed up with Beecham's powders, Adrian started to lay 250 square feet of tiles. He completed half the floor in about five days. We then went in search of grout to Killarney, Tralee and finally Limerick. The Tile Centre in Limerick told us that the grout we wanted was no longer produced and advised us to use a dark pigment in ordinary cement powder instead, which we could easily have bought in Boyles. After a brief visit to my parents we headed back home, a whole day lost for nothing! I grouted most of the tiles myself while Adrian made an airing cupboard, closing in the hot water tank, with some fine old pine shutters that he had rescued from a house being modernised in Killarney.

We had a welcome break on St Patrick's Day when Paul and Susie came to see us. We celebrated with a glass of Guinness in P. T. O'Sullivan's Bar in Killorglin, drunk to the accompaniment of a lone bagpiper playing in the 'square'.

Adrian, his knees sore and aching, finally finished laying the tiles in early April and I did most of the grouting then too, a difficult and uncomfortable task with my big belly getting in the way, but I was determined to finish it before we left for England. When the builder Timmy O'Shea dropped by to see how we were getting on, he was clearly impressed with the professional-looking finish of the floor, and said, "Tis very even and level.'
Adrian was chuffed and so was I.

Susan and I, with Baby Cat in her travelling cage, left by car for England on 26th April. We had sleeping berths on the night sailing from Cork to Swansea. Our finances were again at rock bottom. I realised that my top priority was not to travel for research but to get a temporary job. The day after our arrival in Childrey, I went to the Labour Exchange in Wantage and was advised to go to see Lionel Roberts, who owned Roberts' Taxis near the bottom of Mill Street, opposite 'The Shears' pub and Wantage Mill. The taxi premises were up a slope, above the street on a bare patch of ground. An Austin Princess stood lonely in the yard. The taxi office was a wooden shed – with windows. Hard against it was the car maintenance wooden shed. I found my way into the hut. A woman, who I guessed was the secretary, gave me a nice smile. A tall, skinny man, around 55 years old, was sitting at an untidy table. He was clearly 'The Boss'.

'What can I do for you?' he said in a relaxed, off-hand way.

'I'm hoping you could give me a job, Mr Roberts.' I said.

'I'm Lionel,' he said and, after asking a few questions, said he'd take me on. Rummaging in a drawer for some car keys, he said, 'You can start now if you like.'

His informality was very welcome. I asked if I could start tomorrow instead.

'Be here at half past seven – that's your cab,' pointing out of the window to the Austin Princess standing in the yard.

I was in the yard at 7.30 am the next day, Wednesday. I was introduced to Roger, who did the maintenance on the cars, and to some of the drivers. The woman in the office was Mrs Hall. I took the Princess up into the Market Place. The cabs were fitted with radios working with Lionel's office. I parked on the rank outside Harris's grocery shop, near 'The Bell' pub. Sometimes we parked in the middle of the market place, dominated by the magnificent statue of King Alfred, who was born in Wantage. The work varied from very short journeys from the Market Place shops to the housing around the town or down to Grove, but there were also orders by radio. I collected a woman from a village nearby and took her to the Princess Margaret hospital near Swindon. I had no idea where the hospital was but she directed me.

Back in the Market Place I got orders to drive to Oxford railway station and wait there to collect some girls off a train and bring them back to St Mary's School in Wantage. The day had become hot, and I drove with my window open. After a while I parked outside the station, an old gent stopped alongside me and opened a conversation.

'Nice day. Waitin' for someone?'

Naturally friendly, I said 'Hello' and expected him to go on his way, but not at all. He was vicious about the sins of the government and needed to instruct someone about 'that bugger Wilson ... look what's going on.' I tried to interrupt his flow by telling him Wilson

200

wasn't the government any more, Callaghan was. But he didn't hear. After ten minutes of this I was grateful to see two young women walk out of the station, looking around expectantly. I moved the cab alongside, leaving the old boy a standing figure in my mirror. They got in and I drove off. At five o'clock I considered my day was up, took the cab back to the yard and went back to Childrey.

Next day I arrived at eight o'clock to be told that it wasn't the done thing to go home before 9.00 pm and preferably to stay on 'till midnight. My day was enlivened by taking a fare to Highworth and another to Fawley, high up and deep within the folds of the Berkshire Downs. At 9.00 pm I handed in my takings and went home. On Friday I received my wages: £31 gross, but £25 after tax and National Insurance. As I was leaving Lionel took me aside and very quietly and gently asked, 'How much have I paid you?'

I was puzzled, and had to look at the packet to see. 'Twenty five pounds?'

'No, that's after tax. I paid you £31. How much have you handed in this week?'

I was really puzzled now. 'I don't know, Lionel,' I said.

'Sixty-five quid. Now you're puzzled and I'm not entirely liking this either, but I've got to mention it. I can't really ask you to work more than 52 hours but I've paid you £31, which is nearly half of the sixty-five quid you handed in. So how much petrol do you think you used? Oil? What about tyres, maintenance, tax and insurance, Roger's wages, Mrs Hall's and then something for me?'

I was used to working for British Railways who paid me for rigidly set eight- or twelve-hour shifts, which had four hours paid at overtime rates. Lionel had made things very clear. If he couldn't make a profit after all his overheads, he, and I, would be out of work. Into my mind came the image of my self-employed father, working into the night to finish the repair of a radio to earn his money.

'I'm sorry, Lionel, I just didn't realise'.

'That's OK, Adrian. You understand – I had to tell you,' he said.

After that, for as long as I worked there, I was working fifteen- and sixteen-hour days – into nights.

I liked Lionel. Late, after 10.00 pm, some of us drivers would be there with him in the office, or I'd be there alone with him. A long, skinny man leaning back on his hard chair or leaning forward, elbows on his crowded desk, he was as full of stories as any railwayman I'd met. He had this asthmatic, wheezy, cockney voice. He was the youngest son of a hard-working labouring family. His two brothers were as tall as him. They had been conscripted in 1918 and had both been killed. Lionel had started work aged fourteen in 1935 'dahn in Walf-am-stoh'. He worked for a coal merchant and said he enjoyed ''amping cowl'.

When war broke out in 1939 he was summoned to report for a conscription medical. He decided to be a Conscientious Objector 'because my mother and father never got over the deaths of their two sons and I didn't want to end up killing some German and giving his mother all the grief I'd seen at home. I went to the medical. I could've got out of it easy just by showing him my leg.'

He pulled up a trouser leg. The leg was very thin – he'd had polio. 'I told them I wanted to be excused on Conscientious grounds.'

That put an end to the medical and Lionel ended up in prison. In prison as a 'CO', where he was treated to some bullying, he decided he'd have to do something for the war effort, Hitler being such a horrible man. He decided to volunteer for farm work when he was released. He was told by a Quaker prison visitor that there was a Quaker house or hostel in the village of Blewbury, near Didcot, that took in 'COs', and from there he could get work on a farm. His leg was wizened but straight and he was able to do heavy work. When the war was over, he and his cousin set up in business as coal merchants at Upton & Blewbury station. When the station was closed in 1964 he moved to Wantage and started his taxi business.

I told Lionel how Susan and I had got onto the 'property ladder' by buying a derelict cottage in Kerry. Lionel was interested in my story of the cottage and asked if he and his wife could rent it for a

July holiday. I explained that the cottage didn't have a bathroom but he didn't mind and wanted to pay us rent. There's no record of what we charged him but I guess it was just a token amount.

Taxi-driving brought me in touch with a selection of men and women, young and old, sane and insane, and all gradations in between. There was a chap who worked on the North Sea oil rigs, lived in Wantage and had to be fetched from Didcot station. On the way he grumbled to me about his wife. Even when she was in the taxi he criticised the poor woman and even invited *me* to criticise her looks, her clothes.

Taking women from the International Stores out to the estates or to Grove were short trips, in and out, round and round. Just once, in the midday heat, I became confused. Two women got in with laden shopping baskets and asked for 'Hamfield'. I drove off, along Wallingford Street and turned into Charlton at the 'Lord Nelson' pub. I stopped in Aldworth Avenue. I didn't know why I was in Aldworth Avenue, and where the hell was Hamfield? The women in the back were giggling. I asked them how to get to Hamfield. They laughed out loud. I sat for a couple of minutes, regained my senses, and took them to Hamfield – on the far side of town.

When a Roberts' taxi was booked to a Heathrow run, the 'TAXI' sign was removed from the roof. A driver working these runs was allowed to finish at tea time the day before the run because they would be getting up very early next morning. Heathrow passengers were usually scientists from Harwell, needing to attend a conference somewhere in Europe. The time of 'pick-up' depending on when the man had to be at Heathrow. The Harwell clients seemed always to live down an anonymous, half hidden, narrow track in the back of a remote Cotswold village. The feeling of rising panic as I drove around trying to find the place is something I can still bring to mind. When I'd found him there was then the drive to Heathrow! Oh my! On the M40 down steep hills like the one around High Wycombe was where I first drove at 100 mph to get the man to the airport in time to check in.

I had done an early morning run into the Cotswolds for a 6.00 am pick-up, then to Heathrow and return empty. Entering the Market Place, busy with cars and shoppers, I was driving a smart red saloon car at walking speed with no 'TAXI' sign on the roof. A young woman standing outside Scotts the Chemist flagged me down as if I was a taxi. Automatically I pulled in to the pavement, the young woman got into the cab and slammed the door shut. I must have been a bit tired with the early start and I hadn't eaten since the day before. I just drove away, around the statue and along Wallingford Street. Coming up to the Cottage Hospital crossroads I said to my passenger, 'Where d'you want to go?'

She laid her hand high on my inner thigh. 'I'll go anywhere with you!'

I turned to look at her properly for the first time. She wore non-matching slippers, odd socks and a very tatty cardigan over a worn-out-looking blouse. Her hair was very dirty and uncombed. My immediate thought was she must have escaped from somewhere.

'OK,' I said, 'that's great. We'll go along here.'

I turned right at the crossroads and went back into the town to the police station. 'Now you sit quiet there, I'll be back in a minute.'

I went into the cop shop. 'Are you looking for a woman who's escaped from somewhere?'

'Yes, from Moulsford,' said the policeman at the reception counter.

'I've got her in my cab. You'd better come and collect her.'

They took her away and I drove back to the yard.

Chapter Twenty-one
Midsummer Day

Spring merged into summer. The weather was superb. I had got used to sixteen-hour 'days', driving about the West Berkshire countryside up and across the Berkshire Downs and sometimes into Gloucestershire and Oxfordshire. The day before the great event of our lives, I had to make the long drive to Witney – across the Vale, over the Faringdon ridge, through the town and down into the valley of the young Thames and the wondrously named River Windrush. The fields were wide and silky, rippling with half-ripe corn under the vast expanse of Vale sky, a sky full of towering cumulus. At 4.15 pm I had driven an elderly lady home to Nalder Town and had got back into the Market Place when Scotty (Mrs Hall), the office lady at the taxi office, radioed in.

'Get yourself over to the John Radcliffe. Your wife needs you. You're gonna be a Dad. But there's no need for hurry – she's only just started.'

I turned into the John Radcliffe car park in Headington thirty minutes later. The following afternoon, in an emotional condition, I wrote the history of my daughter's birth, intending to give it to her – I did not know her name at the time – on her 21st birthday:

'My Dear Child, I want you to know of the manner of your arrival into the world and rather than worry long as to how to begin I will start at the end and go backwards. This is a system typical of me as any of my friends will tell you. Well then, I have just eaten some bread and soup having arrived home from the hospital where you and your mother are lying.

Last night, having first donned a medical overall and an elastic trimmed cap that made me look like a medieval Turkish simpleton,

I was shown into a very pleasant room with floral wallpaper. Susan was glad to see me but was very busy with the labour, bravely fighting the pain by relaxing and breathing deeply when every instinct – I would have thought – would have made her want to tense up against the pain. Your Ma was having contractions once every seven minutes...

All through a golden evening, while the sun poured its colour over dark green trees while their shadows darkened and lengthened on the brilliant green lawns, Susan worked away accompanied, watched over, by two dedicated midwives while I sat feeling foolishly helpless by the bedside. The contractions came more frequently, four minutes apart and more painful, lasting for one minute each, though the space between the pains was perfectly calm and comfortable. The midwife told us that the birth was progressing correctly and you would be born at midnight. Susan was unable to hold out against the pain without some relief, and a pain-dulling drug was administered, into her bottom, at 8.20 pm. That entailed her being rolled onto her side, and while in the side position she had a contraction and this may have had the effect of turning you 'nose upwards' inside her instead of the proper position, 'nose down'.

After the injection Susan's contractions became weaker and further apart; she was having the pain without the progress of the labour and as a result grew more tired. To speed up the contractions she was put on a glucose and drug solution fed into her by an injected drip. The process and purpose of the drip was quietly and clearly explained to her before it was carried out, and as the trees outside disappeared into the night your mother continued with her labour. At about 11.00 pm you gave a great leap and it may have been *this* that turned you the wrong way up. You could not bend easily into the birth canal; indeed, you were going to 'bend over backwards' to be born!

You had always been an active baby, kicking hard and apparently turning somersaults though I cannot truthfully report that you overturned coffee cups placed unwarily on your mother's 'bump', because she is not an unwary person and never balanced cups thereon, but had a loaded cup been above one of your kicks it would, without doubt, have been overturned. Sometimes we saw the outline of hands or toes when you kicked out and, indeed, you actually gave her a small hernia with your kicking.

Susan fought her pains. Every three minutes, hour after hour. Sitting by her bed, I could barely keep my eyes open, having been at work all the previous day. But the midwife, checking regularly your heartbeat, Susan's blood pressure, pulse, temperature, frequency of contractions and duration, worked untiringly until, at 2.00 am, Susan was exhausted and the midwife told me, 'I'm going to switch her off for a while so that she can get some sleep.'

Susan was given a painful 'epidural' injection so she would feel nothing below her hips. I was shown into a room and re-called at 4.00 am.

By that time most if not all of the mothers in labour through the various rooms had finished, but Susan, you and the midwife re-started the battle of the most difficult conditions of labour. At 4.30 am the cervix was fully dilated and the second stage of labour commenced; Susan had to push you out into the world. Her forehead was sweaty and some of her dishevelled hair was sticking there. She put a leg against a hip of each of the two nurses while I gave her head something to press back against, then, with her chin down on her chest she heaved, forcing down, till she was red in the face and could hold her breath no longer. Every time Susan had a contraction she gave heaves like that, lying back and relaxing between each effort, eyes closed. From 4.30 to 6.30 am Susan tried to no avail and the midwives, realising that you and/or your mother would be damaged if matters continued like that, called in Mr Bibi, the gynaecologist.

He was a young man, six foot tall, possibly a rugby player, with sandy hair and a beard, who quietly explained to Susan what was going to be done, then we all went along to the forceps theatre. Susan began pushing again at 7.00 am and the doctor cleverly manipulated you face down. At 7.15 am he inserted the forceps into Susan's vagina and slid the ends, like large, flat spoons, around your head. When the next contraction came he pulled your head down, the following contraction pushed you a little further down the canal, and I could see the top of your head; the third brought you to the very gateway of the world.

I was expecting to photograph you being born, but I never imagined how terrible this birthing could be for the mother – the love of my life. What was happening in front of me was awesome, terrifying. 'Poor girl, poor girl. Poor, brave girl.' I was decidedly humbled then and forever after. The face mask hid all but my eyes so that no one could see – although of course no one was looking – how hard I was biting my lower lip to keep my mouth tight shut. An enormous emotion boiling inside me would not overflow. I was shy of crying but the tears were behind my eyes like a lake of boiling water. Luckily, I had previously judged the distance between myself and the table Susan was lying on and had set the focus accordingly.

Before the fourth contraction Dr Bibi took up a pair of scissors and cut downwards from the bottom point of your mother's vagina so as to enlarge the hole to enable your head to pass through. He seemed to cut and cut, but maybe there were four snips in all – a wave of fainting passed through me. At the fourth contraction he said, 'Push, push! There's a good girl,' as Susan heaved. As you came out the midwife moved with astonishing swiftness, accurately and fast. I fired the shutter blindly and he pulled you out with his forceps. It looked as if you had been dragged out like a sack of coal. You were born at 7.22 am on Midsummer Day, 24th June 1978, and weighed 7lb 9oz.

A tube was slipped into your mouth to clear mucus from airways. Up to that moment you had been purple and silent but once the mucus had been cleared from your mouth and throat you let out a hearty yell and you were placed across your mother's tummy, your skin rapidly clearing and becoming pink. Deftly and rapidly the doctor unwound the umbilical cord. You didn't cry again and lay cradled in your mother's arms while the cord was cut. Then you were taken to be weighed in the scales a foot or two away and quickly handed back to your mother, who held you while the afterbirth was expelled.

I stared down at you and Susan silently and dared make no reply to the nurses' urgings of 'Isn't she lovely...?' You were an amazing sight with your poor forehead bruised and swollen from the beating it had received through the long labour, one eye was closed up and you had a scratch on your nose. I fought back the scalding tears and looked at you with love and amazement. I was shaking; your mother was exhausted.

I will never forget and nor will you, having read this, the devotion your midwife showed. When her twelve-hour shift was over at 6.00 am and still you were not born, she turned her relief away so that she could stay with you and see the job through. Because she cared about you, she enabled you to survive and to be born, and you were a stranger to her. Her name was Janet Vaughan and she was a Jamaican. No one of one's own family could have cared for you with greater loyalty, but of course, we are all of one family, white Vaughan and black Vaughan – we are just people.

Eventually, when we – Susan and you and me – were back in the ward, we had a good cry! I went out to buy some fruit and flowers for Susan and walked the mile or so into Headington in a daze. The morning was a perfect summer day. I came back with strawberries and flowers and stayed awhile till Susan bade me go home to sleep. I left for home at about 10.30 am. I drove in a daze of mental and physical exhaustion'.

I could never describe the birth of our first child as eloquently as Adrian; he was there witnessing it and wrote up his moving account only hours later. I was there doing it, too busy to be aware of anything more than surviving what was the most painful experience of my life. I did not come to it properly prepared. I had re-registered with my old GP practice on arriving back in England and had attended antenatal clinics in Oxford, but it strikes me as very strange in retrospect that while I wanted a 'natural' birth I had let myself be booked into the John

Radcliffe Maternity Hospital, a modern Obstetric Unit. During the 1970s medical intervention was routinely carried out in many Obstetric Units.

Campaigning groups such as The National Childbirth Trust promoted and encouraged more natural births. They offered classes to pregnant women to prepare them for the birth, using relaxation and breathing techniques. Sheila Kitzinger of the NCT was a pioneer of natural childbirth, promoting women-centred birthing, and wrote many best-selling books on the subject. Although I had her book 'The Experience of Childbirth', her message seems to have passed me by. Perhaps I thought childbirth would just happen 'naturally', no need for preparation. Perhaps underneath it all, I was scared and wanted to be in the best possible place for medical help if things went wrong.

So when in labour I had little to fall back on. I had read about 'breathing through' the contractions, and the midwives helped me to put this into practice. All seemed to be going well until it all went wrong, when I allowed myself to be taken over. It was decided to intervene in my labour and break my waters to speed up the labour. A trainee midwife practised her skills on me and whatever she did was intensely painful. I screamed in agony and after that my breathing went out of sync with the contractions. Then everything becomes hazy. I remember being given an injection, which made things worse, and I begged for an epidural to make the pain go away. That injection was the most painful thing I have ever endured. I slept for a bit, but when I woke up I wasn't aware of the contractions. When it came to the birth I didn't have the urge to push although I tried when I was told, but the epidural seemed to have taken away my muscle strength. I vaguely remember that the baby was 'face to pubis' and that forceps were used to deliver her.

After the midwives had cleaned me up, removed the catheter and stitched me back together again, I was taken to the maternity ward. It was a bright, sunny place, where everything seemed subsumed in a soft yellow light, curtains gently billowing at the open window. The baby was wheeled there too, her crib placed by my bedside. Adrian and I gazed at her together, full of wonderment and awe, and we had a little cry. The baby cried too. I picked her up and put her to my breast. She *latched on quickly. It felt wholesome and good and I was thoroughly bonded with my baby. This bit I knew I could do well.*

We called our baby daughter Rebecca, a beautiful name for a beautiful girl. As the bruising subsided on her face, her fine, delicate features emerged and her downy skin had a golden glow. She was neat and sweet and much admired in the ward. I was a very proud mother. They kept me in the John Radcliffe for a few days to keep an eye on the baby's jaundice, which explained the glow, then I was transferred to Wantage Cottage Hospital for ten days. Imagine that!

In the event I discharged myself after three days because I didn't have full control over the care of my baby. The nurses were not waking me at night to feed Rebecca. They were bottle-feeding her alongside the other babies in the night nursery. In those days babies were kept apart from their mothers at night-time to enable the mothers to sleep undisturbed. I didn't want to jeopardise my breastfeeding – the more a baby sucks the more milk is produced – and I did not want to feed my baby formula. I felt confident enough to stand up for myself here. I had the book 'Breast is Best' by Drs Penny and Andrew Stanway. Obviously I had received their message loud and clear.

Our little family of three went back to Childrey, where Edith and Owen welcomed us with a small tea party. There was much oohing and aahing over the baby, but I quickly felt tired and went next door to Tudor Cottage. I took Rebecca upstairs. It felt good to be out of the hospital and I relaxed as I lay on the bed feeding her. It felt very peaceful in the sunny under-the-eaves bedroom with its pretty pink rosebud wallpaper and windows overlooking the cottage gardens. In one corner stood the Victorian bassinet where Rebecca would sleep. I had borrowed it from Adrian's sister Lalo and restoring it had given me something to do during the interminably long hours when Adrian was out driving taxis before Rebecca was born. I had painted it white and made some pretty drapes from Laura Ashley fabric, which had white ditsy flower prints on a dark blue background, matching the curtains in our bedroom back home at Meanus.

And so I began my new life as a mother. Edith helped out with practical tasks, but I felt very alone once Adrian had gone to work in the mornings. I had no friends around with which to share the joys and frustrations of early motherhood. I caught myself crying on occasions and in particular one sunny morning when Owen gave me a colander full of beautiful plump pea pods, ripe for shelling. I wanted to shell them ready for our lunchtime meal, Rebecca wanted to be fed, I couldn't do both, and shed tears of self-pity and frustration. Such a silly little thing, but I suppose it was then that I realised my life had truly changed for ever.

Nearly every afternoon I took Rebecca for a walk in her pram. In my mind's eye it was always sunny and we walked for miles around the summer-blown lanes of Childrey. We nearly always stopped in the churchyard for a little picnic and a breastfeed. A herd of black cows munched contentedly in the verdant pasture below and there was a timeless, peaceful quality in the atmosphere. I felt as if I had been transported back to the 1950s; it was only the dead elm trees – devastated by Dutch elm disease – whose skeletons stood gaunt in the fields, which dated the scene.

I remember two visitors from that time. My Uncle Danny, who lived nearby in Wantage, came to see us one evening when Adrian happened to be at home. Being my Godfather and a good Catholic, he felt duty bound to ask when we would be baptising Rebecca. We told him that we did not intend to baptise her. He was shocked and the atmosphere in the room became very tense, and tempers on both sides rose. Adrian and I were adamant and Danny left the cottage very disappointed. I was very upset.

Just before we were due to leave Childrey, a Health Visitor came to see me. She was a tall, plump woman. Her hair was piled high into a beehive style and she wore white plastic clip earrings, the size and shape of chocolate buttons. She was very business-like and brusque, sniffy about the primitive facilities at Tudor Cottage, and commented on the lack of running hot water to the bathroom sink – it had to be fetched in an enamel jug from the Sadia water heater in the kitchen. She said she presumed the facilities would be better in our home in Ireland. I nodded in reply, not daring to tell her that we didn't even have a bathroom, let alone running hot water to a bathroom sink!

I carried on with taxi-driving and at weekends researching and writing my railway autobiography. I was sitting in the Austin Princess taxi in Wantage market place one very hot day when the market stalls were up and all was bustle. I went into a mood – it was so hot – and a piece of writing came urgently into my head. I found a piece of paper in the cab, got out of the car and in two minutes had scribbled out the piece on the hot bonnet. The piece was perfect and was never altered. It became the 'Prologue' of what I was then calling *A Signalman's Life*. A day or two later I handed it in to OPC, the thick typescript so laboriously typed out, asking Colin Judge if he would like to publish it.

On 1st August I told Lionel I'd be leaving at the end of that week. I was truly sorry to leave the little firm. I'd become very friendly with Lionel, we'd spent nights in his office, waiting for the phone to ring, and he telling me stories of the East End of London. He had witnessed the 'Battle of Cable Street' when the Moseleyite fascists tried to march against the Jews, and other stories. I was also good friends with Mrs 'Scotty' Hall, Roger the car mechanic and the crew of drivers.

My big sister Lalo had invited us to stay with her in Devon before our return home to Ireland. So we set off in our packed-tight, rickety, somewhat rusty Sunbeam Vogue. Because of the terrible events in the North of Ireland I felt a bit self-conscious driving a car with Irish registration plates. I thought it might attract Constabulary attention on the 165-mile drive to the little hamlet of Broadhempston, buried deep in the steep-sided lanes of Devon.

We had been there only a few days when Susan began to have abdominal pains one evening after supper, which became worse as the night progressed. I could see her intestines writhing like serpents under her skin. Around 6.00 am Lalo phoned the doctor. He came and pronounced 'appendicitis' and an ambulance was called out from Torquay Hospital. I followed the ambulance in the Kerry car, leaving six-week-old Rebecca in the loving but entirely unprepared, unequipped, care of Lalo. Torquay Hospital could not deal with Susan at once because the operating theatre was dealing with a seriously smashed-up young motorcyclist. Susan was in total agony on a trolley. I stayed with her. She was not allowed to drink anything. I wetted her very dry lips with a wet flannel. A nurse suggested that I leave for a bit as Susan was going to be 'out' for some time. I left around 3.30 pm and went to Newton Abbot railway station, seven miles away. There I came across a retired GWR engine driver, Bob Nicks, and from that meeting I was able to write his biography, *Western Engineman*, many years later. I went back to the hospital and it was 11.30 pm before Susan was taken into the operating theatre.

Oh my goodness, it was all such a shock coming so soon after the birth of Rebecca and in someone else's house! I was beside myself in pain and agony. At last the ambulance came and I was whisked off to the hospital minus my baby. I feel so guilty now at leaving her, the tiny scrap of a thing, and I can't honestly imagine how Lalo cared for her during that time, but I really had no choice. I was unable to hold my baby, let alone feed her.

In the hospital I was examined several times by several different people. The location of the pain didn't quite fit the pattern for appendicitis, so a gynaecologist was called in to examine me internally to see if anything had been left behind after the birth. It hadn't, but the examination brought on bleeding, which was the last thing I needed. Luckily by this time the intensity of the pain had diminished somewhat. Eventually appendicitis was diagnosed and I had surgery, not before time, as apparently the appendix had been on the point of bursting. When I came round I was in a side room and Lalo brought Rebecca in to me. I was so relieved to see her, tears welled up in my eyes. She seemed so little and lost in Lalo's arms. I wanted so badly to cuddle her, but I was so weak and fuzzy after the operation I couldn't hold her for long. My milk had all but dried up too, so the nurses fed her with formula milk and helped me to care for her during the rest of my stay. I put her to the breast whenever I could, and Adrian brought me some Guinness to drink, and although it is not a 'milk stout' it did the trick and brought my milk back in. Before long I was successfully breastfeeding again.

Chapter Twenty-two
Back at Meanus

The ferry sailing for which we had tickets was from Swansea to Cork at 10.00 pm on 15th August, but Susan wasn't strong enough to travel. We had paid for the ferry tickets so I would have to use them. It was agreed that I would go home in the car and Susan would stay behind with the baby at Broadhempston and fly to Cork when she had convalesced.

Poor NIN would be labouring, loaded to the roof with luggage, a pram and Baby Cat in her cage. I felt that very gentle speed was necessary out of respect for the venerable automobile. I calculated a railway-style timetable of passing times based on distance and an average speed of 30 mph. I could have lunch with the others, load up and leave at 3.30 pm, getting to the Severn Bridge at 7.30 and arriving at Swansea Docks at 9.30 pm. I got to the toll booth of the bridge at 7.00 pm. There was a large notice:

15-8-78
B&I Line Swansea-Cork Ferry.
Leaves Swansea at 8.30 pm today

I was horrified. I had ninety minutes to cover sixty-four miles. Urgent mental arithmetic as I crossed above the glorious River Severn far below, stretching away north and south, and gleaming like silver in the lowering sunlight. Arithmetic dictated an average speed of 45 mph. I knew that the M4 was not built around part of Cardiff, nor between Bridgend and Porthcawl. I felt hot in my face, a kind of panic. I would have to whip the poor old engine along at a steady sixty wherever possible. My mouth was dry, my nerves were stretched, wondering how long the engine could stand the pace. On the Welsh M4, English and Irish cars went *whooshing* past, hell for leather for the ferry, the occupants staring at the shabby, Kerry-registered car doing its best in the slow lane. Fifteen miles out from Swansea the horrible drum roll of piston-rod big-ends burst into life. My heart leaped. It was a terrible noise and I was only too well aware of what the 2,000 revs a minute noise was doing to the crankshaft. There was nothing for it but to slow down a bit and keep going. I drove into the ferry car park at 8.30 pm at 30 mph. The customs men at the entrance waved me through without a check or a boarding card! The bows of the *Innisfallen* at that moment started to close. At 30 mph I went broadside around the ninety-degree turn. The look-out man on the deck with a radio phone saw the car skid sideways as I turned for the ship's ramp. I saw him raise his phone and speak into it, the bow was stopped from closing. I drove straight up the ramp into the ship and turned off the smoking engine.

The B&I company's tractor took NIN off the ferry next morning and gave me a tow to get the engine started. With the big ends knocking, expecting at any moment that the crankshaft would break, the poor old car got me home – seventy-five miles including the long climb up to Moll's Gap before dropping down into Killarney. Finally, wearily, with the engine rattle reverberating through my head, I pulled up outside Meanus cottage about midday on Wednesday.

As I opened the car door I almost fell out of the driving seat. I opened the gate and walked down the path as if the concrete slabs were the rolling deck of the *Innisfallen*. I opened the front door, opened the 'stable' door, Baby Cat ran ahead of me to her favourite place on the window sill, and I stepped into a warm kitchen and a huge surprise.

A wonderful 'Welcome home'! Agnes had earlier lit the range and Lionel and his wife had stacked the kitchen table with sixteen jars of blackcurrant jam, sixteen jars of bottled blackcurrants and a few jars of gooseberry jam! I sat down thankfully on the hard seat of a kitchen chair and stared. Lionel and his wife had done all that preserving when they were meant to be on holiday – a very wet holiday. Their kind generosity was overwhelming.

Agnes had heard the rattling racket of my arrival and was soon round with tea and sandwiches and the news that the electricity was 'off' because the Electricity Board workers were on strike. She was boiling water on a paraffin stove, said she had a spare and did I want to borrow it? She was all energy, full of real care and all ears and whiskers for an account of Susan and the baby. I gave her a shorter version of Susan's labour, Rebecca's progress, and Susan's appendicitis operation. Agnes loved the telling of it but there was a small elephant in the room. She had yet to ask her most important question about Rebecca's baptism. I did my best. I told her gently: 'Agnes, you would think me an irreverent hypocrite if I stood there, Godparents on either side, prayers being said and devils urged to depart when you'd know I didn't believe in it. Susan and I just cannot do that.'

She was disappointed but she smiled magnanimously, said, 'Welcome home. I'd better get back to Pat,' and departed.

I was hardly there. The car stood on the road, laden. I ignored it.

John and Pam arrived from Limerick that afternoon. John helped me unload the luggage from the car and Pam put everything away in drawers and cupboards, a task that was beyond me. We surveyed the unkempt garden. Grass had grown long in the vegetable plots, hiding the vegetables we had sown and planted in the spring. John dug out 28lb of onions. The broad beans, marrows and courgettes were plentiful and the carrot foliage was tall and fresh-looking, promising a good crop. The tomato plants were safe from the verdant grass and weeds, growing in my old cold frames, heavy with large, unripe fruit.

The bees were in a dire state with little honey in the supers because the lank, rank grass had blocked the landing strip and entry to their hives and the summer had been so wet. John said that the heather was the next harvest for the bees, so we cut the grass away in hope for a late honey harvest. John and Pam left after dinner and drove away into the twilight in good spirits, but leaving me feeling flat and very lonely. I was at least relieved that John had not brought up the subject of Rebecca's baptism!

I received a letter from Susan the next day to say she was recovering well, but was unable to come home until 25th August. Eight lonely days to fill. A great incentive to be busy. I wanted to hide all the Roberts' preserves as a surprise for Susan and we needed a cupboard. I spent the next few days building one to stand on top of our large pine chest of drawers. I made the wooden framework with mortise-and-tenon joints, quite square and upright; the back and side were pine planks and the front doors were two Victorian folding shutters I had begged from the workmen taking down an old house in Killarney. It measured three feet eight inches wide, four feet two inches tall, and fifteen inches deep. I also got in a good load of firewood from Churchtown with the loan of Jack Chowne's tractor and trailer.

Susan and Rebecca flew into Cork from Plymouth as planned. NIN was under repair, so Linda lent me her car to collect them. There was a throat-tightening, happy-tearful reunion! We were all so pleased that our travels and travails were over and that we were home at last.

Great Western Architecture royalties arrived about the same time as Susan. It was a cheque for a disappointing £380. I thought I would receive £580. The UK Inland Revenue had instructed OPC to deduct tax pending receipt of a certificate from the Irish Tax Office proving residency and liability for Irish tax. I wrote to the Tax Office in Tralee, requesting such a certificate and to ask how to go about becoming tax exempt as a writer. Father-in-law had mentioned in 1972 that authors living in Ireland were tax exempt. We didn't go to Ireland to avoid paying tax but, self-employed now, I earned 'peanuts' by ordinary standards and felt that we should take advantage of this privilege. It appeared that I needed to be a proven resident of the Republic *and* that I was '*producing works of artistic or literary merit or cultural worth*'.

My book on architecture had produced some good reviews, and Henry Dodd, as Trustee of the Kerry Historical Trust, had asked

218

me to produce a history of the railways of Kerry. These should prove that I was a *bona fide* Irish resident author producing literary and cultural works. Henry wrote a testimonial for me to the Irish taxman. So, 'in the heel o' th' hunt', the Irish Inland Revenue granted me a certificate of exemption, which I sent to the Thames Ditton Tax Office in September.

My days settled into a new, gentle rhythm. Everything revolved around Rebecca. When she napped, I nipped outside to plant forty strawberry plants on the top garden, spreading leaf mould thickly between the plants. Henry offered us the free run of his fruit trees so, with Rebecca sleeping in her pram in the sunny orchard, we picked green, yellow, rich red and russet-coloured fruit. It was a magical scene with views beyond the trees right down into the valley to the River Laune and the other way across the jagged, purple mountains. But fruit-picking was not a sensible thing for me to do and I strained my tummy muscles. I would have to take things easier.

Adrian stored the fruit along the top walls of the cottage, which made a handy shelf, and also in the shed. Pears were in abundance that year and ripened after a few weeks, just right for Rebecca's first introduction to solid food. She loved the sweet, white, juicy flesh and opened her mouth like a little fledgling waiting to be fed by the teaspoonful. But pears being pears ripened all at once and we couldn't keep up with the eating, so I made the rest into wine.

We soon got used to the serious, time-consuming task of boiling terry towelling nappies. There was free firewood and plenty of turf for the Stanley range, which boiled the napkins in the old five-gallon copper-and-zinc-lined tea urn we had brought with us from Midford. We dragged the boiled nappies out of the boiling water with wooden tongs and into a bucket before rinsing them at the kitchen sink, squeezing out the water by hand. It was an arduous task and I didn't have the strength to do it on my own. Finally they were hung out to dry on the clothes line. It was a splendid sight to see all those snow white nappies dancing in the breeze in the sunlit garden. Fortunately we were blessed with glorious sunshine in September and October that year. Wet days would be another matter, with wet washing draped all over the house.

Then we were given an electric spin-dryer that was part of a twin tub, the washing machine side having broken. We were glad to accept the gift – it would be much easier to rinse and spin the nappies by machine rather than by hand, and the spun nappies would dry much more quickly inside the house during wet weather.

The spin-dryer came from some Dutch friends who had bought themselves a replacement twin tub. They were a husband and wife team who lived with their two boys in a cottage a mile or two away. They supported themselves by spinning and weaving. She cleaned and carded the wool from the fleece and spun it into yarn using a spinning wheel, and he wove the yarn into cloth on a hand loom. Their cottage had an acre of land and they grew vegetables and kept some animals. They worked fourteen hours a day between their garden, animals, spinning and weaving, as well as selling their cloth and balls of wool under the name 'Black Sheep Wool'. They kindly gave Rebecca a gift of a grey homespun knitted jumper. I thought Rebecca would be too big for it when the winter came, which was just as well because although it was beautifully knitted it was really too heavy and dense for a baby to wear.

The wonderful weather that autumn helped us to remain cheerful when we were getting anxious about the legal situation regarding the cottage. Since March 1977 we had been expecting to receive the title deed to the cottage. Eighteen months later the deeds had still not arrived. We went to see Michael Ahern, our new solicitor in Killorglin. We asked him to find out where the title deeds for the cottage were lying. Mr Ahern's reply, which was a further eight months coming, astonished us.

Our application for a title was awaiting the vendor's signature. The cottage had been built at a time before a record of ownership was required. The vendor's brother was the last of the family to live in it and he had died in 1947. The vendor had to swear an oath and sign an affidavit to establish his ownership. But we had been told that that had already been established! It was all very confusing to say the least.

The size of our overdraft was also a worry during those autumn months, although by now we were becoming used to living on the proverbial 'shoestring' and knew some lucrative work would turn up sooner or later. I wrote to *The Kerryman* county newspaper offering to write history articles. They replied that history was not what the paper wanted, but 'forward looking articles'. Around the same time I got £35 from the Kerry Historical Society at Muckross House – the first instalment of £150 – for writing *The Railways of Kerry*.

The draft of my book about the Faringdon branch came back from OPC with the text reduced by half. A note from them explained that, originally, it was the longest branch line book ever, especially when the branch was only 3½ miles long. To have published the original text would cost three times the usual price for a book about a little, single-track branch line. I was disappointed, but I also realised that my great fault in writing is trying to fit in every detail. As the cuts would not be missed by anyone but me, and as they would improve the chance of selling the book, I decided to be happy.

One day in September Jack Chowne called in and invited us to supper at Churchtown House. The house, maybe five miles from our cottage, is near Beaufort village, and today it is a *very* smart hotel. In 1978 it was a sadly neglected place. Churchtown House, invisible from the road, was a severely plain house faced with cement. It was clearly an 18th-century, Anglo-Irish Ascendancy house: four-square, three-storeyed, grey and grim but nicely proportioned. It looked as if it might have been built with defence in mind. We went round the back, between the grey limestone cow sheds, and knocked on the back door.

Jack let us in. He showed us around the ground floor rooms. The interior seemed to be untouched 18th century. The family dining room was lit from large front windows. A mahogany dining table larger than a billiard table had ten Chippendale chairs around it; the dullness of the surface was evidence of it not having been used for a long time. There were grimy antiques worth thousands of pounds standing in dusty corners. On each side of the great front door at the end of the wide hallway stood two five-foot-tall Blue & White Chinese Temple jars. They had been there so long, untouched, that even the umbrellas they contained might have been of great interest to the V&A. I expressed amazement at such a heap of neglected wealth.

'There's 'Old Master' paintings hanging in the upstairs rooms,' Jack said, off-handedly. 'The owner's only interested in what the place can earn. The money the place makes goes to him in England.'

Susan and I looked at each other. The unspoken thought transferred. That was the fate of old Ireland, but here it still went on in the right house for the period.

The most lived-in room was the kitchen, its flagstone floor showing centuries of wear. In the middle of the large room was a big, scrubbed, deal table. A high, wide alcove accommodated a big range. The meal was cooking appetisingly in a large cast-iron casserole pot. The room was pleasantly warm, solidly antique and 'right'.

During dinner Jack asked me if I wanted part-time work, three hours on Saturday mornings and the same length of time on Sunday afternoons for £10. This was to help with the milking of the Churchtown herd of a hundred cows. My job would be to bring in the cows for milking from where they were feeding on kale, move the electric fence onto fresh kale, feed the calves and, after milking, get the cows back out to feed. He also asked me to help clear brambles in the walled garden.

Jack said, 'The brambles are hiding some old hives. The hives are rotting. The bees have filled every space in them and they've been building comb in the open air. Honeycomb is hanging from briars with bees flying about everywhere. If you can clear it you can take all the honey away with you.'

222

After clearance, the area would be concreted over and calf-rearing sheds built on it. For each calf the sheds contained, the government would pay a subsidy.

After the meal I needed to go to the lavatory. Jack pointed to the side door. 'Out there and up the stairs – it's the door on the left of the first landing.'

The staircase was grand but dimly lit, leading up to a spacious landing with several doors facing. As I stepped onto the landing a terrible sense of fear washed over me. True fear. I got a grip of myself, used the loo and went downstairs as fast as I could, bursting through the door to the bright lights of the kitchen. Jack and Susan looked up, startled.

'Are you OK?' asked Jack.

'No, not really. I had a horrible sensation on that landing. It came all over me like a paralysis. I was really scared. Like there was a ghost. Is there a ghost?'

'Ah, I didn't say anything,' said Jack, a bit too casually for my mood just then. 'Not everybody feels that, and I didn't want to set you up to be imagining things. Sorry. Here, have some whiskey.'

He passed me a glass of Bushmills and told me the story.

'A long time ago, a married couple were visiting the house and a priest was a guest as well. The husband got up early for a walk around the estate. He took his shotgun in case he had a chance at a bird or a hare but he had no luck there. He came in and went upstairs, opened the bedroom door and found the priest in bed with his wife. He used his gun on the priest. That bedroom has been locked ever since.'

Susan looked frightened and said in a small, scared voice that she too had felt an overwhelming sensation of fear when she had visited the lavatory earlier, but had put it down to her imagination.

I went to Churchtown House the following Saturday, taking my bee-keeping overalls, protective helmet and smoker equipment with me. After getting in the cows, I fed the calves, moved the electric fence through the kale and got the cows back into the field. After that Jack decided he would wield the chainsaw and we went out into

223

the jungle that had been, long ago, a well-kept kitchen garden. With angry bees whirling around me in brown clouds and wearing my protective equipment, I cut through the billows of brambles for yards in each direction, breaking off attached random honeycombs and setting them to one side. I dragged the thorny stems to a bonfire Jack had started. Eventually all that was left were three gaunt, rotten, tottering hives, three sections high, the land all around just bare earth sprouting hundreds of dark, spiky stalks. The sight looked like a slum clearance with three houses left for demolition.

The awful thing was that the bees were going to be destroyed. The hives couldn't be carried away, they were too fragile. So, feeling guilty and consoling myself by thinking there was no point in the honey being lost as well as the bees, I looted stacks of the comb honey in wooden squares. In all I removed about 60lb of honey, the best combs of which I sold for £20 and the rest was for us to eat through the winter. Poor bees.

Susan was offered a job for a couple of weeks in October, managing Henry Dodd's salmon smokery and shop while he went away on holiday. She was paid £15 a week, which was a welcome boost to our finances. I looked after Rebecca while Susan was working and tried to do all the right things with her, but it didn't come easily to me, especially changing poo-piled napkins and wiping bottoms!

On the evening of Tuesday 5th December a truly awful gale developed with such heavy rain as we'd not seen in Kerry since we'd arrived. For three days and nights the rain fell 'whole water' and the wind roared at 100 miles an hour over the roof. We lay awake in bed for some time on the first night. I was worrying about the roof and wondering about flooding coming in off the road. The rain never stopped, but the house did not flood – my flood channels worked – and the roof stayed on.

We got used to the noise and we were fast asleep on the third night of the gale. We were woken by a terrific *BANG!* In a great fright I flung off the blankets and swung myself out of bed. *SPLASH!* I was ankle deep in icy cold water. I recoiled onto the bed with a yell. The room was pitch dark, the wind was roaring and the rain was drumming fiercely on the roof. My confusion was complete. I stood up again and shuffled through the water to the light switch. The cement floor was three inches deep in rippling black water where it wasn't flashing back a reflection of the light. The water table after three days of rain was so high that it had risen under pressure through the cement floor. The kitchen floor, tiled all over, was dry and there was nothing disturbed to show what had caused that great bang. I went into the porch and opened the front door. It opened inwards, of course, but I couldn't get out of the house because the foliage of a large branch off a nearby pine tree completely blocked my way.

There was no point in going back to bed. Susan got up, bringing our clothes into the kitchen. We dressed, lit the range and sat around. Quite quickly then the gale subsided, the rain stopped and Saturday dawned in peace and sunshine. I opened a kitchen window, climbed out and sawed the huge branch into liftable bits. The preceding three nights were like a bad dream. In the bedroom the flood water subsided back through the floor almost straight away, but the room took much longer to dry out, even though the Stanley burned almost night and day on the other side of the bedroom wall. Luckily we could sleep in the sleeping loft with Rebecca in her cot in the kitchen below.

I was becoming very fed up with the weekend work at Churchtown farm. The work was exhausting and I was coming home soaked through each time, but after a couple of months of weekends I was able to give in my notice, as I had been offered another job. Alan Jones, an Englishman who lived with his mother at Meanus Cross, came to the cottage and offered me a five-day-a-week job as his assistant in his car repair business. 'I can only pay you £40 a week,' he said apologetically.

That was a small fortune to us.

I was experienced with car engine repairs, but knew nothing about repairing and spraying car bodies. Still, I was useful to Alan. A lot of his work was repairing bent bodywork and I could apply filler and rub it down as well as anyone else. We worked happily together. He was glad of some company and I was glad to work in the comparative warm and dry and to be bringing home a regular weekly wage.

Chapter Twenty-three
The school bus

The 2nd January 1979 was the coldest day in Ireland since records began. The Reeks were thickly covered with snow down to the hundred-foot contour. In England it was the worst winter since 1962-63. To compound the misery, in January the Government of James Callaghan had departed from its agreements with the trade unions and placed a limit of five per cent on wage rises. This led to the greatest shut-down of the UK since the General Strike in 1926. Agnes, intensely Catholic, told me, quite forgetting I was English, as she liked me too much, "Tis a visitation on England from God for their hunting down of the priests in 1540.'

On 9th January I received an early birthday present from the English Tax Office to say that from now on OPC could pay me my royalties without deduction of tax. I wrote away at once, asking OPC for the withheld tax. We needed the money. We owed the Allied Irish bank £560, and our credit limit there was £600. We owed Boyles, the ironmonger and builders' merchant, £115. All that debt was a heavy mental drag. It was also depressing that I found myself too tired to write in the evenings after working all day for Alan. But I carried on until I could find something else. It was a struggle trying to combine my writing with money-earning work to see us through from day to day.

For my birthday Linda invited us to a meal, so in the most cheerful of moods we drove NIN up onto the lower slopes of great Carrauntoohil to Mealis for my birthday dinner. Turning right at Meanus Cross, driving up the narrow, uphill road, a pair of headlights turned out of the Mealis road ahead. I slowed down and ran the nearside wheels onto the grass. The other car slowed down and stopped alongside. It was a Garda car. The window was lowered. The driver said, 'What the hell are you doing? You nearly had me off the road… Oh, that's you, Mr Vaughan. OK, so. Good night.'

The car sped away leaving us completely puzzled and astonished.

The steep drive up to Mealis was too much for poor old NIN and it started to emit blue smoke into the passenger space. We had one bicycle between us, so we were going to be a bit stuck to get about as a family. NIN had to be got to Mr Quane's scrapyard from whence it had come, as I reckoned I might be able to part exchange it for a repairable car there. Cars were so expensive in Ireland at that time that this seemed the only affordable option. Alan Jones said he would follow me to the scrapyard so I would have a lift home, or if I bought a car there he could tow it home, but until he could oblige me NIN stood forlorn by the roadside.

One morning a young man, twenty at most, came along and asked to buy it. I told him it was only waiting to go to the scrapyard, it was a wreck. He insisted and was waving a fistful of money at me – fifty pounds. The more I told him the truth, the more insistent he became. So I took his money and gave him the key. He drove away with blue smoke coming from the exhaust pipe. Susan and I went indoors. Five minutes later we heard the car coming back. A very angry young man strode up to me.

'This car's a *wreck*!' he shouted, red-faced. 'I want me money back.'

'Of course – but I did warn you,' says I, handing him back his fifty notes.

When Alan was available, I drove NIN with all the windows open to Mr Quane's scrapyard. The scrap car emporium was somewhere about the Kerry-Limerick border, on a remote, high hill overlooking the River Shannon. The view from the yard was magnificent. A modern factory, with a tall chimney beside the great river, was 'lost' in the panorama of the Shannon flowing westwards widening into the distance, and the greenery of County Clare stretching away to the northern horizon. I was admiring the view when Mr Quane's assistant came up and stood beside me. He was about eighteen with tousled hair and clothes *de rigueur* for scrapyard working. He was, however, of a romantic state of mind, possibly a poet. I asked him what the factory down by the river was for. He said, ''Tis the Plant. They pay great wages there but I'd lose me life if I went into that.'

An impressive remark that has stuck with me.

Mr Quane was a remarkable scrapyard man. He was of slight build, with a mild face, wore lightweight, gold-rimmed spectacles and walked with a stooped back. In Oxford's High Street he could be taken for a professor of Greek. He showed me a 1973 Hillman Hunter Estate. It looked to be in perfect condition.

'It is,' said he. 'It looks great, but there's a small problem with it – the big-ends are gone and the crankshaft will need machining.'

'How much would you want for it?' I asked.

'Would you think £400?' he said.

'That's on the high side with the work it'll need.'

Mild Mr Quane was a kindly man. 'Ah, but I'd give ye £60 off for your Vogue.'

So there it was. We tied a rope from the Hillman Hunter to the back of Alan's car and towed it back to his workshop.

Meeting Alan had been a great good fortune. Not only did he lend me £300 to buy the car, he had the equipment to lift the engine out. We dismantled it together one weekend. We found that the cylinders had not long before been re-bored and the pistons were new. Whoever had reassembled the engine after re-boring had had a great affinity to his native soil. The crankshaft was scored with grit embedded in the white metal bearings of the connecting rods. While the crankshaft was away being reground I bought a new clutch and brake shoes. When everything was fitted I had a car with a 1725cc engine in good condition for £400.

At last the withheld tax arrived. It was an Inland Revenue cheque for £391, which came via OPC! An accompanying note told me that the Tax Office had sent the cheque to OPC and told them to send it on to me. Talk about the '7th Cavalry'! It was a relief also because it arrived just before the onset of a postal strike in Ireland, which lasted on and off for several months. We had no telephone, so all communication with the outside world and English friends was by letter. We suffered a certain amount of stressful frustration waiting for replies.

Luckily another letter also arrived just in time. I had written to CIÉ (Córas Iompair Éireann), the state transport company, in Tralee to ask if there were vacancies for school bus drivers. The reply I got was that there were no vacancies, but they would train me to drive the bus and when I'd passed the test I would be called upon to drive when a Killorglin vacancy arose. I made an appointment with CIÉ and went to Tralee on the appointed day.

There were four others waiting for the Instructor. He shortly arrived driving a school bus. We climbed aboard and he introduced himself as Mr Ashe, but we could call him Paddy. He was in his forties, about five feet seven inches tall. Black hair, blue eyes, stocky. The bus, he said, was forty feet long, eight feet wide and could carry sixty-seven children. The wages would be £40 for a five-day week of twenty-five hours. Paddy put one of the men in the driver's seat and told him drive away and he'd give directions.

When I got my chance to drive, I immediately discovered how 'heavy' the steering was and that the gearbox was so antique that it was not 'synchromesh' – just a plain gearbox. Just like my pre-war Morris Eight. Going up through the gears was like normal, but to change down the clutch pedal was depressed and the lever pulled into neutral, then the engine had to be revved up sufficiently to match the revs that the lower gear would like, and the lever pushed into the lower gear. It was an additional skill that pleased me very much. I asked Paddy about the bus. It was a 1940s Bedford lorry, engine, gearbox, chassis and rear axle. The Irish Government had bought dozens of them and had the bus bodies built on. During my instruction I drove the forty-footer around housing estates as if I'd always driven that sort of vehicle. I could see that Mr Ashe was impressed. Paddy said, 'OK, you can handle this. Let's go and look for the Dingle Railway.'

In five minutes we had discovered each other's interest in steam railways. Paddy's father had worked for fifty years on the Tralee & Dingle Railway. I was delighted at my good fortune to have discovered a T&DR man, albeit at one remove.

So we left the housing estates behind and headed out along the Castle Gregory road. Along the way Paddy expounded on his philosophy of driving. He said, 'Never argue about whose right of way it is. If you come to a crossroads and there's someone coming towards you, left or right, don't charge out because you think it's your right of way. Just let him go by. Going along on these narrow roads, look over the tops of the hedges; if you are going uphill and there's a car parked on the opposite side of the road, near the brow, look underneath the car to see if some car is going to swing out and be on the wrong side of the road on the brow. Take notice of everything. *Read the road.*'

Paddy told me that his father had worked as a Guard on the Tralee & Dingle Railway. He said that his father, during the War of Independence against the British Government, had carried in his railway van, ammunition and food and whatever the freedom fighters might want in those remote mountain places. Paddy and his older brother grew up with the Dingle trains. Like me in England they'd ridden the footplates, learned how a steam engine worked and eventually were entrusted to drive and fire the locomotives. By that time the passenger trains had long been withdrawn. But a monthly cattle train, empty to Dingle and loaded coming back, survived long enough for the boys to drive over the Slieve Mish Mountains while the crew relaxed in the bar at Castlegregory Junction.

It was not long before I passed the official driving test and in April I was appointed a Killorglin school bus driver. The bus stood in what had been the goods yard of the railway station. I enjoyed everything about it. Its engine was inside the bus by my left leg, under a long metal hood large enough for a young lad to sit on if he wanted to talk. The steering column rose massively to a two-feet-diameter steering wheel that took some strength to turn. Sitting in the driving seat, eye level was eight feet above the road.

I cycled into town every morning around seven o'clock. Killorglin was silent, not a light in an upstairs window. Opposite the old goods yard was Tom Melia's supermarket and a row of shops paralleling the road. Diesels have a pre-heater on each cylinder so that the engine will start in sub-zero temperatures. I pressed a button on the instrument panel and watched till the pre-heater indicator went out, then I turned the ignition key. The diesel started with a clattering roar. I'd look across the road at the dark line of shops with living quarters above. Not a light came on.

My first route was the Cromane run. Cromane was a scattered settlement of cottages lining the road that runs north to the end of Rossbeigh Strand. The scenery was dramatic, especially when there were great cloudy stormy skies, with the sun breaking through the gaps pouring a beam of light onto the huge dark bulk of the Slieve Mish Mountains to the north, the Kerry mountains to the south, lining that wonderful extension of the Atlantic Ocean – Dingle Bay.

The bus was not a fast vehicle. It lumbered heavily along in whatever gear it was in. I liked the sturdy, practical, ringing, knocking, rhythmic rattle of the diesel. My passengers were eleven years old up to leaving age. Some children waited in gateways outside their cottages, others sat on the low wall dividing the road from the strand. At first the children climbing into the bus looked at me, a completely new face, with surprise, but doing the run with them twice a day we became friends. Leaving Cromane for Killorglin I would have a full bus.

The bus ripped along the dead straight road at 30 mph, the engine a kettledrum rattle, the body bouncing over low, hump-backed bridges crossing creeks in the grassy flatlands. In Killorglin the children would file off politely, lugging their enormously packed leather satchels, many with a friendly 'Thanks' or 'Bye'.

One afternoon, as they came climbing aboard, a young lad sat down on the engine cover.

'Are you English?'

'I am,' I replied.

'Do you know Kilburn High Road?'

'No, sorry, I've never been there.'

'But you're English!' He went to his seat, very puzzled.

Coming in from Cromane, there were always cars in a more or less continuous line parked on both sides of the road and at teatime home-going workers buying the evening paper or a piece of bacon, making double parking the order of the hour, with an occasional treble parker here and there, so that the wide road became a narrow, meandering path, like a rivulet through mudflats. I drove my school bus into this channel every weekday about five o'clock, 'threading the eye of a needle,' I thought proudly as I piloted the bulky bus around shoals of cars and guided its width between the rocks of a 1965 Morris Minor and a 1979 Ford Cortina whose treble-parked drivers where having a conversation across the shallows.

One afternoon a tractor and trailer came out of the butcher's archway right in front of the bus and proceeded slowly, carefully, in front of me. It was on the *entrail* run. On the flat trailer were a dozen forty-gallon drums, each one overflowing with the bloody debris of a recent slaughter. The driver's caution wasn't enough. Windpipes swung like chains, grey and blue intestines wriggled like live things with the trailer's movement, and, falling, coiled in piles between the brimming drums. On top of one stuffed barrel a skull lay upside down, stripped to the bone, raw and bleeding, its eyes still terrified. Lying at the end of the trailer, on the floor, were what appeared to be stomachs, semi-transparent bladders half full of some dark liquid that slopped and swirled until one fell off, burst and was dragged along the road, the liquid lining the surface till the bladder was empty. A white terrier dog, who someone loved and maybe called 'Spot', rushed into the road, rolled in the stuff and ran off – red.

I had followed for the length of the crowded street before I realised my mouth was half open, yet no one else seemed to notice the passing of this Gothic horror. The tractor passed straight over the crossroads and I, thankfully, turned to the left and left again into the station yard. As I push-pulled the big steering wheel and the bus swung slowly round, my line of sight fell directly onto a bright yellow Ford inside which sat an elderly woman, her face caked with old make-up, irretrievably wrinkled, who was holding in one claw-like hand – nails red, each finger comforted with a gold ring, her shrivelled wrist embraced by several gold bracelets – a mirror. In the other hand she had some tweezers and, oblivious to the world, with the most fastidious precision and the utmost concentration, she removed a tiny eyebrow hair that had trespassed beyond the pencilled line.

Around this time, Linda's father, John Scott, came to see me. I had visited his machine tool factory in Killarney several times and admired the workmanship – the taps and dies of many sizes gleamed like silver jewellery. John wanted me to photograph, as a job, the different types of taps and dies for the company's catalogue. The photos had to show the tools on a white background without shadows. I used a wooden-bodied single lens reflex, a Marion 'Soho', dating from 1922. It used a 120-size roll film. The lens was a splendid optic manufactured in August 1915, and produced wonderfully sharp, clear, 4¼ x 3¼-inch negatives. The problem was to arrange lighting so that there were no shadows. I got it right in the end and John was very pleased with the results. He began to call in occasionally from Killarney, coming down the Beaufort road, and sometimes gave me more photography work.

While Adrian worked hard to keep us afloat financially, I was busy looking after Rebecca and in between stoking the Stanley, preparing and cooking the meals, washing the interminable nappies and planting up the garden for the coming year. I enjoyed being a mother, but it was not an easy role to slot into, as any new mother knows. There was so much to learn and worry about and never a moment to oneself. Rebecca started to crawl soon after Christmas and crawled madly all over the place so I had to keep an eye on her all the time. Soon she had learned to pull herself upright, an achievement that sent her shivering and rigid with excitement. She had the usual teething troubles, but didn't grizzle too much if she could be distracted. She was greatly interested in Baby Cat and was forever head butting her and pulling out handfuls of fur. But Baby Cat sat all prim with a simpering look on her furry face and put up with it. She was a cunning feline and knew her patience would be rewarded with an extra titbit.

Rebecca loved music and Adrian often played something on the Dansette in the mornings as she ate her breakfast in her high chair. She especially enjoyed listening to the Chieftains and banged her spoon excitedly to keep time. One day a parcel arrived from Paul and Susie. It was a mixed classical record with Carolan, the great Irish harpist, on the first track. Adrian put Rebecca in her listening (high) chair and played the music. Rebecca drew herself up ready to listen – she must have been expecting the Chieftains because her expression changed wonderfully when she heard what it was, and after a moment she said 'Ooooh!'

Rebecca also loved fruit; she had devoured the pears in the autumn and in June we had strawberries. Rebecca was very, very fond of 'bawbish', as she called them, and ate one or two every day as they ripened. Eventually we had enough to make a delicious strawberry and cream flan and pounds of strawberry jam.

For the summer season I worked mornings in the antique shop. Adrian looked after Rebecca and tried to push on with building the bathroom extension at the same time. One day when she was about fifteen months old I was in the shop and, looking out of the window, saw Adrian draw up in the white Hunter estate car. He came running towards me with a bundle in his arms and thrust it at me. The bundle was my baby, blood all over her face. I thought her eye had been gouged out and nearly fainted. He said, 'Quick – we have to take her to the doctor!'

I don't know how I managed to lock up, but I did, and once in the car I realised almost immediately that her eye was still intact and she was bleeding from her eyebrow. She had two stitches put in. Adrian explained that Rebecca had come running into the cottage from the garden straight into the handle of the wheelbarrow, which had been standing in the porch, full of cement. Her eyebrow was the exact height of the open-ended tube of the wheelbarrow handle. Luckily the

235

diameter was wide enough to miss her eye. The incident made us both feel very guilty.

In June I went to England by myself to retrieve the *Signalman's Life* manuscript from OPC. They had done nothing with it for a year, probably because it was far too long for their formats. I needed to find another publisher. The offices of OPC were in a converted semi-detached house close to the roundabout where the Oxford Eastern bypass joins the A40 coming in from London. I went into the shop, but Colin Judge was not there. His office was upstairs. I asked the shop assistant to accompany me there because I wanted to find the typescript of my book and take it away. There it was, a two-inch-thick pile of foolscap paper, gathering dust. The shop assistant gave me a carrier bag, in it went and I departed for London. I was booked to stay with my sister Frances, in Ifield Road, SW10.

When I arrived there she had Penelope Betjeman staying with her. She and Penelope were very good friends. Penelope should have been on her way to India but the plane had broken down at Heathrow and she had been told to come back to the airport the next day. Penelope and I were well acquainted because we used to ride out together back in Childrey in the 1950s. I told her that I was looking for a publisher and she said in her squeaky voiced, upper-class drawl, 'Well, in order to write you have to have something interesting to say!'

I was sure I had plenty to say and handed her my manuscript, which she had the generosity to sit down and start to read. She read several pages of the first chapter and said, 'I really like this. John would love it too. Tomorrow I will take you to our publishers and then go on to Heathrow.'

Next day she took me to John Murray's offices in Mayfair. We got to 50 Albemarle Street at ten o'clock. I was expecting an office building. There was no office, but an 18th-century dwelling house. Spearheaded railings that lined the pit of the basement rooms curved around on each side of the well-worn stone to the steps leading up to a finely panelled door. There was a brass letter box, an 18th-century brass knocker and, above the door, a glass panel with glazing bars reminiscent of a spider's web. Penelope used the big door knocker and the door was opened by the doorkeeper. This gentleman recognised her at once, friendly words of greeting were exchanged, he retired to his mahogany and glass cubicle in the hall, and she led me up a grand staircase. On the way we passed Lord Byron's underpants framed like a picture, on the wall.

Murray was a family firm, established by Mr John Murray in Edinburgh in 1786. By 1979 it was probably the oldest publishing company in Britain. There was hardly a famous man or woman author of the past who had not been published by the John Murray house. They'd published Austen, Darwin, Byron, both Sir John Betjeman and Penelope, and now they might publish me! All because Penelope Betjeman's plane had broken down at Heathrow.

Penelope introduced me to the senior Murray, 'Jock'. He was working in an unchanged, smallish 18th-century room. The low light in there actually enriched the wonderful antiquity of the room. He was elderly, slim, of medium height, his face lined with age, yet, bright, lively and as friendly to me as if I was an established author. Penelope left for Heathrow, Jock Murray poured two glasses of whisky and gave one to me. He asked me about the book. I launched into my favourite subject – life on the steam railway. He seemed genuinely interested. As we talked I was able to surreptitiously pour my whisky into the soil of a pot containing a tall plant. When he'd heard enough he picked up my typescript and said, 'I'll take you to Simon Young; he's one of our directors and a very fine editor. He'll look after you and your book.'

Chapter Twenty-four
Suspected terrorists

John Murray sent me a formal letter of acceptance for a *Signalman's Life* and in August we went to England so I could visit the publisher and search out the railwaymen I had worked with to ask their permission to mention them in the book. We stayed at Childrey and I went to Oxford to see Don Kingdom, my best engine driver friend, who had conferred many privileges on me; I travelled several thousand miles on his footplates. I had written a lot about our time together and I wanted to make sure that was OK with him. He was very pleased to see me and as to my request he said, 'That'll be fine. If anyone asks I shall deny every word.'

I went to Uffington, to the council house where signalman Elwyn Richards had lodged. I knocked on the front door. It was opened by a rheumy-eyed old woman of stature short and stout.

'Yes?' she snapped. She was fitter than she looked.

'Hello. I'm a friend of Elwyn's. I worked with him at Uffington signal box. I want to ask his permission to write about him in a book I'm doing.'

She smartly folded her arms, cocked her head up and to one side to look at my face.

'We don't give no permissions here,' she said, with terrible officiousness. She was about to slam the door when the situation was saved by her ancient husband. He came hobbling with all speed from around the back of the house and restored his wife to civility. Elwyn had lived with them while he worked at AERE Harwell, but then his mother had died so he had retired and gone to live in his mother's house in Glamorganshire. He had left an address so I was able to write to him.

Next I went to Stanford-in-the-Vale to find Harry Strong. It was a Sunday, early on a sunny evening. If he was still alive he would be in his eighties, but if he was not then surely his widow would be alive. I parked against the kerb near some bungalows for the elderly. A group of possible inhabitants were standing on the pavement. I walked over to them.

'Hello, sorry to butt in. I'm looking for Harry Strong. Can you tell me where he lives?'

They — a skinny, mean-faced-looking man, two big middle-aged women and a much older woman — froze. Mouths opened, they stared at me in what was obviously a shocked silence.

'I'm writing a book about my time on the railway. I worked with Harry at Challow station. I'd like to write about him and I want to ask him if he would mind. Can you tell me where he lives?'

'Right!' boomed one of the big women, angrily. 'You have just given Mrs Strong here,' she said, pointing to the oldest woman, 'a severe upset. She is sick and weak from her loss and you come round here,' her voice warmed up as she got into her stride, 'barging in, interrogating her about her sad loss. We'll have to know a lot more about this.'

Completely thrown, I turned to leave but the skinny man darted in front of me. 'You'll make it worse if you leave now. You'd better come inside.'

In the bungalow they were all sitting down, Mrs Strong in an armchair, looking very cheerful. What I'd said outside had sunk in. The two large women, one of whom was Mrs Strong's daughter, were sitting bolt upright on hard chairs looking daggers at me. The skinny man stood. I stated my case again, directly to Mrs Strong, who smiled encouragingly. I asked her if she had any photos of Harry. She got up to search. There were cries of protest from the two Guardians on the chairs. They were very mean and distrustful. They asked me where I lived and, wanting to do something to annoy their miserable selves, I said, 'Ireland.'

There should then have been the sounds of the opening bars of Beethoven's fifth. How I enjoyed the looks on their faces, but Mrs

Strong got up and came back with a couple of battered photos, which she gave to me. I said that I would copy them and send them back to her. She said she didn't want them back. Sharp intakes of breath and indignant gasping noises from the chairs. My father copied the prints and I took them back to Mrs Strong the next day. She was sitting on her own and we had a lovely talk about Harry.

We were back in Meanus when a most terrible event occurred on 27th August 1979. Lord Mountbatten was fishing off Mullaghmore, Co Sligo, with him was his grandson and a local lad, when a bomb exploded within the boat, killing all three. On the same day eighteen soldiers of 2nd Parachute Regiment were killed by two roadside bombs. Both were IRA actions. In the days following these August murders we had a few local people stopping their cars and coming into the garden to apologise.

In September we were invited by Timmy and Anne to the christening of their son in the Roman Catholic parish church of St James in Killorglin. St James is a massively constructed stone building in the heavy Victorian Gothic style, consecrated in 1891. I whiled away the time inside, casting my eyes over the awesome weight of timber forming the roof. Having not long before cut a few rafters for the cottage roof, I think I understood what a magnificent achievement it was to get hundreds of tons of wood up there so perfectly cut and jointed together. The walls were tens of thousands of tons of stone, cut out of the living rock in a quarry, then shaped – by hammer and chisel? – to plane surfaces. Behind the altar there was the reredos, an intricate lacework in alabaster. I'm not sure that it was to my taste, but I admired the vast input of human skill to construct it.

When built the church represented the stony power of Catholic doctrine over the population. I thought it was no longer quite like that. Many Irish Catholics in 1979 were taking matters with 'a pinch of salt'. I knew that priests were not always addressed as 'Father', but nicknames were used – 'Mick' or 'Pat'.

Susan and I went back to Timmy and Anne's house for drinks and food and I got into conversation with the child's grandfather.

240

He was a dear man. He had gone to England in the 1930s and worked for a civil engineering company, some of the time working on railway improvements during the war. He went to Mass every Sunday and carried out all the observances a layman Catholic should, but at the same time had a remarkable cynicism about it all. He said he didn't like to hear a priest being chatted to as 'Mick' or 'Jimmy', but he had a store of anti-priest jokes. So when it was announced that Pope John Paul would make a four-day visit to Ireland on 28th September, I wondered what sort of reception he would receive.

Pope John Paul was to visit, among other places, Dublin, Drogheda, Knock and Limerick on the final day. Nine coach loads of Killorglin-ites went to Knock and to Limerick. I was hoping I might be conscripted to take any overflow in the school bus, but it was not to be. In all, an estimated 2.7 million people turned out to see the Pope.

There were lots of 'Pope' souvenirs for sale: posters, T-shirts, coins. The Church spent four million pounds on the dressings of the tour. The red carpet the Pope walked on in Phoenix Park cost £250,000 and we supposed it would afterwards be cut up into inch squares to be sold to the pilgrims. The *Irish Press* thought that the visit was being vulgarised, and to make their point suggested that His Holiness could have commercial slogans on his robes: 'The Pope Drinks Coke', and 'Rothman's Cigarettes' stickers on his 'Popemobile'.

The end of the Pope's visit was marked by him saying Mass on the race course at Limerick. Part of his message to the Faithful was that a husband should not be lustful for his wife. He should approach sexual intercourse as a duty – not fun. The contradiction then was that artificial birth control was a mortal sin, but it was not sinful to calculate when one's wife was temporarily infertile, then engage in, by definition, lustful sex.

With the bathroom finally finished and operational, we set out yet again for another trip to England on Friday 14th December. It was becoming clear that I needed to spend a lot of time in England researching and working on my railway books. We planned to spend the week or so before Christmas staying with Paul and Susie in The Old School House, Radstock, so that I could meet Simon Young, the editor at John Murray, who lived in nearby Bradford-upon-Avon. Christmas would be spent with my sister in Devon. We were to leave from Rosslare, first calling at Scott's Tools to pick up three suitcases heavy with boxes of taps and dies. They must have weighed a hundredweight each. John Scott had asked us to take them because they were a fulfilled order to go to England but had been thwarted by yet another postal strike. They would be collected from us by his son James. We drove off the ferry at Fishguard at 2.00 am with a long and tedious journey ahead of us. I had a Christmas parcel to deliver to my great friend John Morris, who lived in the village of Crundale, near Haverfordwest. I pushed the package through John's letterbox and we got on our way.

We spent a pleasant day with Paul and Susie in their house in Radstock, and next day, Sunday the 16th, they took off at 8.00 am with Christmas presents for his family in Hastings. Susan, Rebecca and I were in the front room. Susan was playing with Rebecca and I was reading one of Paul's books. We were waiting to go for lunch with Simon Young and his wife. At 11.00 am there was a knock on the front door. The door had two glass panels and, before I opened it, it crossed my mind that there was no silhouette of the person who had knocked on the other side. I opened the door. It was flung open, throwing me back into the hallway. There was a rush of dark uniformed men with large boots – I saw them before any faces. In two seconds I was flung back against the wall, looking down the barrel of a revolver. My vision was intensely concentrated on the gaping barrel and, a little distance back, the chambers within which glinted the copper noses of .38 calibre bullets. It was a Webley. I remembered firing them when I had trained as a weapon and drill instructor.

Someone was shouting, 'Police! Do not move! Stay where you are!' Big boots went thundering up the stairs. Policemen barged into the front room to the considerable alarm of Susan, if not also Rebecca.

'We have reason to believe that there are arms or explosives in this house.'

With this crisply factual accusation, my brain had something solid to concentrate on. I thought for a few moments and said, in the first quiet voice of the incident, 'There's no arms or explosives here, but there are three suitcases in the next room full of taps and dies. Is that what you're looking for?'

Some policemen thundered into that room while I, gripped by a policeman on each side, was rushed outside to the one-time school playground where our Kerry-registered car was parked. A policeman pointed through the rear window of the estate car.

'What is that?' he demanded – as if he already knew.

I looked. It was my father's home-made battery charger and electric toy train controller. I was taking it to him to mend. My father was a radio engineer. The battery charger had been built in about 1947 when there were tons of ex-government electrical equipment being sold. It was a metal box. Black, crackle finish, about ten inches tall and ten inches square. It had two chromium-plated carrying handles. The top side was a panel of shiny black Formica, carrying a big, ex-government ammeter, a chromium on/off switch, a black fuse box and a red light that came on when the instrument was in use. Most frightening of all was the voltage control knob, a two-inch-diameter disc. It was on a tall metal spindle, making the disc about three inches above the top panel. To a passer-by who recognised the car's Irish registration number, the voltage control disc on its stalk might have been seen as a plunger to detonate a bomb. Perhaps a passer-by had come to these conclusions and phoned the police? It was just the sort of thing that an IRA bomber would leave on show!

By this time I had recovered from surprise and was getting 'ticket collector feelings'. Hackles rising, I opened the hatchback.

'Stand back – do not touch that!' shouted the policeman in charge.

I ignored him and lifted the thing out. 'This is a battery charger and electric train controller made by my father out of ex-government surplus.' I went on to explain how one would use it. Then I put it back, shut the hatchback and deflated the policemen.

I was taken back to the house. The policemen asked about the taps and dies. I told them who had made them, why I had them, and that they'd be collected by James Scott who was coming from Birmingham. They said they would confiscate the suitcases and I was marched down the path from the front door to a waiting police car. As I progressed I saw policemen crouching behind bushes – and there was one on top of the church tower – they all had Lee-Enfield rifles. On the drive to Radstock police station I saw that the roads had been sealed off. But not in time to stop Paul and Susie going to Hastings, apparently. At the start of the questioning I asked about them.

'They are being followed,' I was told.

At the police station every single box of heavily greased taps and dies was opened, emptied and repacked. It must have been an awful mess. They found no weapons, of course, but they weren't going to let me go. The questioning went on and on – in circles. Around one o'clock I was asked, 'Did you once work on the railway hereabouts?'

'Yes, at Frome and Witham,' I replied.

At last I was 'free to go'. Next day I heard through the grapevine that a new radio operator had come on duty at 1.00 pm at Bath police HQ, and as soon as he heard my name he said, 'Ask him if he ever worked on the railway here.'

The answer I gave went back to him and he said, 'Oh! That's Adrian. I often used to call in on him at Witham in the small hours.'

And so I was let go, but only after they'd soothed their embarrassment by giving me a strong telling-off for bringing in anything heavy from Ireland. 'It might have been a bomb.'

While I was in Radstock police station the police had also arrested Tom Chapman and his daughter. Tom was a church bell ringer with Paul and Susie. Tom and daughter had arrived outside the house while the police were still there. They had come to deliver

244

Christmas presents. He and she were on a powerful motor bike, clad in classy black leathers and big crash helmets. Clearly terrorists. Before they had even dismounted they were swooped on from behind and stuffed into a police van. Tom, the owner of Radstock printing works, was put in a cell in spite of all his protestations of identity and innocence. He was visited by the Superintendent of Radstock District who called out, 'Tom! What the hell are you doing in here?'

'I don't bloody know — ask that silly bugger behind you. He arrested me.'

I was driven back to The Old School House in a police car with the suitcases repacked. Susan and I were both in a state of shock, which we did not recognise. We ought to have cancelled our lunch with Simon Young, and instead sat down with cups of tea and waited for James Scott to arrive from Birmingham to pick up the suitcases. I phoned Simon to tell him we had been raided by police under the impression that we were the IRA, and that is why we would be arriving late. We left a note for James with Simon's phone number — and we left for Bradford-on-Avon, nine miles away. Only a little while after we had sat down for lunch — delayed for the whole family — James rang asking for the tools. Susan had to leave with Rebecca to drive back to Radstock to hand over the suitcases. I carried on with a rather shocked Simon and his wife, trying to talk about my book with a large elephant in the room! Susan returned to collect me and we left the puzzled and astonished Youngs. We had considerably upset the even tenor of their day; the embarrassment was general. We were not thinking straight, and as we drove the enormity of what had happened to us grew like a great purple bruise.

We talked over and over about the events. How did the police know that we were carrying the machine tools? Had there been a false tip-off? If so where had it come from? We were dreading the arrival of our friends, breaking the terrible news to them and making them feel as shocked and embarrassed as we were. Both of them were well known in the town; they were members of the

245

church bell ringing team and regarded by all as a very respectable couple. And to make it more embarrassing for everyone concerned, Susie was the sister of the Rector of the parish church, St Nicholas, next door!

While we were just sitting, waiting, turning it all over and over there was a loud knock at the door. It was a bit early for the Dyes. Was it the police again? I hurried to the door, heart racing. Opened it. A man was standing there, notebook and pencil in hand.

'Somerset Guardian. Have you any comment on what happened here today?'

'No,' I snapped quite loudly, being under stress.

'Oh, but surely you'd like to give your side of the story?'

'No comment,' I said, and slammed the door shut.

The Dyes arrived, coming through the front door with happy greetings. Then we broke the news. Susie, in a state of shock, telephoned her brother. It transpired that not only had the police sealed off the roads leading out of the town while the armed operation was going on, the congregation in St Nicholas's Church had been evacuated during the Sunday morning service!

Next day the headlines in the local papers were 'ARMED POLICE EMPTY CHURCH' – *Somerset Guardian* – and 'CHURCH EMPTIES IN IRA HUNT' – *Western Daily Press*. As a classic example of press standards, the *Somerset Guardian* reported exactly what had happened, right down to the last line. 'A bearded man refused to answer questions.' How sinister was that? The atmosphere in the house was very difficult as everybody came to terms with what had happened.

After a solitary breakfast, Susan and I left the house with Rebecca and drove to Bath. Susan did some shopping and I went to see Ivo Peters, a fellow OPC author. Back in Radstock, we parked in the old playground about lunchtime and decided we should leave to give our friends some time to recover by themselves. Inside the house the conversation was stilted, but Paul did say that the police were sending a detective round in the afternoon to explain what had happened.

Detective Constable Meade arrived and was invited by Paul into the front room. Susan and I were sitting there. Paul went over to a chair next to Susie. Constable Meade was rude. He opened his talk with an eviction order to Susan and me. 'I have come here to apologise for the upset you' – looking at Paul and Susie – 'have had, but I am not apologising to those two' – pointing at Susan and me. 'They will have to leave the room before I start.'

Paul was furious, and said very firmly, 'You will not order people about in my house, Constable – they stay here.'

'OK. But I must emphasise that I am not apologising to them.'

Susan and I were very cross. It was unjust. It was an insult. I had been released from police interview without any charge and was innocent of any crime. But we could not protest. Paul and Susie had enough to put up with, without us making a fuss. Meade didn't really talk about anything we didn't already know; there were no real explanations for what had happened. After he had departed we told our friends that we would pack our things and leave too.

Chapter Twenty-five
Derry witness

It took us a long time to recover from the shock and injustice of that police raid. It was so upsetting, unsettling and embarrassing for all of us. Not least for Paul and Susie who, in the aftermath, had to field questions from family, community and work colleagues. Because we didn't want to jeopardise our friendship with them further – we all needed space to recover – we left them earlier than planned and went to stay with our friend Martin Brown and his then wife Joy, who lived in Thatcham. They were very kind to us but they were busy preparing for Christmas and I felt in the way. Then there was more drama! Rebecca and I were coming down the stairs at their house when Rebecca suddenly stumbled and grabbed at a stair rail to stop her fall. She let out the most agonised cry and slumped on the stairs. We couldn't work out which bit was hurt and she couldn't explain, but she was clearly in a lot of pain. We took her to the surgery in Thatcham and saw a doctor almost straight away. I have no recollection of what happened next but I think she was treated for a partially dislocated shoulder. In any event she was no longer in such pain and we took the poor, pale little waif back to our friend's house. I so badly wished we were at home. My equilibrium was shattered, but we were not yet finished with drama on that ill-fated trip.

We drove down to Devon through magnificent downland and river valley scenery to stay with Adrian's sister and her two teenage children for Christmas. We were well received and Christmas Day got off to a good start but as often happens at family gatherings, the atmosphere soon deteriorated. This was partly because Rebecca, no doubt reacting to all the stresses we had been under, started to scream, periodically and piercingly, which put us all on edge and especially irritated the teenagers.

Next morning at the breakfast table there was a heated political discussion that quickly veered towards an argument with raised voices and entrenched positions, but no-one actually fell out. Throughout the morning the teenagers kept to their bedrooms and I did my best to entertain Rebecca who was clearly feeling miserable. After a difficult lunch, during which hardly anyone spoke, there was an explosion of tension and an unhappy falling out. We decided to leave.

It was very disturbing to leave someone's house under a cloud yet again – the second time in just over a week. And there we were on a cold Boxing Day afternoon with an eighteen-month old child in the car and nowhere to go! Darkness would soon be drawing in and we couldn't drive very far as we had little petrol and there were no garages open. Nothing was open. It looked as though we might have to spend the night in the car. Motoring along the road towards Exeter, Adrian saw a pub that thankfully did appear to be open. He pulled into the front yard and went inside to order some sandwiches – sadly we had left several pounds worth of food behind. The barman was reluctant to make anything for us, but Adrian pressed on and described our plight. Hearing this tale of woe he went off to make some sandwiches and a customer, overhearing the conversation, said incredulously, 'You are going to sleep all night in a car with a baby?'

'Yes. No choice,' Adrian replied.

This man was aghast and said he would phone some friends who owned a hotel. The friends were very kind and put us up for the night in a room in their own suite. It cost us £12.50.

The next day we phoned our friends Jane and Jim who lived at Witham Hole, near where Adrian once worked. They were happy to put us up for as long as we needed. So we headed east in the teeming rain. Jane and Jim didn't seem in the least put out by Rebecca's shrieking, which thankfully calmed down as time went on.

Jane invited some friends around for supper that evening and I put Rebecca to bed upstairs. I read to her and settled her down, stroking her hair until I thought she was asleep, but as soon as I started to creep out of the bedroom, up would come her little head and she would be out of bed in a flash, her little feet thundering across the room towards me.

249

This happened several times. I could hear the murmured conversation downstairs and I was desperate to join in. But this was the reality of motherhood, forever putting oneself last. Finally, Rebecca fell asleep — she must have been exhausted — and I crept downstairs, looking forward to a drink and some grown-up time.

The kitchen was bathed in soft yellow candlelight, several people were seated around the large pine table, drinking and conversing. And there, in the centre of the table on a large decorated platter, was a pig's head glistening in the candlelight, with an apple stuffed in its mouth. It felt most surreal.

Before returning to Ireland in the New Year I had another meeting with Simon Young at 50 Albemarle Street. The typescript was on his desk when I walked in. After the usual pleasantries, he said, 'We can't publish *War and Peace* in one volume, Adrian. It'll have to be two books.'

With that he picked up the thick wad of my book, held it upright between the palms of his hands, searched for the centre of the wad with his thumbs, inserted them, and divided it into two. He put them down separately on the table. I was surprised and must have looked doubtful because he said, very cheerily, 'That's good for you, Adrian — *two* advances!'

He was actually *pleased* that the typescript had been easy to divide into two books and was amused that I did not realise that this was possible. I signed the contract for the first volume, which Simon wanted to call *Skylarks at Challow*, and left No 50, £750 richer! I wrote seven books for John Murray before the business was taken over by Hodder & Stoughton. After that I never again worked with a publisher so keen to give me money.

The journey home was uncomfortable for Susan; there was something wrong with her seat, which made her back ache. There was also a problem with the car. The distributor moved during the journey across Ireland, the engine making a terrible 'pinking' noise, burning more petrol than it would otherwise have done. We were exhausted by the time we stopped outside the cottage at midnight.

We creaked stiffly out of the car and turned up the path. There was something leaning against the front door – a carrier bag full of groceries from Linda and a note of apology for the terrible ordeal we had endured at the hands of the English police. That certainly raised our spirits.

Next day John came round with a bouquet of flowers, as large as his embarrassment, apologising profusely for what had happened. We were grateful, of course, but the whole sorry episode had been no more their fault than ours. Agnes brought our mail round – and another great booster for morale: a £180 cheque from OPC! I was able to bank £930 in all. I felt as though I was getting somewhere at last.

On 9th January I started rewriting the first volume of the book. It is always the way that, reading back over one's earlier efforts, one can see a better way of writing a sentence. Working with an iron typewriter, a page would be written out several times as changes were made, typos corrected and a fresh – hopefully – perfect page could be produced. That day was the first of months combining work on the house, repairs to the car, driving the school bus, and hours on the book. At some time during the interminable rewriting, the title was changed from *Skylarks at Challow* to *Signalman's Morning*, and the second volume would eventually be called *Signalman's Twilight*.

Susan's back was visibly bruised when we got back from England. The bruise and the ache subsided slowly, but she felt poorly generally. She thought she might be pregnant. Rebecca was teething four teeth. Poor little Becca. She was in pain and miserably bored. Susan wasn't feeling well and I was trying to concentrate on the book. The difference in Rebecca and indeed the whole cottage was amazing when Susan's parents arrived with her youngest sister, Siobhán. She was delighted to play and distract Rebecca all day long. Joy was unconfined all round.

Through January the weather outside was bitterly cold with thick, white frosts each morning. The bitter cold had an asthmatic effect on me. Many days I worked till midnight. I would wake up in the night with asthma and thoughts windmilling around about the book. I'd get out of bed, relight the range, make tea and poke around with pen and paper.

One day I decided to go to Tralee to buy a £33 return bus fare on Slattery's bus as I needed to do some research in London. The car wouldn't start. There was something wrong with the starter motor. I took the motor off, freezing cold, out on the road. It was jammed somehow, so I took it to bits and got it working. We went to Tralee next day to purchase the ticket and to buy, on hire purchase from the Electricity Supply Board (ESB), an automatic washing machine. We would definitely need it. Susan was definitely pregnant. Boiling nappies was not something she wished to repeat.

A few days later the cylinder head gasket on the car failed, and water got into the oil. I took the head off and took it to the mechanics to be machined – plate-glass flat. I took the sump off to clean out the buttery yellow slime that had been oil, and bought a scrap distributor off a Morris Minor. When I put on the skimmed head I inserted the alien distributor, bolted everything down tight, adjusted everything and after all that the car worked perfectly.

At the end of March I sent off the finished typescript only to get it back after a couple of weeks with more suggestions for rewriting. From January through to March one or both or all of us was ill. It was a very trying time. Driving the school bus was also proving very stressful. In the last three months I had only five-to-ten-year-old children. They just would not stay in their seats. They wandered about the central aisle, and even came up to me. Coming up to stops outside a house, I had to shout back down the bus to get them all back in their seats and *beg* them to sit still until it was time for them to get off. I asked the Headmaster of the primary school to come to the bus before I left Killorglin and tell them to keep their seats and do what I told them. All to no avail. If a child was standing up in the aisle when I had to make an emergency braking, the child would be thrown forward and badly hurt. So in the end I handed in my notice to CIÉ. Paddy Ashe was disappointed and so was I.

I was pregnant again – it didn't come as too much of a surprise. We'd had our fun over Christmas, finding ourselves in need of a certain amount of stress release. But the early pregnancy took a greater toll on me than I had expected and then I went down with 'flu. As I emerged shakily from this illness, and feeling in need of some extra support, I came across a lovely Irish/American woman who lived in Killorglin. She was Kathleen O'Connor, daughter of Chub O'Connor, also known as Chub Connor, the TD (Teachta Dála), a member of Dáil Éireann, the Irish Parliament, and owner of one of the builders' yards in Killorglin. She had lived in America for many years, but had come back to Killorglin with her family. Her youngest child was around five. Although Kathleen was only in her early forties she was just the sort of experienced motherly figure that a new mum could call on for advice and support. She told me about La Leche League in Ireland, a voluntary organisation, originating in America, which provided information and support for breastfeeding mothers.

Meetings were held in Killarney in members' homes. Women who attended were at various stages of pregnancy or were breastfeeding, some expecting their first baby and others, like Kathleen, with large families already. They were a tremendously supportive group of women, mainly from middle class backgrounds; none of them as far as I remember had careers or jobs of their own. Kathleen wasn't the only American. There was the wife of an American Baptist minister. She said they'd come to Killarney to convert Catholics to the true religion.

'We've been here five years, and when we've made enough converts we'll build a chapel. But so far we haven't made any converts.'

I related this conversation to Adrian. He said that a Baptist attempting to bring Calvinism to Catholic Killarney seemed like an insincerity of purpose, like a refrigerator mechanic going to Iceland to sell refrigerators!

The start of April brought lovely weather and the Holy Week concerts in Killarney. We went to the cathedral to hear the Ulster Orchestra and the great Irish solo violinist Geraldine O'Grady play.

She set out on a very difficult piece, intricate millisecond fingering – beautiful. We were all spellbound. One man was excited beyond bearing. He sprang out of his seat, clapping loudly, energetically. The conductor swung round and glared at the entranced clapper. That brought him back to earth and he crashed back into his seat. Geraldine played through as if nothing had happened.

On Good Friday, with Susan and Rebecca I drove out to Mountain Stage and Caherciveen intending to photograph Kells and Caherciveen viaducts and the short tunnels after Mountain Stage. Between there and Kells Viaduct the railway ran on a narrow ledge along the face of a cliff, maybe 200 feet above the sea and 30 feet above the road. Between Glenbeigh and Mountain Stage I made a snap decision and turned left down a narrow lane to explore. Driving the school bus I'd seen a little settlement down there with a tiny church.

We left the car and walked down the sunny lane. We came up to a detached two-storey house standing in a fair-sized garden. The cement-stuccoed roadside wall had a blacksmith-made little iron gate. A tiny child, two years old, was standing behind it looking out, and the Granny was leaning over the wall, enjoying the sun, the peaceful day and her little granddaughter. Both were pleased to see us.

Granny said, 'Hello, good morning. Happy Easter,' and we replied in kind.

'Are you visitors?' she asked.

'No, we live near Killorglin.'

Conversation in Kerry always flourishes with the curiosity of seeing strangers. Rebecca went to the gate and the two little girls held hands through the bars. The sound of wellingtons clumping along came into earshot and the Grandad with a fine collie dog at his heels came up to our group. More smiling greetings. We congratulated each other on the fineness of the day.

He asked, 'Where are you from. Are you visiting?'

He was pleased to know we lived near Killorglin. We had a truly friendly craic. After a few minutes he said, 'Wait there awhile now,' and went over to the grassy bank lined along the top with fuchsia hedge. He began ruffling around in the grass with his fingertips – and found a nice brown egg. He worked away until he'd found four. He brought them back and handed them to Susan. His wife beamed a big smile. 'Now – there's your Easter present,' he said.

Killorglin Historical Society planned to have an exhibition in the CYMS (Catholic Young Men's Society) Hall over one weekend and I was asked to provide some pictures. Eugene O'Sullivan, estate agent and a member of the Killorglin mountain rescue team, invited me to give a talk on 'The Railways of Kerry'. He must have heard of the work I'd done for Muckross House on the subject. A surprisingly large number of people turned up at the hall. My opening sentence was, 'The capital for building the Farranfore-Caherciveen railway was guaranteed by the parochial rates.'

From the back of the hall, a tall, skinny, ginger-haired man leapt to his feet and shouted angrily, 'And do ye think that was right?'

His accent was that of Ulster. I was taken aback and was getting myself together to explain the benefits that would come from having a railway, but Eugene was quicker. He smacked his hand down on my shoulder and whispered urgently, 'Leave it.'

Then he turned to the audience and dismissed them. To my surprise they all rose and quietly filed out. They must have been afraid of that man, but I was never told who or what he was.

Walking away from the 'CY' Hall I passed the opening of Cahillane's muddy alleyway, which ran along the backs of large houses, the fronts of which faced onto the market place. A group of young children, six to ten years old, were leaning against the wall of a shed, one of many forming the other side of the alleyway. There were three bullocks standing close to the opposite wall. The children were very interested in something across the alley. I turned into the passageway. The little ones were calmly watching the killing, butchering and skinning of a bullock! The three cattle outside were no more than ten feet from the scene, quietly awaiting their fate. One glance was enough for me. All I could do was hurry away.

About that time I was out with my camera, looking for landscapes to photograph. I was on the Board o' Works road. It had been built by hungry, semi-starved men during the terrible famine of 1846-47. I came upon two men out for a walk and fell in with them for the craic. One was in his late twenties, short and stout, the other was ten years older, tall, thin and sandy-haired. I'll call him Michael, and the younger man Donal. They had the strong, grating accents of Northern Ireland. They were friendly enough to let me walk with them and, being surprised to hear my West Berkshire 'Want-ij' accent, Donal asked if I was on holiday. I launched into my story – as is always my failing.

Donal told me they were from Derry, now living in Killorglin. He was a carpenter with a wife and two children. Donal seemed calm, normal. Michael had a lean and hungry look; he looked dangerous somehow. We came to a little bridge over a stream tumbling down off the Reeks and stopped to lean over the parapet. Michael had softened slightly and was telling me that he worked for the Post Office, operating a switchboard somewhere in the district. A yellow wagtail flashed into sight, landing on a stone in the brook. Michael leaned forward, intent, watching. It certainly was a nice little bird with the water just washing over its toes. In a flicker of yellow wings it was gone and Michael slouched again. 'You won't see many of them,' he told us. ''Tis rare.'

We walked on, downhill, heading back to Meanus Cross. I was wondering why these two had moved to Kerry. For a peaceful life, I supposed. 'That was an awful thing up there in Sligo, Mullaghmore last year,' I ventured.

Michael and Donal stopped instantly and Michael, seething immediately with bitter anger, shouted, 'He got what he deserved! He showed that the British still occupy Ireland. Well, not any more.'

We walked on in frigid silence. I felt literally shaken at his fury. I remembered the angry, sandy-haired man who had challenged me in the 'CY' Hall. He had been in the darker part, at the back. Maybe this was the same man? It was as if he had a split personality. Delighted with yellow wagtails on little wet stones and delighted

256

with the death of Mountbatten and two little boys. When we got back to the cottage, Michael walked on but Donal stopped with me at the gate. He was not angry.

'Maybe I shouldn't have said that up there?' I said.

'Well, 'tis true what he says, but you weren't to know.'

'Well, I know now. Can I say to you that I would like there to be a 32-county Ireland with equality for Catholics and Protestants all over. There's lots of people in Ireland and England who think the same, but bombs in pubs and shooting policemen make it impossible for the rest of us to support the cause.'

Donal exploded. He whipped round to face me and his words ring in my head to this very day. He snarled in that Northern Irish accent so effective in anger. 'Who wants your fucking help anyhow? If you'd a' been born in the Bogside like I was, you wouldn't mind shooting a few o' the bastards! You could be sitting at home in the evening, the front door crashes in and the 'B' Specials are into the house. They're trashing the place. They say they are looking for arms but they are just trashing you because they can.'

His trauma was fresh in his mind.

'Whoa! Whoa! Donal,' I said, holding up both hands. 'I'm sorry – I knew nothing about what you've had to bear. I know now. I'm sorry for your troubles.'

He relaxed, we said 'Cheerio' and he walked on to Killorglin.

Donal and I became friends. We took the occasional walk up the lanes towards the Reeks. He loved to be out in the countryside and he knew the names of flowers and birds. We passed the time of day if we met in town and that, I saw, was not what many or any of the townspeople did. Some people crossed the street, I noticed, rather than walk past either of them. When Donal's children took their first Holy Communion, I photo'd them in their special white dresses and made prints for their parents to frame.

I added that eye-witness account to what I'd seen on BBC newsreels in the 1950s, the Orangemen marching through Catholic streets in their dark suits, bowler hats, orange pinafores and rolled umbrellas, while their huge drum thundered contempt. Even as a twelve-year-old I did not like what I saw.

Chapter Twenty-six
Finished!

Adrian had rebuilt and plastered the front garden wall, put up two cement gate posts he'd made, and fitted a new gate. Having done that he wrote in his diary for 19th April 1980, 'I could say the house is completely rebuilt and apart from making some new units and repainting the kitchen, the task we began in October 1975 is done.' Five years and seven months of laborious work, learning as we went along, fitting the work in alongside trying to be self-sufficient, writing books, earning cash to keep us afloat, travelling backwards and forwards to England and having a baby. Much of my mental and physical energy was now taken up with the ever-increasing demands of an energetic toddler. Ideals of self-sufficiency were being squeezed. But I wanted to grow as much for ourselves as I could and planted up the garden in the spring, often working well into the twilight after Rebecca had gone to bed in the evening.

Timmy asked me to help him cut turf on his own bog, as he needed a 'brincher', and in exchange I could take away enough turf for our own use. After we had both finished our day's work and had something to eat, I'd drive to Killorglin and collect him. I drove into the town on Confirmation Day at about six in the evening. In the market place were dozens of girls and boys aged around eleven in their best suits and dresses, now 'Soldiers of Christ' by virtue of the gentle slap on the cheek from the Bishop. The Confirmation ceremony was lengthy, tiring and boring for children, so there were tensions to release. With money in their pockets from parents and grandparents, the boys and girls were queuing to get into Mary McCarthy's shop or Champs, each coming out with a fistful of sweets.

Daylight was lasting longer as May moved closer to June, so we worked on the bog well into the twilight before packing it in. Small figures on the vastness of the bowl of the bogland. A thousand acres sunk deep within the silence of the encompassing mountains. Coming home from the bog that evening and turning into the Meanus road at the Bianconi Inn, I saw Bishop Kevin McNamara's red Fiat Mirafiori parked outside. I knew it was his because, where one normally saw a lounge jacket hanging on a coat hanger in the car, there was a gorgeous red damask chasuble, embroidered with gold thread. He was worn out at the end of the lengthy Confirmation service, with all that slapping, then saying Mass, and was in the Bianconi enjoying a pint or maybe something stronger. I thought it was a great human ending to a long day.

On the last evening, having cut enough turf, with the sun behind the Slieve Mish Mountains, we made for the car. Headlights on and the car bumped and trundled down the stony track to the main road. Turning right I'd driven a mile and a half towards Killorglin when the engine checked and stuttered and stopped. Out of petrol. We got out of the car and started walking. We had not gone far when welcome shadows appeared in front of us accompanied by the sound of a lorry coming up behind. We turned to face it and the lorry pulled up alongside. The driver was the young carver of gravestones from Killorglin with his wife, his brother and a child. He and Timmy knew each other so we climbed into the load-carrying part of the lorry and headed onwards for Killorglin. A mile and a half further on, the familiar sounds of a shortage of petrol! We freewheeled tight into the roadside verge and all got out onto the road. The five of us went on, mother carrying the child. We were quite happy. It was a chance for a conversation. We had walked a mile when we were passing a house just as the owner was getting into his car. Timmy went into the garden and we gathered round the car. Timmy asked the question.

'Yerra, o'course, get in,' says our man.

Timmy in the front and four more into the back seat of a Morris Minor!

Ten minutes later we were in the town. Jack O'Shea was knocked up. Old Castrol tins were filled with petrol and in Timmy's car we went back out along the road. The night was dark and cloudy but there was a gap in which shone a *sliver* of a crescent moon with four attendant stars placed all in a straight line from the crescent of the moon. We all agreed that it was a good reward for our troubles.

Adrian had rewritten the first volume of his railway memoir and was hugely chuffed when he phoned Murrays. Simon Young congratulated him and said they wanted to sign him up for the second volume and give him another advance. Simon said he enjoyed the dialogue and the way Adrian teased out the stories. There was some minor criticism, which meant that Adrian had to rewrite part of it yet again and concentrate on making more of 'mannerisms to characterise the people speaking'. He set to on the typewriter with renewed enthusiasm.

Adrian also needed to earn some money as apart from my little income which came from working one day a week in the Killorglin shop we had no cash to survive day to day. Henry offered him a few weeks renovation work on a small cottage he owned, and after that Adrian got a part-time job, working for a friend of Linda's. Tadhg was a lean, gaunt, wild-looking guy who always wore an IRA-style beret. He and Adrian would hold intense political conversations whenever they met, and maybe Tadhg was pleasantly surprised to find that an Englishman was sympathetic, up to a point, with his views. Tadhg and his father ran a small garden maintenance business in Killarney.

Adrian's job was to cut grass. He was supplied with a petrol-driven lawnmower, which he carted about in the back of our estate car, to various domestic gardens and holiday homes in and around the town. The pay was only £1.25 an hour, but it was cash in hand and we were glad to have it. The lawnmower spewed out fumes and Adrian's asthma got a great deal worse. He kept at it for a couple of months until one day he came home utterly exhausted and aching. He fell into bed. He later woke, drenched in sweat with a temperature, red eyes, a sore throat and a dry cough. He could hear the lawnmower hammering in his head. Enough was enough! I am quite amazed looking back that he kept at it for so long. Health and safety was not much of a consideration in those days.

Henry asked me to make some curtains for his cottage. The fabric was a light, woven material in vertical stripes of oranges, yellows and beige. I sewed them on my ancient Singer treadle sewing machine but the fabric was difficult to handle and I found it exhausting. One evening I sat up until well after midnight to finish them off as I wanted to give them to Henry when I went into work the next day. He paid me for the curtains and said that I could keep the remainder of the fabric. Lucky me – I don't think he realised how much was left over. Years later I was able to make myself a decent pair of curtains out of it.

Next day I went into Killarney to help Linda in her newly opened Salad Bar. Adrian went off to do some work of his own and Rebecca stayed with me. While I was stacking a shelf I suddenly had the most terrific pain – I nearly fainted. I was six months pregnant at that stage and it was as if the baby had somersaulted inside me, ripping something apart in the process. Linda couldn't take me home, as she was terribly busy – the place was going like a bomb. I couldn't get hold of Adrian. All I could do was go upstairs to the stock room and lie down – in considerable pain – on the wooden floor, trying to keep Rebecca amused until Adrian could rescue us several hours later. I went to see Dr Billy (Prendergast) that evening. My blood pressure was high, I had a urinary tract infection and a temperature. I had clearly overdone it.

We met several interesting people through Linda, not least Stan and Helen Moore. Stan had fitted out the Salad Bar with his excellent bespoke woodwork. They lived in a handsome, two-storey stone house in enviable remoteness in the Black Valley situated at the southern end of MacGillicuddy's Reeks. To get to it from Meanus one drove to Beaufort then south through the Gap of Dunloe, a single-track dirt road between the Reeks and the Purple Mountain. The scenery through the Gap is awesomely spectacular – the narrow road winds through jagged stony outcrops and rocky grey mountains towering up on either side, passing around five lakes interconnected by the River Loe, which tumbles through the gorge. Near the southern end the rough road rises so steeply that the view from the car is of the car's bonnet and the sky.

Our first drive through was very scary because we did not know if the road turned sharply right or left immediately after the summit. In fact, the road led straight on and dropped into the valley below and on to our friends' house.

Like us, Stan and Helen had come from England, seeking an alternative way of life in Kerry. Stan was a fine artist as well as a woodworker. I got on very well with Helen. It was good to share experiences of being mums and bringing up small children in rural Kerry. It was difficult to find like-minded friends who were also mothers in the local community or to arrange what would now be called 'play dates' for the children. Rebecca enjoyed playing with the boys. They were, as Adrian said, her 'sparring partners'. The sad news was that after seven years of life in the Black Valley, Stan and Helen were planning to return to England, but we enjoyed some good times together before they left.

On Sunday 29th June Adrian drove us all to the Macroom Mountain Dew Music Festival. This open-air rock festival was the first of its kind in Ireland. It had been started in 1976 by an enterprising group of local people who wanted to revive the town's flagging fortunes with something different: an outstanding musical event that would attract international as well as Irish visitors. The annual festival lasted for six years and starred world famous artists including Marianne Faithful and Rory Gallagher. It was a glorious sunny day, the best the summer had to offer so far, and we lazed about in a huge grassy field together with thousands of others, enjoying picnics and listening to The Chieftains in the sunshine. I cannot remember any other performers, but Van Morrison headlined in the evening. To my regret, we didn't stay to listen – I was exhausted and Rebecca had grown tired and fractious.

One afternoon when Susan and I were visiting Stan and Helen, Stan told us about the indomitable O'Sullivan sisters, Nora and Joan. He had found them when exploring in his early days in the valley. He did some repairs in their cottage and got to know them and to be trusted by them. They were born in the cottage and lived all their lives there, the last house west in the Black Valley. They were in their late seventies and late eighties but they still clung on to their farm and sold sheep and cattle.

Stan said, 'Apparently they own half of Carrauntoohil. I'll never forget the day when we were talking about the mountain and they asked me if I would like to buy it. They said, 'The days of traipsing up and down the mountain are gone, so why would we want it? Ah go on … you will … the price of a car…' Shall I take you to see them?'

So off we went along a rough track for about two and a half miles, rising across the face of the lower slopes of the Reeks with Carrauntoohil away in front to the right. The cottage had no garden, it just stood there, alone in the wilderness of the mountains, in sight of the summit of the pass, where the land then falls into the Ballaghbeama valley. There were some turf-cutting banks away from the cottage and cattle and sheep scattered around.

Stan knocked on the door. It was opened by an old lady who clearly knew Stan well. She invited us into the kitchen, the main room of two or three. Stan introduced us to Nora, who had brought us in. She was tall and slim to the point of gauntness, except that her face was smooth and young. It was the shock of seeing how swollen were all her knuckle and finger joints that gave away her age. Sitting at the plain deal table was her older sister, Joan, almost chair-bound. The room was of spartan simplicity. The antique poverty of the room was relieved by an electric light over the table and a small electric cooker – the electricity had reached the Black Valley only in 1977. Over the fireplace hung a framed picture of Jesus, showing his Sacred Heart, and on another wall was a framed print of Jesus holding a rosary. I had been brought up by oppressively religious Catholic parents and was familiar with Catholic iconography and statuary, but I had never seen Jesus portrayed with a rosary. Nora saw me looking at and said, 'Isn't that marvellous? Our Lord invented the rosary and there He is holding it.'

Nora and Joan were practical, common-sense people, in some respects quite in touch with the world, but their religion was the most common sense and practical thing they knew. What was most important to Nora was to attend Mass every Sunday in the ultra-modern church on 'The Fossa'. Every Sunday she walked two and a half miles from the cottage, come rain or shine, to where a friend was waiting to pick her up, drive through the gap and on to Fossa. Once a month the parish priest came out to the cottage to give Joan Holy Communion. I wanted to photograph the sisters but they wouldn't let me, although a friend of Stan's did eventually take their photographs.

I also wanted to photograph Eddie Moriarty. Friendly as he was in practical matters, I didn't like to ask and it would be an intrusion to point a camera at him without first asking his permission. His nephew, Brendan, was approachable, so I told him that I wanted a photo of Eddie and asked if he would ask Eddie on my behalf. Brendan agreed at once and clearly understood my careful approach.

About two weeks later I saw Eddie going past on a large, grey carthorse with a very unkempt mane hanging down its neck. Eddie was *whistling!* Anyhow, I got on with what I was doing and two minutes later he came back – still whistling. The reason for his exceptional behaviour burst upon me. I dashed into the house. 'Eddie wants his picture taken! Where's the Rollei?' Finding that and the exposure meter, I dashed out onto the road followed by Susan and Rebecca. Eddie was riding his sixteen-hand ploughing horse bareback, steered by a rope to the bit. He leaned right over sideways, no saddle to grip with his knees, and with his right arm swept Rebecca up onto the horse's withers, saying. 'I'll have the wee wain up here.'

And like that I took his photograph.

Early in September Paddy Ashe came to the cottage driving his CIÉ-issue blue Citroën with a gear lever that projected from the dashboard. He asked if I would like to do some bus driving on a temporary basis. The other Killorglin bus driver had reported sick. Would I take on his run until he came back to work? We needed the money so I agreed at once. The sick man kept his bus at his house –

which explained why I didn't know of his existence. Paddy and I went to the house and took the bus away. Paddy took me over the two routes of that bus, which I did not know. One went up into the narrow lanes of Glencar, the other went through Milltown to Castlemaine where it turned west and went out for some miles along the Dingle road. The Glencar run was great fun because the lanes were hardly wider than the bus and climbed high up to the Board of Works road along the lower slopes of the Reeks and down through Kilgobnet to Meanus Cross and so back into Killorglin.

There was a T-junction on that route where high hedges were scraping the bus as it approached the right turn. That was a *five-point* turn: forwards and backwards and forwards, scraping the hedge, heaving on the two-foot-wide steering wheel. On the Castlemaine run, the last set-down was some long way along the Dingle road. After that there was no room to turn for two miles. After crossing a little bridge, there was a rough gravel track joining the road ten feet above the river – just enough room to reverse the bus. Looking to the left-hand mirror as I swung the bus around backwards into the narrow gateway, watching the left-hand rear wheel curving round on such an angle that as I straightened up it would run along the brink of a horribly shaky looking gravely cliff edge, with a stream ten feet below.

One morning, driving into the station yard after the run, I was greeted by the man I was standing in for. He looked to be in good health so I asked him if he would be taking back his job. 'No, ye're welcome to it. I've me grocery store. I'm getting £65 a week on the sick and I'll stick to that as long as I can.'

I was very surprised and was just managing to stumble out 'Thanks' but he was turning away and walking out of the yard.

Chapter Twenty-seven
Born in the Poor House

I was listening to a drama on BBC Radio 4 one afternoon when my ears suddenly pricked up at the name of Constance. I remembered my father telling me about one of Ireland's famous heroines, Countess Constance Markievicz. She was born into the Protestant, aristocratic Gore-Booth family in 1868 and as a young woman married Count Markievicz, from whom she later got a divorce. Constance was courageous and determined. She eschewed her life of privilege, developed a strong social conscience and became a political activist. She took part in the Easter rebellion of 1916, fighting for Irish Independence against the British. Sixteen leaders of the Rebellion were executed, and although Constance was sentenced to death it was reduced to life imprisonment because of her sex. She was later freed under a general amnesty. Countess Markievicz was the first woman to be elected to the Houses of Parliament in 1918, but together with the other elected Sinn Fein MPs she refused to take her seat.

I thought Constance would be a fine and fitting name for a baby girl if we had one. I also liked the name Maeve, coincidentally the name of Constance Markievicz's only daughter. Adrian liked my suggestions and I don't think we considered any other names apart from Edmund if we had a boy.

I had decided that I should give birth in St Finbarr's Maternity Hospital, Cork. Looking back this seems a little crazy as Cork was a two-hour drive from home, but it was the only option. Tralee Hospital still didn't allow fathers to be present at the birth and home births were not really an option in Ireland at that time, even if I had the confidence to make that choice.

On 29th September I had a 'show', and knowing that we had such a long way to drive we decided to leave before contractions started, although I had been having false contractions – Braxton Hicks – for days. We left Rebecca in the capable and willing hands of Agnes. It felt such a wrench leaving my little girl behind, but she was excited to spend time with her beloved 'Aggie'. Nothing more had happened by the time we got to Cork, so we had a pleasant meal in a place called 'The Penny Farthing'. It was good to have some adult time together – goodness knows when that was likely to happen again!

I started contracting for real in the evening after walking the corridors of the hospital for what seemed miles, clinging on to Adrian's arm and willing myself to get started. Adrian went off at eleven o'clock to sleep in the car in the car park. He came back to the Delivery Room at two in the morning. And so my labour progressed slowly through the night. I had Adrian by my side and I was so much better prepared than before, but I did lose it eventually and asked for pethidine for pain relief, which my midwife had been pressing on me for some time. A big mistake. I felt woozy and lost control. Gas and air saw me through, just. I know I was in a state. I remember seeing Adrian, who had disappeared behind a camera at this stage, and feeling very cross with him. My feet were up in stirrups. Three assistants supported and encouraged me or administered gas and air, while my midwife was busy down below warning me not to push just yet. She stepped aside for the doctor to cut me and at last I could bear down! Finally, after what seemed an eternity of pushing, my lovely Constance was born. I don't think I even saw her before she was whipped away. I sank back onto my pillows with relief.

Adrian hugged me. We were overcome with emotion and exhaustion. One of the midwives handed Constance back to me wrapped in a pink blanket. She was a big, heavy baby. I heard someone say, 'She weighs 10lb 3oz.' Ouch – no wonder it was so hard to push her out! Her poor, purplish face was bruised and swollen, all squashed around the eyes. I put her immediately to the breast and she latched on straight away.

St Finbarr's Maternity Hospital was not far from 'The Penny Farthing' and Cork City centre. We drove to it as the sun was going down. It was a grim, fortress-like building with high walls made of the hard grey limestone blocks one sees used in old official buildings and railway stations. I was reminded at once of the 18th-century Royal Navy barracks and hospital in Devonport, with which I had had more than a passing acquaintance. The staff were as kind and welcoming as the building looked forbidding.

Bringing forth Constance was hard for Susan. She was surrounded by four expert women who did their experienced best for her, but to me the birth seemed so mechanical, so regulated. She was flat on her back with her legs up in those 'stirrups', which were suspended from chromium-plated bars. Then they called a doctor to cut her. I was close to fainting. She was strung up and helpless. It looked like a torture chamber. Susan was under instruction to 'push' for forty-five minutes – I timed it – before the baby's head emerged, and Constance was drawn out. It was 9.15 am on Tuesday 30th September.

When they'd taken the baby away for washing and weighing, Susan and I hugged and wept. Susan was completely exhausted and I felt totally at a loss for words to thank her enough for what she had gone through. So we were just there, worn out but of course she far more than me. After she had been sewn up and cleaned up, she and baby Constance were taken to the maternity ward. Susan drifted off to sleep and I slipped quietly away and went out to look around this formidable and huge old building; only a part of it was in use as the maternity hospital.

Wandering about, climbing high external staircases, I met the friendly caretaker and boiler attendant. He was pleased to find someone interested in the building and wanting to know more about it. The reason for its truly grim appearance was that it had been built in 1841 as a 'Poor House', or, as we say in England, a 'Workhouse'. He took me into one of the unused rooms. A wide and lengthy barrack room with a high ceiling; where ranks of beds could have been placed there were rectangular, single-bed-sized depressions in the wooden floor. My guide told me that they were the beds of the paupers. Each slot in the floor would have been filled with straw.

That night I slept in the car again. Next morning I was woken by a pair of nurses, one of whom was knocking on the window. They were very solicitous, asked how I was eating and how long I was going to sleep there. I said I would be going back to Killorglin that evening.

'Would you like some breakfast?' I was asked.

'I would so, it's very kind of you.'

'Wait there now and we'll see what we can do.'

The two young women were back in fifteen minutes with a cooked breakfast on a plate, covered by a dish. Their smiles were wonderful.

After eating I found where to take the plates, then went into Susan's ward and asked where I could find a shower. I was taken left and right turns along endless corridors wondering if I should ever find my way back. With breakfast inside me and a good wash on the outside, I went back to the ward. At lunchtime I went into Cork for some food and to buy Susan some flowers, and found a beautiful white cyclamen to give her.

I got back to the cottage at eight o'clock and went straight next door to collect Rebecca. Of course she was in bed and asleep. Agnes told me how well behaved she had been. 'She follows our prayers and says 'Amen' at the end of each one. She's had plenty to eat with ice cream after the main meal. She's been very good.'

I thanked Pat and Agnes and told them about the new baby, but I was tired, Rebecca was asleep, so I went home. Next day I had to drive the school bus, but got around the course briskly and was knocking on Agnes's door at nine-thirty. Agnes opened it and at once said, 'You're early about.'

It was half past nine and that wasn't early for either of us. 'I've come to collect Rebecca, Agnes,' I said.

'Oh, but I have to wash and dress her – we're getting ready for Mass,' and she walked out of the hallway leaving me standing there, feeling irritated and uneasy. I didn't really want Rebecca to go to Mass. But what could I say?

Pat came along and said cheerfully, 'Don't be standing there – come and sit down.'

I went and stood awkwardly in the room. Pat talked about how fine the day was, but I couldn't do the small talk. I felt he knew that I was unhappy about Agnes taking Rebecca to Mass. There was a changed atmosphere between two good friends and me. I excused myself with, 'I'll go away from you now Pat – I need to do things at home. I'll be round later to fetch Rebecca.'

Agnes came round to the cottage as soon as she got back from Mass. She brought a packet of stamps I had dropped, but no Rebecca! I thanked Agnes and, feeling rather agitated but trying to be polite. I said, 'I'll come back with you now Agnes and collect Rebecca.'

'Oh, why is that?' she asked in a puzzled voice.

Now I felt an alarm that overtook politeness. 'Why?' I said. 'Because I'm her Dad, Agnes, and I haven't seen her for days and I'd like to take her for a walk, have a talk, tell her about her new sister.'

Agnes didn't want to let go. 'But she's very happy with us and no trouble at all.'

I realised then that she didn't *want* to give her back, at least not at the moment. I spoke as calmly as inner panic would allow. 'Agnes you have been very kind and helpful over the last few days. I don't know what we would have done without you. But I need to see her now and I'll take her with me when I go to Cork to fetch Susan tomorrow.'

'Well, all right,' said Agnes in a quiet voice, 'but you must bring her round when she asks for Aggie's house.'

I didn't reply to that, and she turned and walked quickly away. I followed to fetch Rebecca. I did feel sorry for Agnes. She was a very loving person, she had no children of her own, and she had been very helpful to us ever since we'd come to Meanus. Maybe I was just tired but it seemed to me that she was indoctrinating Rebecca and she shouldn't be 'taking liberties', as Pat would say.

271

I hadn't reckoned on being unable to sit down after the birth. I expected discomfort, of course, but this was more. This was more than sore, it was excruciatingly painful, as though I had been sewn up with barbed wire. I mentioned the problem to the midwife who discharged me, but she didn't seem concerned. Apparently the stitches would dissolve away in due course. I couldn't put any pressure on my bottom and had to sit sideways on one buttock. I couldn't sit all the way home like that, so Adrian put down the back seats for me to lie along the length of the car. The baby stayed sound asleep in her Moses basket for the whole journey, and Rebecca and I snuggled down together under a blanket. An unthinkable thing to do now, but in those days it was not a legal requirement to wear seat belts while driving or for children to be strapped safely into their own car seats. We never considered the danger.

My mother came to stay after a couple of days and we put her up in the sitting room on an Army-surplus camp bed. Mum was a big help in looking after Rebecca and she stoically dealt with the interminable washing, including the nappies, which now went into the machine, washed at the highest temperature.

To begin with Constance slept most of the time in between demand feeding every couple of hours or so. One morning she was fast asleep and Rebecca had gone out for a walk with her grandmother so I decided to make a chicken pie for lunch. I boiled the fowl on the range, prepared the other ingredients, made the pastry and assembled the pie. I was still in my dressing gown and halfway through felt really weak and wobbly, but pushed through. What on earth did I think I was doing so soon after giving birth? A chicken pie from scratch? I don't think I've made one since.

I remember only one visit from a midwife after I arrived home from hospital, but I think she was then taken ill and I had no further post-natal support at home. After ten days of agony, still unable to sit down without feeling as though I was being pricked by several sharp needles, I went to see Dr Billy. He located a nasty knot with some treacherous loose ends in the stitch work that had not melted away and cut it free. The relief was enormous.

Rebecca was fascinated by her little sister. She was very gentle towards her and tried to share her raisins or toys or tricycle with her, but she couldn't understand that the baby was too small to play so we had to keep a careful eye on her. Constance quickly became very pretty and at two months she was a placid, smiling, gurgling baby. Rebecca started to vie for our attention. She liked to do things she knew would annoy us like hitting down hard on the keys of the typewriter. If she thought we hadn't noticed, she came to tell us what she was doing. Or she would roll on the floor and scream, so we'd pick her up and give her a cuddle. She wasn't really one for cuddles, though she would tolerate mine, but if Adrian cuddled her she would pull his beard hard and tell him to 'Go away, Daddy.'

In the evenings, when Rebecca was in bed, we sat in the sitting room and enjoyed a good fire with wood got from up the road. Adrian often sat at his desk, hammering away on the typewriter, while I fed the baby. She spent a long time at the breast, but I didn't mind – I loved this bit the best. The connection between us, the comfort and calm of our love.

In between breastfeeding I knitted garments for the children and eventually, when Constance was older, I worked out how to breast feed and knit at the same time. For me that was blissful too. One memorable evening Adrian and I made love in front of the sitting room fire; it was a snatched five minutes between the baby going to sleep and waking up again. That was the tricky reality of early parenthood.

In November I got a formal card from John Murray Publishers informing me that my brilliant editor Simon Young had left the company and one Duncan McAra would take over as editor for Simon's books. I was very upset. Simon was a brilliant editor and my very kind friend. He had worked with me on what was now *Signalman's Morning* ever since it was taken to Murray. I was worried as to whether the new editor could be as good as Simon. At Christmas I was very pleased to receive a handwritten letter from him, written as a friend. It was the last time I heard from him.

I was still driving the school bus and 'keeping the wolf from the door'. I liked driving the clumsy old bus with its heavy steering and 'crash' gearbox along difficult routes. I was not on the primary school runs but working with twelve-to-seventeen-year-old boys and girls on my old Cromane run. We got on very well together. There was a teenage girl known as Deep Purple. She was a fan of the heavy rock band of that name. I remembered them from the late 1960s for their very heavy rock music, with lots of screaming but some wonderful guitar riffs, and was surprised she was 'mad' on them in 1980. She came onboard each day from a little cottage in a narrow lane. She always looked abstracted, didn't come up the steps with a smile and a 'Hi' as the others did. From September to the last school day of the year she came on board wearing a purple overcoat.

On Monday 8th December I set off for Dooks and Cromane. I arrived back in the station yard without finding a single child waiting for me. I went across to Tom Melia's supermarket and asked why there were no children for school. The lady at the cash desk smiled and gave a little laugh.

'Ah, 'tis the Feast of the Immaculate Conception. It's a Holy Day of Obligation – there's no school because everyone must attend Mass today. We heard you going off at breakfast time and realised you wouldn't know that.'

The next day 'Deep Purple' was in tears as she walked towards the bus from her garden gate. I was alarmed and asked her what was wrong. She looked at me for the first time, the very essence of misery, eyes red, tears streaming, and whimpered, 'John Lennon's been murdered!'

He had been killed the day before, the news only now filtering through because of the time difference between continents.

The last day of the school term was on Friday the 19th. I was on the Cromane run, and after I'd completed the morning round-up and delivery the bus went into the station yard and I went across to Melia's supermarket to buy Christmas decorations for the bus. I bought yards of tinsel, silvery and coloured. I bought balloons and a roll of four-inch-wide coloured paper, like a loo roll but proper paper, then cycled home with it.

At home I cut off a twelve-foot strip of the roll and wrote in coloured crayons in very bold fat letters 'HAPPY CHRISTMAS TO THE CROMANE BUS CREW'. I left home early for the afternoon run so as to use up all the tinsel on the chromium vertical pole at each seat, tie the balloons on everything and Sellotape the banner to the wall of the bus above the windows. By then it was time for the boys and girls to start appearing into the yard. I had the door open but they gathered outside and called me to come out. I went down and with much cheering and laughter they presented a very surprised bus driver with a large box of chocolates and a bottle of whiskey. So thank goodness I had suitably decorated their bus. I stood aside feeling very emotional, proud and happy as they filed aboard and the whoops and shrieks started as they saw what I'd done for them. We had a great ride home, a bus full of excited, happy people. I put my foot to the floor once we'd left the Caherciveen road and were on the long straight heading for Cromane. We hit the little humpy bridge a mile down the road. Up went the back of the bus and those on the back seat bounced up to head-butt the roof. I often wonder, forty years on, if any of those bright young people remember me and the Cromane bus.

Susan and I met Richard McGillicuddy (pronounced 'Mac-le-cuddy') through Henry. Earlier in the spring I had asked his permission to photograph the grand avenue of trees, lined with hundreds of daffodils, leading to his grand house called 'The Reeks'. He was pleased I'd asked and gave his permission. That Christmas I printed a postcard of the view and Susan used it to make a Christmas card for Henry. Henry put it on his mantlepiece with all the others. During the Christmas season he had a party for the local aristocracy, which included Richard McGillicuddy. Richard saw the card picturing his house and instantly became angry. How I know that is because the next day he actually knocked on our door. We cheerfully invited him in and were then given a serious dressing down because, he said, we had infringed his privacy. We were astonished, of course, but I recovered after some seconds and was saying, 'But you gave me permission…,' but he was already striding out of the cottage.

I came across Tom O'Sullivan a few days later. Tom worked on McGillicuddy's estate. He looked grim and shrugged. 'I'd expect nothing else from him. That's how the man is and always has been,' he said. 'Ye wouldn't be knowing it, but when we have to address him, or if ye're answering a question from him, it has to be, 'Yes, or No, The McGillicuddy'.'

Having supper with Pat and Agnes one evening, I told them the tale. Agnes said, 'Poor Richard, it's his mother's doing. When he was a growing child she found him playing with the children of the family at the lodge house at the gates of the drive. She forbade him to talk to them or anyone beneath his station in life.'

Chapter Twenty-eight
Hunger strike

Over the winter we gradually adjusted to our new family routine. Life was very different with two children, and it was hard to juggle the demands of a new baby with those of an energetic toddler. Constance went from being a placid baby to a very bonny one. She laughed delightedly at Rebecca's antics, waving her little arms and legs up and down in excitement every time her sister did something silly or funny or annoying. But a problem was developing. Her bottom had been very sore since Christmas – maybe it was the nappies, dried stiff out of the washing machine and not boiled to kill off the germs, or maybe it was an early indication of allergy, because the soreness appeared in other places too, like an eczema. I tried letting her lie without a nappy and applied cod liver oil ointment, which helped.

By the middle of January Constance was miserable. I felt very distressed that she was so poorly and unhappy. Dr Billy prescribed a hydrocortisone cream but I was reluctant to use it. Kathleen suggested I cut triggers from my diet such as dairy foods. I took a Vitamin E supplement to help with healing and in the end, split open the capsules, spreading the oil directly onto her sore skin. Gradually the inflammations cleared, but Constance didn't return to her former jolly self. She wanted to be held nearly all the time and grizzled whenever I put her down. Something was going on that we didn't understand. Maybe she was in pain.

Rebecca, in trying to keep my attention focused on herself, developed a good line in climbing up me if I was sitting down, draping herself around my shoulders from where she would climb onto my head and cover my face. This always seemed to happen when we had visitors, especially when Agnes called by or when I was feeding the baby. The best way to get a few minutes peace was to give Rebecca something

277

mechanical to do, like screwing screws into holes with a screwdriver or fitting spanners into nuts on the bicycle. She loved mechanical things.

She also loved poetry and was very fond of reciting poems especially when Aggie came round because Aggie was impressed, then invariably would want to whisk Rebecca away to Mass, which meant sweeties afterwards. It annoyed Adrian when Agnes took her to Mass, but I didn't think it could do too much harm, so she went. Once, after she came back, we asked what she had been doing in church, and she said, 'I bin to Holy God.'

Adrian took Rebecca outside one evening and recited the first couple of verses of 'The Highwayman' by Alfred Noyes, to her as they watched the clouds scuttle across the face of the moon. She was excited by the language and the rhythm, so 'The Highwayman' became part of her repertoire. She was in the bank one day with Adrian. There were a lot of people waiting to be served, so Rebecca decided to entertain them and, spreading her arms wide, recited the first verse. There were delighted smiles all round. When they left the bank Rebecca saw an old Kerry farmer go trudging past dressed all in raggedy black. 'Look!' she said excitedly, 'a highwayman!'

Rebecca was a double handful, bursting with life and calculated mischief to enliven her day and give herself a great laugh. If we had to go on errands further afield, Killarney or Castlemaine, Agnes often looked after her. Agnes had trained her to use the 'holy water' dip just inside the front door. Rebecca would be blessing herself with the water as she came out through the door. Sometimes she'd get more on her fingers than necessary and would flick it onto the window of the room where Pat was sitting, to bless him too. Maybe she thought he needed it. Agnes said she was worried about Pat as he kept having bad pains and wouldn't rest but went off to hide down the field so she wouldn't see them happening.

I found being a father a totally alien experience. I wasn't prepared for it at all. For me, growing up at home in Reading was oppressive and often harsh. I discovered at the age of six or seven the steam railway. I could spend all day with kindly engine drivers and signalmen. And my father could get on with his home-based work in peace. I realised one day that I was as intolerant of a bright little child as my father had been of me, especially at mealtimes. A lady who lived along the road a little way and had spent her working life helping children with learning disabilities, said to us: 'Rebecca is exceptionally bright so you'll just have to give her a free rein and put up with her humour as best you can.' So I loosened up, saw the joke and laughed with Rebecca.

Susan called me indoors one morning. 'Come and see what Rebecca is doing!'

I hurried in and there was Rebecca, sitting in the water-filled sink with her doll and that morning's breakfast crocks. 'I'm doin' the washing up,' she said with a big cheeky grin.

The day before my fortieth birthday Christy O'Riordan delivered a large, square parcel very neatly wrapped in Christmassy paper. It had been sent from Germany and we knew no one in Germany. It was a mystery and slightly worrying. I opened it in the garden. The contents were German sweets, and they are the most extravagant in the world. There were 'cigars' of dark chocolate filled with marzipan, whole blocks of marzipan looking like Semtex, chocolates that were obviously filled with a liqueur, and a pirate's treasure of 'gold' discs looking like Spanish doubloons, but under the wrapping was chocolate. There was no covering letter. We were thoroughly mystified. Rebecca unwrapped one of the 'coins'. She didn't have many sweets, but knew what these were even so.

Then I remembered the German tourists who were long-distance walkers. On a scorching August day in the previous year I had been working in the garden, and some walkers were about to pass when they saw the tap I'd attached to the gate post and stopped to ask for some water. I fetched cups, and they sat on the wall to drink and rest. They were Germans and a pleasant craic ensued before they went on towards Killorglin. Ever since I was aged in single figures I would like to talk to anyone I met, particularly strangers. I would 'bend their ears', and after they'd managed to escape I would be embarrassed by my talk. In Ireland, though, casual chatter with a passing stranger was not embarrassing because Irish people enjoy talking.

That evening a mother and son from Bristol, newly arrived for permanent residence in Kerry, came to dinner. The German sweets had come at just the right time. I had made their acquaintance in my usual manner. She was cycling into Killorglin when I was sawing firewood in the garden. I told her to call in 'for a cuppa' on her way home. She came back with her bike handlebars laden with four plastic bags of groceries, and the bouncing they were getting threatened disaster for the food. Indoors, over tea and Susan's soda bread, she was free with her biography.

Her name was Pauline, her son was Peter. She was 57 and had been married twice. Her first husband was an RAF fighter pilot who had been shot down during the Korean War. Her second husband was a radio repair man, and he'd died. After the disruption of the second half of the 1970s in England, she'd had enough so she had bought 20 acres at Coolcumisk. She said they were then living in a corrugated-iron shed while her son built their permanent cottage. They intended to grow food, keep chickens, be self-sufficient and live in peace.

Pauline invited us to come to see their place sometime. Completely intrigued, I jumped at the invitation and said, 'We'll take you back there now, bike and groceries an' all.'

The last of the road was a steep and stony track. 'Here we are,' she said, quite happily, as we rounded a bend.

The corrugated-iron shed was fifty yards ahead. I was thinking, naturally enough, of a sturdy little building with maybe a pitched roof and a front door. What they had was something with a flat roof swathed in heavy white polythene that lay in heaps and was held down by eighteen-inch cement blocks and tied all around the top of the walls with yards of rope. It wasn't a corrugated-iron shed – it was an amalgamation of bits of different iron sheds.

Up the slope further, and to one side, on a levelled piece of gravelly ground, there was some building going on. Peter was up there laying concrete blocks on a cement base. I looked for signs of foundations having been set in. There was nothing to suggest that Peter had dug a foundation trench – no spoil that would have been produced from digging a trench. A double wall of concrete blocks was being laid on a rectangular cement base, and there were no wall ties between the inner and outer blocks and no damp-proofing membrane. The cement platform seemed very small for the base of a cottage, never mind a house. The whole thing looked very dodgy to me. I asked Peter if this was all the cottage was going to be. 'Oh no, I'm just building the first room here – there'll be more later on.'

'Oh,' said I, for once at a loss for words.

Signalman's Morning was scheduled to be published in June 1981. We made plans to be in England for the publication and to carry out the publicity that John Murray would arrange. I received an outstanding royalty payment of £638 from OPC, which was immediately sent back to our English bank account to help finance our trip. We hoped to stay in Tudor Cottage as before and rent out the Meanus cottage for holiday lets, which would also give us an income while we were away. We spread the word among friends and family and advertised in a couple of English publications. Kathleen agreed to manage the lets as a caretaker for a modest fee. Drawing on her experience of managing the lettings in Bath, Susan drew up a list of useful information for holidaying tenants. She also drew up a list of all the little jobs that I would need to do to make the place more attractive and comfortable for people on holiday who would not be used to the more basic conditions of living in the Meanus cottage.

With the prospect of letting out the cottage, we realised that the sleeping loft over the range end of the kitchen was dangerous; there was nothing to stop a body falling from the outer end. The open end would have to be secured with wooden railings and a central gate. I thought the upper space would then be quite a traditional 'feature'. I went to Chub's yard and bought some lengths of three-quarter-inch beech dowelling, a three-quarter-inch drill and a length of two-inch-square wood for the frame of the gate. I took the greatest care to make the frame precisely rectangular while using

281

mortice and tenon joints. The top and bottom bars were drilled to take three-quarter-inch dowel. With a short, stiff saw, a chisel as wide as the hole to be cut, everything plumb and true, and with some light taps with the hammer, the tenon went firmly dead straight into its mortice. That was satisfaction. When it was finished Rebecca moved out of her cot and up into the sleeping loft to sleep with the gate secured. We kept a night light on, she had a potty up there and was quite snug and cosy.

It was Confirmation Day in Killorglin on the last day of April and I had been asked by a couple of families to take some photographs of their children. The day would be commemorated with coloured prints of scrubbed, pressed and bored boys and girls. It was a Thursday, trying to rain but never quite managing it. The first to arrive at the church were the photographers, one with a wife and daughter to supply sandwiches and secretarial services, each with a 35mm Nikon and a flashgun. The professionals arranged themselves across the paving outside the church like a line of trawlers waiting for a shoal of fish. One man had a chair and a table of frilly ironwork, the latter surmounted by a bowl of plastic flowers. Children could rest one hand on the table, or an elbow, depending on their height. That constituted his open-air studio. He had a portfolio of mounts. The prints inside showed almost identical boys in suits and girls in dresses, their pink faces staring out as plastic as the plastic flowers on the table. Only the shape of the frame or the mount varied – oval or rectangular.

I had come to the church with my Rolleiflex and Weston Master meter. 'No one doing black and white?' I asked.

'Yerra no-ah. The people went off that years ago.'

One of the professionals, seeing my camera, asked if I had colour film. I told him, no, just FP4. He was amazed but nostalgic. 'I didn't think I'd ever see a man using a Rollei *and* black 'n' white film. They are nice cameras.'

A strange crying sound filtered through our conversation. I walked out to the pavement. There were some families with their children standing around talking. The awful sounds were registering and families in their best clothes turned to the direction the sounds were coming from. Trotting desperately up the slope of the road was a young lad, maybe fourteen or fifteen years old. From a distance he seemed to have raspberry jam all around his mouth, which was open, giving out a whimpering sobbing and sometimes a howl. He drew closer and I saw his mouth was a mass of blood. He drew near. Quite terrified, like a hunted animal, looking ahead only, crying out past the stiffly dressed confirmation-ees. There was a line of cars to my right, the boy swerved across to them and, as if he was entering water, he just dived under the one nearest. Everyone there realised he was hunted. We all looked left and saw his hunter.

He was about forty-five years old of average height and stocky. Nothing else seemed 'average'. He was naked from the waist up. His massive torso hairless, broad shoulders, massive biceps and forearms, his head shaved and shiny on a thick neck. He was menace personified. He came on at a loping trot, his arms at his side, large fists clenched. I stepped into the road to photograph this Yul Brynner-type person, saw the murder in his eyes and stepped back onto the pavement. But blood from his nose was down to his chin. Had the young lad done that? Then there was a high-pitched wailing and round the bend at the bottom of the slope came a woman.

She was middle-aged with her hair drawn up in ropes over her head. Her face was brown and weather-beaten, and probably beaten in other ways too. Her body was baggy from child bearing, wide, squat hips spreading a ragged tartan skirt. I thought she was barefoot but she came closer and I saw she had leather soles strapped to her brown feet. She was trying to run but holding her left hip as if it was painful while holding her right arm out in front of her, as she called out to the back of the brute disappearing away from her, 'Ah, I swear to God I nivver thought I'd see the day, runnin' through them at the church on their Confirmation. Come back! Come back!'

A clergyman of some rank, identified by the red piping on his black clothes and a cheerful red bobble on his biretta, crossed the road in front of the distraught woman with never a glance. His two curates followed. The car carrying the Bishop of Kerry came out of the presbytery across the road from the church and Bishop Kevin McNamara got out and went inside. The importuning jarvey photographers drove in among the crowd, flashing coloured cards. 'Do ye want a photograph?'

'No. Not till after,' was the usual reply.

I was still on the pavement and was startled by the half-naked giant rising up off the road close by. He had been looking underneath the line of parked cars but the lad had slipped away after he'd gone by. I wondered if the boy could ever go back to his caravan with that brute waiting for him. It never occurred to me to call the Gardaí and no local person would bother them with 'Traveller' troubles.

The Gardaí in Killorglin town ruled with a light touch, a relaxed and helpful crew – although there was that strange incident we had in 1979 on the road going up to Mealis. In summer, tourist mega-coaches and articulated lorries were sometimes gridlocked in the town. The main road from Tralee and from the opposite direction, Killarney, met head-on to turn onto the long, narrow bridge over the Laune. Over the bridge, across the crossroads and up the hill into and through the tiny triangular market place and into Upper Bridge Street, a narrow throat of a street past the Garda station out to the Caherciveen road. Traffic coming from Caherciveen, finding that narrow passage blocked, could continue straight on past the church, then turn right down to the crossroads where traffic off the bridge was standing because the market place was blocked.

I was in the town one morning and saw a Garda car slipping away along Langford Street. I walked down to the bottom crossroads. A huge lorry was blocking the crossing. The driver was sitting in his cab having an early lunch. He saw me with my camera and suggested I climb onto the roof of his cab and photo the happy scene across the bridge.

The Gardaí could be kind, helpful and sympathetic. I was outside Henry Dodd's antique shop with a Garda a couple of yards uphill of me. It was around midday. On the other side of the market place a line of cars were parked facing downhill. In the middle, right outside the door of a bar, was a black Morris Minor. The street door of that bar opened and a very drunk man staggered out. He managed to cross the pavement and fell against the Morris. Supporting himself with outstretched arms against the bodywork, he made his way round to the driver's side door, opened it and fell in onto the seat. He started the engine and released the handbrake. The car rolled forward a few feet and came up against the car in front.

I looked to my left to see what the Garda would do about this. He heaved himself off the wall, strolled across and entered the bar. A minute later he came out with two strong men. I strolled across the road and leaned against the bar wall to watch. The two men went to the front of the car and the Garda went to the steering wheel; the men pushed the car backwards as the Garda steered the car out onto the road. 'Put your handbrake on, Michael,' says he.

The Garda turned the wheel for down the hill. 'Now start your engine. Can you find first gear, Michael? That's it, so. Now let the brake off and the clutch in and go away home like that.'

The car rolled off down the hill, in a remarkably straight line, retarded by bottom gear. The whole thing seemed well rehearsed.

On 1st March the name Bobby Sands came out on the RTÉ news. He was an IRA man in the Maze prison and he had started a hunger strike with the purpose of having his and the other IRA prisoners' 'political prisoner' status restored. Bobby was born into a Catholic family in 1953, on the Rathcoole estate, on the northern edge of North Belfast. In 1969 he began an apprenticeship as a coachbuilder. Protestant bigotry would not allow a Catholic to better himself and he was intimidated by his co-workers to such an extent that he had to leave. In 1970 the 60% Protestant element on the Rathcoole estate began to intimidate the 40% of Catholic residents. That intimidation developed into mob violence, and in 1972 Bobby's parents' house was invaded and trashed.

Bobby joined the IRA. In 1976 he took part in the bombing of a furniture company's showroom, was arrested in possession of four hand guns, and in 1977 he was sentenced to fourteen years in the Maze prison. At that time they had 'political prisoner' status; they did not wear prison clothes, they did not do prison work, they were allowed one visit a week, a letter and a parcel. When that status was removed they became criminal prisoners. Bobby went on hunger strike for the return of their original status. By May the 1st tension in Ireland was acute as it had been broadcast that Bobby Sands was near to death. There was a fear of reprisals from the IRA when he died. On the 5th Agnes came rushing round to us bearing the news of his death and telling us that she was afraid for our safety. 'The whole country is holding its breath.'

Every leading public figure, including trade union leaders, was calling for 'calm'. Susan and I were sorry for Bobby Sands and we didn't share Agnes's anxiety. I went into Killorglin to see what was happening. Chub Connor had told me that Killorglin people had been largely pro-Treaty in 1921, the only town in Kerry to be so. In the Civil War that followed the signing of the Anglo-Irish Treaty, the town was attacked for three days by anti-Treaty forces. I walked all around the town and saw only one person openly showing any symbol of mourning. Donal had a black ribbon with the Irish tricolour pinned to his jersey. I did not see a single black flag in the town. My impression was that the town was quiet. Perhaps someone had gone around the shops and pubs a day or two earlier and spread the word about the advisability of closing business until after the funeral.

Killorglin remained quiet – as far as I know – until the dance at the CYMS Hall on Saturday 16th May. An argument over the 'Castle' bar not closing on the 7th led to a fight that poured out onto the street, resembling a 'scene from the North' (of Ireland). It was such a near riot that Killorglin Gardaí had to call for reinforcements from Tralee. On that same night Judge Robson, a retired British judge, who lived in a house at Caragh Lake, was visited by a group of men carrying petrol. They broke in. He set his dog on them. The dog was shot. The judge and his wife went out of the back door and ran to a telephone while the men poured petrol in the hallway and set fire to it. Teddy (Chub) O'Connor was Chief of Killorglin fire brigade. He told me that while his team was dealing with the fire, a Garda murmured in his ear, 'You know this is an IRA fire, don't you?'

To which Teddy replied, 'Maybe. But it still has to be extinguished.'

Chapter Twenty-nine
Signalman's Morning

We planned to be in England for nearly four months and left on 22nd May 1981. We planted potatoes and shallots in the garden before we left and painted the cottage inside and out to leave it fresh for our summer visitors. We left Baby Cat behind to fend for herself as there wasn't enough room in the car with the children, the baby paraphernalia, the typewriter and the luggage needed for a long stay away. Agnes promised to give her some milk and we knew she would easily catch enough rabbits to feed herself. Kathleen wrote in the middle of June to tell us that Baby Cat had taken up semi-permanent residence with Agnes, but when she detected new arrivals at the cottage she would saunter round with her tail held high in the air to make herself known to them in her charming feline way. I hope they enjoyed her company.

We had found four sets of holidaying tenants, including my sister Bernie and her boyfriend. It was a pity we didn't have more bookings, but nevertheless £315 (minus expenses) was a respectable income from a few summer lets. Kathleen wrote that the bees had swarmed from the hives on the top garden, which frightened our first visitors and stopped them from picking the huge crop of strawberries growing up there. Kathleen was worried that the bees might sting someone, but luckily there were no further incidents and all the lets went without mishap. Which was just as well as it had never occurred to us to take out public liability insurance. The mindset was very different in those days, and more trusting.

It was three years since we had last stayed in Tudor Cottage and I hadn't appreciated then quite how old-fashioned the place was with its lack of hot running water to the bathroom, or a washing machine. Clearly I had moved on from the days when things like that didn't matter. As the mother of two young children, proper bathing and clothes-washing facilities assumed a much greater importance than before. Edith took charge of the nappies and washed them in her 'Baby Burco' electric wash boiler. Not much different from boiling nappies on top of the range in that one had to haul them out of the boiling water, rinse and wring them with reddened hands, before hanging them out to dry. For me boiling nappies was an exercise I didn't wish to repeat; for Adrian's mother it was a way of life and I was grateful to her for taking them on. I took the rest of our washing to the laundrette in Wantage.

Then I met Jean who offered me the use of her automatic washing machine. Jean and her then husband, Charlie, lived in Dog Lane, Childrey, with their three children. They were a Scottish couple who had moved south because of Charlie's work. I met them through the village playgroup that Rebecca attended. We fell in straight away and Rebecca palled up with Jean's youngest child Lyndsey. Taking the washing round was a great social occasion for me. We mothers drank coffee and chatted while the children played – or argued – and the washing got done. We also looked after each other's children. I had Lyndsey to give Jean a break and vice versa. The two girls were full of energy, noisy fun and cheeky retorts, not the easiest children to look after, and we joked that no other mothers would take them on.

I also enjoyed the friendship of the wider group of mums who took their children to playgroup. On sunny days after a session we often wandered round to the playing fields so the children could let off steam on the swings and slides while the mothers chatted, keeping half an eye on their boisterous offspring. Constance was super-mobile by then and a much happier baby. She had started crawling in April and by June was almost walking. One day, sitting chatting to a group of mothers, I suddenly realised that my nine-month-old had climbed the rungs of the ladder to the top of the slide. I leapt up to grab her just in time. Less chatting and more keeping an eye out for me in future!

This easy, supportive camaraderie between us young mums was something I lacked back home. Rebecca had been attending a playgroup run from a private house on the outskirts of Killorglin. Parents dropped off and picked up their children by car so there was little *opportunity for a friendly exchange, let alone making friends. I began to realise that life in Kerry was quite an isolating existence for a young mother with two small children. We received wonderful support from Pat and Agnes and Kathleen of course, but it wasn't enough to fill all my needs. I expressed how I felt to Adrian. We began to talk about the possibility of moving back to England. It wasn't the first time we had discussed it. There were many reasons for thinking about such a move, not least because the Meanus cottage was now too small for our family of four.*

The 17th-century Tudor Cottage was uncomfortable and gloomy and there wasn't enough room for me to work in peace away from the children. But Peter Gill, who lived opposite the cottage in a modern house built by himself to his own design, kindly gave me the key to his front door and the use of his dining room table to write on. Peter was hardly ever there – he went to work each day and went sailing at weekends. I was rewriting *Signalman's Twilight* for John Murray and articles for a very new magazine, *Steam World*, owned by David Wilcock.

Our shabby old Irish estate car, MZF, attracted suspicious observation in Wantage market place. A policewoman constable made several passes of the car with me and the children inside. She stared fixedly at us. It was obvious to her that I was clearly a *bearded man with wild hair* and the children were not mine but merely a poor disguise for an IRA man driving a car with Irish number plates. It was well known that the IRA were careless about subterfuge! But recently five soldiers had been killed by an IRA bomb in Northern Ireland, one of whom came from Abingdon, so feelings ran high at the sight of Irish plates. One afternoon I was writing in Peter Gill's house. The dining room had a vast glass window overlooking the lane. I saw a Panda car come *very* slowly past my parent's cottage. Heads craned to the left. It must have turned in the wide space of 'The Hatchet' pub and Les Noviss's garage and came slowly back. But nothing further ensued.

The day after the inspection by the Wantage police, a phone call summoned me to Murray's at 50 Albemarle Street to meet John Gammons, their publicity manager. *Signalman's Morning* would be published on 27th June and he was arranging a great deal of publicity for the book, starting with a book signing session on that day in Mr Miller's book shop in Mill Street, Wantage. I was duly astonished that so much fuss was being made of my book. I was quite unused to being taken seriously by energetic, well-educated people. I had my first 'publisher's lunch' in a Dover Street restaurant with John Gammons and Duncan McAra, my new editor. The talk was mostly of what Gammons was organising *for me*! Back at No 50 I asked John Murray if he would be interested in a railway book for children twelve to fifteen years old. 'I could use my knowledge of GWR history to make a story around some period.' Murray told me to speak to his children's books editor, Osyth Leeson. I went upstairs to her office. She liked the idea and asked for an outline of the story.

I left 50 Albemarle Street feeling wonderful. In December 1954 the headmaster at Springfield Road School in Wantage had told me, 'There's nothing more we can do for you, Vaughan. Don't come back after the Christmas holidays.' I was a month away from my fifteenth birthday. I had failed the '11-plus' exam; now I was a failure. To be taken seriously in the matter of writing books for a great publisher was an overwhelming, intellectual success.

I stayed overnight with my sister Frances. Next day, before I travelled home, I went to Sutton, in Surrey, to 'Lens of Sutton', owned by John Smith, the most famous commercial provider of railway photographs. He had travelled the entire country for decades, photographing every station. He had done a great service for the nation. Passers-by gave me directions and soon I was outside his humble shop in Westmead Road. The shop was not well lit, practical rather than pretty.

'Good morning,' said a stumpy little man naked to the waist except for the first string vest I had ever seen in use, shabby trousers and a very old cloth cap. This was John Smith. A legend in the railway world. I told him what I needed and he wrote down my order on a printed form. I asked him how he went about this lifetime work.

'I'd take my bike on a train to a starting point and then cycle. I cycled from Midford station to Bournemouth West and photo'd every station on the 'Somerset & Dorset'. I used a Zeiss 'Super Ikonta' with a 'Tessar' lens because the negative was a decent size and the three-by-two proportions fitted well onto a postcard print.'

I told him I used a 'Super Ikonta' too. He was delighted to meet someone who understood photography. We talked on and I left his shop with a job. He gave me a large wad of old postcards he'd bought and asked me to make copy negatives.

I threw myself into visiting railway friends, into the world of John Murray and publicity, with an energy that astonishes me utterly forty years on. The rusty but quite trusty Kerry car over a single weekend carried me from Childrey to Pontypridd, Cheltenham, Bath and Bristol in that order. On my way south from Cheltenham to Bath I saw a Morris Mini pulled onto the grass verge and a woman and small boy standing beside it looking lost. I pulled in just in front of the Mini and asked if I could help. She said the engine had 'gone sort of jumpy', she'd been scared and switched it off. I opened the bonnet. A sparking plug lead had come off a plug. I put it back on. She took a pound note from her purse and offered it to me. I said, 'Thanks, but you don't owe me anything.'

She had seen the state of the rusty hatchback door tied down with baler twine. 'Come on, take it, you look as if you could use it.'

So I did.

On the Friday before the launch of *Signalman's Morning* I drove to Swindon station, saw the Area Manager, Mr Brown, and asked if I could visit the 'Panel' signalling room because I was an ex-signalman and hoped to see some old friends. He kindly took me along. The building was ugly and the interior not well lit and grimly sterile. I was reminded why I had left railway employment. Two of the three men there, Ronnie Astridge and Derek Main, remembered me and were pleased to see me. The Panel control room had opened in 1968. Ronnie named five Panel men, names I knew, who had died of heart attacks before they retired. I told them about *Signalman's Morning* being published in Wantage the following day and the laughter began as stories of life in the mechanical signalling boxes were remembered.

Next day I did the book signing session at Miller's bookshop, then to Swindon for a prearranged signing session at Launchbury's bookshop. There were still thousands of ex-railwaymen and steam age railway enthusiasts who remembered the humanity of the steam-hauled railway and shared the way I felt about it. The book sold well at both shops and soon it was selling well all over the country.

Murray's publicity campaign took off on the following Tuesday. Peter Claydon invited me for interview for his BBC Radio 2 programme *Round Midnight*. Next day I was in Bristol for a TV interview to be followed by Southern TV. On Thursday I was interviewed on *Kaleidoscope* by the presenter, Paul Vaughan. At 50 Albemarle Street, John and Jock Murray, Duncan McAra and salesmen gathered to listen to the interview. On Friday I was in York being interviewed on late evening radio and was so tired that I heard myself using some barrack room words. But I didn't seem able to stop them coming out, here and there. It was only as John Gammons drove me away from the studio that the full horror of that episode dawned on me and I said so to him.

'Don't worry,' he said, 'they have a delay system so they can bleep out that sort of thing.'

Penelope Betjeman bought the book and took it to her husband, the then Poet Laureate, who was in hospital. She said he was very pleased with it. Charles Causely, the most wonderful poet of the 20th century, reviewed *Signalman's Morning* on 1st or 2nd July for a newspaper I did not record. He did not like the 'technicalities' of the railway I wrote about and criticised as 'two-dimensional characters' my descriptions of the railwaymen who were my schooldays friends and whose kindness caused me to want to work with them on the railway. I only knew them as railwaymen, there was nothing more I could write about them. However, Charles Causely also wrote that he 'liked my style of writing' and said it was the 'poetry of railways'. He picked out for compliment my mention of the coal merchant at Challow, Frank Shepherd, whose cheeks were 'as red as rear lamps'.

Over the years I occasionally received letters from readers telling me that *Signalman's Morning* had inspired them to join British Railways and become a signalman. The imperative to write about my time on the railway was the affection I had for the old hands who had welcomed me into their circle when I was a boy. 'Ordinary' people they were to the world and to themselves, but to me they were special. 'Ordinary' people often seemed to me to have lived extraordinary lives.

I came home from London one day in July and as I swung the car across the road to go up the steep slope at the side of the cottage I saw a shabbily dressed old man sitting on the lower part of the high bank on which the cottage stood. I parked, went back and sat beside him. I asked him if he needed any help. He said he was just taking a rest walking between agricultural jobs. He didn't look strong enough to walk, let alone work, so I asked him to come into the kitchen and have a cup of tea and a bite to eat. Sitting down with a plate of bread and cheese and a cup of tea, he revived somewhat and began to tell us about himself. After he left I wrote down what he'd told us.

'I was born in Coalpit Heath near Bristol before the war. I was eighteen when some Gypsies turned up and stayed around for a few days. I was attracted to them, they had a horse and caravan. They were nice people, Mum, Dad and some children. When they moved on they allowed me to join their family. They made clothes pegs, sharpened knives and garden tools. In the evenings we'd have a fire started with the shavings and chippings of wood from their clothes peg making. I slept under a sheet of canvas, supported by hoops of willow stuck in the ground. We worked on farms in Somerset and picked strawberries in Kent. We'd go from one farmer to the next, the farmer would tell us where he thought we'd get work. I went off on my own eventually. I always tried to find some shelter at night. I'd sleep in a church porch. If the church door was open I'd go in and curl up on the floor of the pulpit. Less draughty. Before the war there was plenty a strong man with a pram to hold his kit. I've seen men pushing a pram with a woman sitting on top of what they had. But today I don't have a pram. Just this pack. If I was pushing a pram now there'd be some young chaps as would tip it over. It's dangerous for the likes of me nowadays and there's too many cars on the road to have a pram. It's not as safe as it was.'

Finishing his story, he got up and thanked Susan for his food, heaved his pack onto thin shoulders and made for the front door. Susan offered him a good shirt. 'No thanks, Mrs. I've just been given one and there's no room in this for anything more.'

We saw him out onto the road and watched his little figure walking up the hill through the tunnel of trees.

One day while Adrian was away on his publicity tour, I went to fetch Rebecca from playgroup, leaving the radio switched on. Adrian was due to be interviewed on Radio London and host a phone-in about his book, and I didn't want to miss the programme. The radio was an old-fashioned wireless set, about two feet wide by eighteen inches high, the size of a small television set. It sat on a shelf by the hearth in the sitting room of Tudor Cottage. As we walked in through the back door, Adrian's voice drifted across towards us. Rebecca looked at me with complete astonishment.

'That's my Daddy,' she said and, not finding him in the sitting room, she rushed around to look for him at the back of the wireless. She was so excited, and wound Constance up too, both of them laughing and shouting and tearing about that I missed most of the programme.

It was exciting for us too that there was so much interest in Adrian's book. But with that 'up in the air' excitement came some down-to-earth discussions about where we were going to live in the future. It seemed increasingly obvious that Kerry was not the best place for us to live if Adrian was to become a serious writer of railway history. Constant trips to London would be required for research. We couldn't keep going backwards and forwards between the two countries with two little children in tow. We could only afford to be in England because of the generosity of Adrian's parents letting us stay in Tudor Cottage rent free. We were grateful to them, but living next door to Edith and Owen wasn't without its problems either.

One day Rebecca must have done something to annoy Owen and he followed her back into the kitchen of the cottage, doubtless to complain about what she had done. Rebecca whirled around on him and shouted, 'Get out of my house and go in your own!'

Owen was thunderstruck, and having no understanding of little children took this personally and was furious with her, accusing us of letting her 'get away with it'. Adrian was unhappily transported back to his own childhood, and the children naturally picked up on the ensuing tensions.

Constance was a strong, sturdy-looking child with big brown eyes and an amazing smile. She had been walking herself around the furniture for several weeks and on 12th July she stood up and took her first step unaided. By ten months of age she was walking completely independently. She was full of energy and happy but she was too distracted to feed much during the day. She made up for it by continually feeding through the night. As soon as I drifted off to sleep after feeding her she woke up crying, wanting to be fed again. Just cuddling and soothing her or letting her cry didn't help, and I was too tired to work out how I could change this dysfunctional pattern of night-time feeding that we had drifted into, and so it went on. At six o'clock one morning, after a sleepless night, I was so exhausted I broke down in tears.

Adrian got up, dressed both the children, gave them breakfast and spent a couple of hours walking them round and round the village and onto the playing field – Constance in her pushchair and Rebecca standing on the rail behind – something he repeated many times that summer to give me a couple of hours of uninterrupted sleep. That morning, in desperation I drove into Wantage to buy a feeding bottle and some formula from the chemist. I felt very bad about this and was concerned that I might be judged for 'resorting to the bottle' by

Kathleen and Le Leche League. Nonsense, of course, but sleep-deprived people don't think clearly. In any case I needn't have worried as Constance wasn't in the tiniest bit interested in a hard plastic bottle with its alien rubber teat. She wanted the warm, soft touch of her mother's breasts, and who could blame her?

Constance was growing apace and needed increased sustenance, but she wasn't interested in solid food. I tried tempting her with little spoonfuls of baby rice or puréed fruit, but after a tiny taste she would clamp her sweet little mouth firmly shut and screw up her face in a grimace of disgust. I think in retrospect that she would have benefitted from the modern practice of baby-led weaning where soft, manageable chunks of food like banana, cooked broccoli or carrot are left in range for baby to pick and choose. It makes sense that a baby who is used to breastfeeding on demand should also choose to eat the food she found tempting, by grabbing it herself, rather than be fed something strange on the end of a spoon.

We mulled over ideas for finding somewhere else to live, and at first thought we could find another tied cottage in England. We could let the Meanus cottage to holidaying tenants and use it ourselves for a holiday home. We answered an advertisement for caretaking a huge old house in a village nearby while the owners went abroad. We were invited for interview and went along with the children. It was a beautiful, rambling old place full of antique furniture and fine old bits and pieces, but I couldn't imagine living there with the children. The preciously antique environment would be far too constricting for a boisterous young family, and we didn't think we could afford the running costs of such a large place, even if it was rent free. But looking at the caretaking opportunity was an interesting exercise that made us realise that what we really needed to do was sell up in Ireland and buy somewhere of our own in England. It was a painful realisation to come to after all the years of hard work getting the Meanus cottage habitable. It seemed like disloyalty to up sticks and move back to England when Ireland had given us the opportunity to put our own roof over our heads unencumbered by a mortgage.

Shortly afterwards we had Sunday lunch with Adrian's friend Keith Montague from the Public Relations Department, Paddington, and his wife Ros. They gave us a slap-up feast and we enjoyed a rare afternoon of relaxation and talk while the children played and squabbled. Keith told us that he would be leaving his job at Paddington as he was in the process of buying a coach company in Norfolk and the family would be moving there by the end of the year. We told them that we were thinking of selling up in Ireland, but wondered if we could command enough money from the sale of the cottage to buy somewhere outright in England. I can't remember whether it was Keith or Ros who suggested that Norfolk was the place to go for cheap property with the added bonus of relatively close proximity to London.

Norfolk? There was something romantic-sounding about the name that resonated with me and I felt unaccountably attracted to this place I had never been to in my life. I knew nothing of Norfolk except to occasionally hear it talked about on the radio, and even then I had been moved by its mention. My feelings defied explanation, but Adrian was equally enthused with the idea of the place. From that day onwards our plan was clear: we would sell up and move to Norfolk!

Chapter Thirty
Up for sale

It was time to go home. By ten o'clock on Monday 6th October we were loading our stuff into MZF. Finally, Susan and the children squeezed into the back seat and, after handshakes and hopes for a safe journey from my mother and father, we set off. The time was 10.30 am. Pembroke Dock was 204 miles away and the good ship *Innisfallen* would leave for Cork at 10.00 pm. We had left much too soon for good sense but there was nothing more to do or say to keep us – we just wanted to feel we were on our way home. We rolled into Pembroke town at 4.30 pm in pouring rain and a strong wind. Now we had five hours before we could board the ferry, stuck in the car as darkness deepened, the wind rocking the car and the rain teeming.

The crossing was abominable. The *Innisfallen* struggled through mountainous seas. Heaving itself up a wave and falling off the top to hit the sea below with a thunderous shaking 'boom' – like hitting concrete. We were ten hours on the crossing, two and a half hours late into Cork. Constance had the best sleep of her life. Ten hours solid. We arrived at Meanus, worn out, at midday. The cottage was spotlessly clean and warm inside. Kathleen was waiting, the range was lit and a meal cooking. We sat down with her and ate her spaghetti bolognaise. Susan was exhausted from 280 miles of driving and the rough sea crossing. She thought she was becoming ill and decided to go to bed. Kathleen left. I cleared up and looked after the children. They'd slept well and felt fine.

Next day Susan was semi-delirious, in pain and close to fainting all the time. She had mastitis. She felt hot and cold at the same time, under the blankets with a hot water bottle. I went into Killorglin to ask Kathleen for some advice. She came back to the cottage and brought rosehip syrup, honey, some oranges and Disprin. She advised Susan to let the baby feed on the affected side at least every two hours and to gently massage the area of the mastitis. On Sunday Susan was feeling much better and in the afternoon her Mum and Dad and sisters turned up bearing gifts

Kathleen's intervention helped me to get better very quickly. Now we had to set our minds to making arrangements to see us through the winter and prepare ourselves financially for our move back to England. We both needed to find work. The cost of living was sky high in Ireland, a fact brought sharply home to us on our return as it seemed comparatively cheap in England. Money just melted away with an inflation rate of more than 20%. Food and petrol in particular were very costly.

Henry couldn't give me any work, the antique shops where closed for the winter, and indeed his business had suffered from a 'dearth of tourists' that year. But through Henry I eventually found two jobs. The first was working for 'The McGillicuddy' and his live-in girlfriend Virginia at The Reeks, cleaning and ironing for three hours a couple of mornings a week. They were kind employers and Virginia in particular was friendly and considerate. She was quick to praise my bath-cleaning skills and declared of the bath in Richard's bathroom that she was surprised to find it gleaming white; she thought it had been naturally scum-coloured!

At the end of November a French woman, Isabelle, who lived in The Dower House at The Reeks, called in to see us. She was looking for someone to care for her daughter Sarah for three hours every afternoon for £50 a month. Sarah and Rebecca knew each other through playgroup and as they seemed to get on I thought it would be a nice little job for me. I took it on condition that Isabelle would do the fetching and carrying as Adrian needed the car for any work he might pick up.

Isabelle and her husband were an odd, rather exotic-looking couple. She was in her late thirties, tall, dark and very chic. She was an artist who painted portraits of pets and children. He was an Egyptian journalist, probably in his mid-sixties, shorter than her with a modest

300

paunch and scruffy in an intellectual, abstracted way. They both smoked heavily. I looked after Sarah every weekday afternoon all through that winter and for a week in the spring while her parents went on a road trip to Donegal, prior to leaving Ireland for good. Sarah was a quiet child, who responded to almost anything we said with a shy nervous giggle. I don't think she understood much. English was not her first language. But she had a calming influence on my daughters, who were very bright and completely irrepressible and noisy!

The family were moving to Italy. When they left they asked me to clear and clean up The Dower House. They couldn't pay me but offered in exchange 85 bags of turf, some firewood and anything else left behind in the house. We went up there on the day they left to see what I had let myself in for. The place was filthy. I doubt if they had cleaned it in the year they had lived there. We found lots of food, meat, coffee, cigars, but no booze – they had drunk every lost drop. There were only empty bottles.

Among the beautiful clothes left behind were three fine coats, including a magnificent three-quarter length, double-breasted navy blue coat for Adrian, which he wore for years afterwards. Some OshKosh dungarees for the children and a beautiful cream blouse and a tweed skirt for me. I was particularly taken by a beige and brown soft woollen scarf. I scooped everything up and put it in the car, but when I got home the scarf was missing. The next time I went to The Dower House I looked for it in vain. Then, one day in Killorglin, I went into the antique shop and there sat Henry with the scarf neatly tied around his neck! I couldn't help smiling as I imagined him and 'The McGillicuddy' scrounging around in The Dower House looking for non-existent booze and having to make do with the remnants we had left behind.

1982 found Ireland close to insolvency. The national debt was seven billion Irish pounds (punts) and rising. The November 1981 election had produced only a stalemate government. The cost of living was rising fast, as was unemployment. VAT would soon be increased on top of rising prices. It felt like another reason to leave. We had done a good job in restoring the cottage and had learned a great deal. We would miss living in this wonderful place with its helpful, characterful community of friends, but it was time to move on. Friends in England sent us copies of *Exchange & Mart* and the *Eastern Daily Press* so we could research property prices and contact estate agents.

I asked the lovely young woman working in Chub Connor's office if she would be interested in buying the cottage. She was getting married and she knew how much I'd put into the renovation. Her eyes widened in astonishment at the suggestion. 'Why would we be wanting to live in an old place like that?'

So in February we placed the sale of the cottage in the hands of a German estate agent, Mrs Bachem, based in Killorglin, who had been recommended to us by Henry. She advertised in Europe. We thought we'd have a better chance selling to Europeans. Our price was 20,000 Irish pounds (punts).

Susan was working part-time and I was doing various odd jobs. What we earned barely got us through a week. Eggs were £1.30 a dozen, a grapefruit, if you could get one, cost 50p, and road tax for the car was £84 a year. We didn't pay it! I needed to up my game if we were going to pay off all our debts and earn enough to pay the costs of moving. I offered my photographic services locally. I had used a colour print film at Killorglin's pantomime and grossed around £100 from selling the prints. I did colour photography at Confirmation and First Holy Communion days, which brought in a lot of orders for prints. I also photographed the men at work inside John Scott's factory. I made ten ten-by-eight-inch prints, which he took to an exhibition in Dublin.

I also photographed the wedding of Pat, Kathleen's son, to Anne Marie, Christie O'Riordan's daughter. I knew young Pat a little; he was a very handsome young man, but until that day I'd not met Annie Marie. She was astonishingly beautiful. In the course of the festivities I learned that they would be emigrating to Colorado, USA, shortly after the wedding. I had no right to be shocked, but shocked I was. We were invited to the farewell in April and I brought my camera along. A super car was waiting for them. It was loaded with piles of wedding presents they were taking with them to their new home. I attempted to take some photos but it was impossible. This was an emigration, economically a very comfortable emigration but still equal to a funeral in grief. Anne Marie was crying, Christy and Pat were in a tight embrace, and Mrs O'Riordan had her face in her hands. Having experienced this modern emigration's grief, I understood properly why, in Ireland, the nostalgia is for people – not things.

On the other side of the world the Falklands War was about to take place. The Falkland Islands were and are a British possession in the South Atlantic, 300 miles east of the coast of Argentina. Argentina invaded them on 2nd April 1982. The Argentines had always claimed the islands. The Thatcher Government withdrew all British naval presence in the South Atlantic, presumably to save money. The last ship to be ordered out of the South Atlantic area was the British Antarctic Survey's HMS *Endurance*. It seemed to the fascist dictator Galtieri that Mrs Thatcher had gone away leaving the back door open. And so the 'burglar' saw his chance. The British 'Task Force' set out to reclaim the islands as soon as the Government could hire enough civilian ships to augment the few naval vessels available. On 27th April Rear Admiral Woodward, Commander of the Force, being interviewed on BBC, emphasised his soldiers' enthusiasm for the battle by saying that they were 'mainlining' – a reference normally associated with injecting heroin. I thought it strange.

Susan and I had been introduced to Donald Cameron at a party at Linda's. His mother, Mrs Cameron, was Chairwoman of the Falkland Islands administration in London. She invited us to dinner at her house in Beaufort. The conversation was, of course, mostly about the Argentine invasion. I asked her how it was that she was head of the Falkland Islands administration.

'I own a large part of the island – I inherited it from my husband. Before this invasion, Britain didn't care much about the Islands. I had a job to get funds for pencils from the Government.

303

Now Her Majesty's Government is spending millions to get the islands – and my land – back.'

The war created a tsunami of emotion in much of Britain. On 6th May the Conservative Party won hands down in the local elections.

Meanwhile in Killorglin, six Republicans, one of whom was my friend Donal, together with a guest from Derry, created a memorial to Bobby Sands on the first anniversary of his death. They nailed black flags to every pole in the Market Place and two posters – 'Mrs Thatcher wanted for Murder' and 'In Loving Memory of Bobby Sands. You can kill the revolutionary but you can't kill the Revolution.' Thousands of men and women in Derry and Belfast were to a greater or lesser extent traumatised by persecution because of their religion. It was that often violent repression that caused the 'Troubles' of Northern Ireland.

During April I had received a £550 royalty cheque from John Murray, which paid off our debt to the Allied Irish Bank and left some change. Shortly afterwards I posted off to Murray the first draft of my children's book about a railway navvy and his family, *The Tunnel and the Ring*, hoping for an advance. On 24th May I received a letter of rejection from Osyth Leeston. I was very disappointed.

All through the spring and summer I did various painting, renovating and gardening jobs for customers in Killorglin and at Caragh Lake. Mrs Leavis at Meanus Cross wanted her window frames renovated. I was very pleased that she was able to pay me £2.50 an hour when I had only asked her for £2! Her back garden was open to the view of the Reeks and the great mountain of Carrauntoohil. She would bring out tea and biscuits and we had some very pleasant talks. One story she told was from a time she lived in Crosshaven. I wrote it all down when I got home.

She said there was a very wealthy inhabitant who spent a lot of time in Hong Kong. His house was in a narrow street with houses opposite. One room in the house was fitted out as a 'strong room' but there were valuable things in other rooms too. One day two men stopped their car outside his house. A woman across the street noticed and watched from her bedroom window. The men entered the house empty-handed, and came out each carrying a large and very heavy suitcase. One man put his suitcase down to help the other man get his suitcase into the car. That man then drove the car away to turn, leaving his companion standing with his suitcase.

A few seconds later the car driver called his friend to help him – the car had got stuck while being turned. The man went away to help, leaving the suitcase behind. The watching woman seized this opportunity, dashed downstairs and captured the suitcase. She struggled with it across the road, hid it behind her front garden wall, then leaned over the wall to await events. The car came back. No suitcase. The men crossed the road to her. 'Did you see anyone passing the while?'

'No.'

'Not someone with a heavy suitcase?'

'Not at all.'

The men, considerably annoyed, drove off in a hurry. The woman took the car's number and phoned the Gardaí.

At the beginning of June a French couple came to view the cottage and went away hoping to raise the money to buy it. On 28th June our solicitor Michael Ahern wrote to say that the title deed to our cottage had been converted into absolute. We had the deeds after seven years of waiting! Michael Ahern had worked very hard on our behalf to get the title deeds. The reasons for the long delay were complicated and included a claim on the property by distant relatives of the vendor.

Mr Ahern said that we would need a wayleave for the septic tank from Eddie Moriarty, to put with our deeds, something that, of course, had not occurred to us. I arranged a date with Eddie and on the appointed day went in the car to collect him. I drove into the yard and found the house locked. Brendan's car was gone. I looked around a bit desperately and saw Eddie reclining on piles of straw, his back resting on a bale, reading *The Kerryman*. He had probably been there for some time because he had a bucketful of the papers

305

beside him. He now struggled slowly upright and brushed straw from his Mass-going clothes, as much as he could reach, anyhow. Tall, thin and bony he was, his craggy face furry with grey stubble. He had on a black jacket that had seen thousands of Masses and funerals pass, black trousers, worn thin and shiny, patched and stopping short at his ankles, ankle-length black boots and a very soft flat cap on his bumpy head.

Inside Michael Ahern's office Eddie agreed that he and I had a 'gentleman's agreement' about putting the septic tank on his land and said he would sign a paper to that effect. Michael already had a wayleave written out. He offered it to Eddie, asking him to read it before he signed. 'I don't want to read it,' said Eddie.

Ahern read it out to him. Part of it was that I had to pay Eddie for the grant of wayleave. Ahern suggested five pounds. Eddie said, 'I don't want any money. I have money enough. I don't need any more. I'll just sign it – so.'

On the way home Eddie told me that his father had told him that the road we were on was a 'Famine road'.

'Women were paid fourpence a day to carry the earth to make this embankment over this floodable ground by Annadale. The bridge we've just gone over and the one above, near my place, were both blown up during the 'Tan war'.'

Eddie had been a teenager during the War of Independence, then through the Civil War. I wish now, writing this, that I'd got closer to him over the years and got him to talk about what he and his father and grandfather had experienced. He truly was a very remarkable man.

With our home-made 'For Sale' sign outside the cottage, we celebrated Rebecca's fourth birthday with a party in the garden. Friends from Le Leche League brought their children. Pat and Agnes came too. A huge bowl of plump, red strawberries fresh from the garden formed the centrepiece on the table and Rebecca was the centre of attention. We gave her a school satchel for her birthday present and she spent the day with it strapped to her back. She was very excited at the thought of going to school. Pat played the accordion and we all danced in the sunshine, Rebecca with her satchel swinging out behind her. When I saw Agnes gently jigging Connie around the garden to the tune of 'Saddle the Pony', I felt a pang of regret that we might soon be leaving. We would miss our kindly neighbours and surely they would miss us too?

Constance, or Connie as we now called her, was growing up fast. She was a bright, chatty toddler, still breastfeeding although I was slowly weaning her. She was gradually taking to solid food and usually now waking only a couple of times a night. She would nurse for a short while, then go back to sleep, so my sleep improved too. By twenty-two months she was speaking short sentences and had a good understanding of language. I thought she was quite a wit even at that early age! I would say to her, half-jokingly, 'It's time you were weaned.' She would reply, quick as flash, 'I'm not weaned.'

Or we would tease her with, 'You're a silly billy,' and she would reply, 'I'm not a silly billy,' but if we said 'You're a nice girl,' her reply would be, 'Yes!' You couldn't trick her.

I've never been a businesslike person but gradually I came to realise how well I was doing with photographic work. I liked having the jobs for their interest! There were holiday homes being built out at Glenbeigh and Rossbeigh Strand, so one evening in July, leaving the children at home with Anne's girls babysitting, I drove out there with Susan hoping to get a commission. I didn't, but Susan and I gave ourselves a compensatory supper of cockle and mussel soup and some Jameson in The Towers Hotel, and afterwards watched as the sun set over Dingle Bay. At ten o'clock we were entering Killorglin and got stopped by the Gardaí. We weren't speeding but the Gardaí were not locals and they took a dislike to MZF, with which they were unfamiliar.

It was just as well they did examine the car. There was no obligatory annual inspection of a car in Ireland in those days and, together with being hard up and very busy, I had become used to the lack of a tax disc, the balding tyres, the lack of a horn, indicators, safety belts and handbrake that they discovered. A Garda said, 'Do ye have a driving licence and insurance?'

'Ah yes, I can help you there, Officer,' said I.

There was relief all round. 'Well here's your ticket to show them into the barracks within the next three weeks. On you go now – and get something done about that car!'

Next day I parked MZF just next to the Garda barracks and showed the portly Sergeant my ticket, licence and insurance certificate. The good man went pink and mumbled, 'Arra, I wouldn't be worrying about it,' and wrote in his ledger that I'd shown my papers were in order. I went outside into the sun with a light heart. That was anarchy at its best. But we'd soon be travelling to England so I set out to get the car into 'shipshape and Bristol fashion' condition.

We sold the cottage to a German couple, the French people having fallen through. We heard the church bell tolling the midday Angelus as we signed the contract in Michael Ahern's office on the Iveragh Road. The Germans were keen to live full-time at the cottage. I wondered about that as the only way of living they had ever known was an apartment in a block of flats in Berlin. However, they didn't want to move in until *Weinachtsfest*, which suited us and would give us time to buy somewhere in England. They agreed to our request to stay there until 15th December.

Susan had researched Norfolk house prices and it seemed that £20,000 would buy a nice place. We had optimistically been thinking along the lines of a ruined rectory. We were such simpletons. We did not know that, since March 1979, the Irish pound was no longer at par with the British pound. The Irish punt was then 'floating' independently on the money markets.

On 25th August we went to sign the Deed of Transfer of ownership at Ahern's. An assistant solicitor dealt with us. He asked us to sign the Deed, which would hand over the house to the new owners in return for IR£20,000.

'Where's the money?' I asked.

'Ah, 'twill be here in the morning.'

Our trust in Irish conveyancing had been eroded by all the problems we had in securing the deeds to the cottage. We didn't want to get into difficulties selling it and were reluctant to sign.

'We'll sign in the morning, then.'

'Ah, don't worry, it'll be here. Sign now.'

We went back next day, signed, and received a banker's draft less an amount of IR£395 for solicitors fees and IR£700 for estate agents fees. The estate agent charged us 3.5%, which seems an outrageous amount in retrospect. I went direct to the Allied Irish Bank and had the money paid in. It transpired that the sterling value was £15,250.

That was a bit of a shock and disappointment. We would need £250 for the expenses of going to Norfolk to look for a house so that would leave us with fifteen grand. Dreams of old rectories disappeared. Then the Irish Currency Control would not let us withdraw Sterling until a month before 15th December, the date by which we had to leave the cottage. Being now aware of 'exchange rates', I was very worried come then that the Irish punt might be worth even less against Sterling. Irish inflation and uncertainty was not slowing down. So I explained to Exchange Control that we would be leaving for house-hunting in England imminently and needed Sterling as a deposit on the chosen house. We were allowed to take out a Sterling draft of £4,000 to cover expenses and a deposit. We were told, 'When you've a house bought, send the Allied Irish its address and the address of the estate agent and we will immediately release the balance in Sterling.'

Chapter Thirty-one
The vision

One night, shortly before we were to leave for England, I dreamed of a water tower, brilliantly illuminated. There was a central, wide-diameter column rising to a huge cement drum holding the water. Within that were a series of narrow, square-paned windows. At the periphery of the drum were a ring of supporting columns. At the base of the central column there was a yellow front door, which was opening and shutting allowing happy, laughing people in and out. The vision was crisply clear and sharply focused. Then it was gone and when morning came I woke and immediately told Susan what I'd dreamed.

We left Meanus at 6.40 pm on 27th August to catch the night ferry to England. We planned to be away for about ten days and get back in time for my sister's wedding in the middle of September. We reckoned that with such a tight budget we could only afford a B&B perhaps once or twice; the rest of the time we would sleep in the back of the estate car.

We had with us about half a dozen sets of property particulars for houses for sale across Norfolk. I reflected on these as we drove along. We wanted somewhere rural, a cottage needing some restoration but habitable while the work went on. Ideally it would have three bedrooms and a large garden. My favourite was a beautiful, detached stone farmhouse, needing renovation and situated in West Norfolk. It was the house of my dreams, but now at £20,000 it was out of our price range. The least favourite was a three-bedroomed semi-detached cottage, old but with an ugly 1950s extension. It was in a North Norfolk village selling for £15,950. There were several cottages in the £13,000-£15,000 price range, all of them terraced, all quite small, some of them pretty

310

but not really what we wanted. The moment of truth was dawning. What on earth could we buy with our limited budget? Had we been carried away by ill-informed enthusiasm? I hoped that estate agents would have more properties to show us when we got to Norfolk.

After stopping overnight in Childrey, we headed east. We couldn't have chosen a destination further away from the West of Ireland! The journey was long and tedious, and it was difficult to keep the children entertained. They were fed up with travelling. Finally we reached the Barton Mills roundabout on the A11.

A huge green sign at the end of the dual carriageway indicated 'CROMER A1065, NORWICH A11'. I have often noticed that British road signs only carried such information as local people would understand. Never having been east of Piccadilly Circus in my life, I was lost for a panicky moment, then chose the A1065. Later I found out that 'Cromer' was actually the road for Brandon, Swaffham, Fakenham and Holt. Words have always interested me. Driving north in Suffolk and Norfolk I was struck by the sounds of the names of towns and villages. They sounded so different from what I was used to in the west. I thought sounds meant a different original language.

Five miles along the road we drove past the ultimate modernity: a vast American air base at Lakenheath. Skirting around that, along a road through flat, dried-up-looking heathland sometimes lined with wind-twisted pine trees, we came to Brandon on the border between Suffolk and Norfolk. There was a very nice signal box at the railway level crossing. We drove on northwards, a forest on either side, past the Hilborough 'Swan', the only habitation on the road for many miles. The road became winding and hilly through empty countryside until we got to a handsome town – Swaffham. Then out again into wide-open, lonely landscapes, past venerable Castle Acre village and its ruins away to the left, and the 'George & Dragon' pub to the right. In the sixteen miles to Fakenham we had passed by one village and through another. Susan and I were feeling worried. Where were the country cottages we so desired?

We arrived at the attractive market town of Fakenham and I called into the estate agents, Spalding & Co, on Oak Street to register our interest as potential buyers. It was slightly worrying to find they had no cottages in our price range on their books, apart from the property particulars we already had. I made an appointment to view a house in the village of Helhoughton, east of Fakenham, the next day. Wanting to explore the area we decided to start with the coast and drove to the harbour town of Wells-next-the-Sea. Here we parked up and perked up. Sitting on the harbour wall eating fish and chips was just the tonic we needed after our long journey. Wells-next-the-Sea was a charming little seaside town with fishing trawlers moored at the quayside and narrow streets lined with colourful shops and cottages. We drove from the quay down a long straight road to the car park by the lighthouse station and the beach. The children played for a while on the sands, which stretched out into the distance, interspersed by shallow lagoons and overlooked by an embankment of pine woods with a long row of multi-coloured beach huts at its feet, the likes of which I had never seen before. There was a slight breeze. The water in the lagoons rippled and sparkled in the sunshine. It was a delightful place to be and our spirits were much lifted.

North Norfolk was a revelation. We had come to the right place if only we could buy a house. We drove out of the town and turned left along the coast road. All the way along the road the sea and the marshes were glimpsed or in full view. That brought us to Stiffkey. The winding, narrow road and flinty cottages were astonishing to us wannabe blow-ins. Then came Morston of the yachts, Blakeney and its great windmill and huge mediaeval church on a rise, looking out over the North Sea, and Cley-next-the-Sea lined with handsome old houses backed up by a huge windmill. Susan and I were in a state of continuous 'Wow!' This was the place to be, or as near as we could get to it. We told each other that houses here were going to be beyond our budget.

Two miles further on we came to a widely scattered village called Salthouse. The road was at sea level. The village pub, the 'Dun Cow', was by the road at the start of one of the two narrow lanes about two hundred yards apart, rising gently to a low ridge. An ancient church was just a little way up the rise. Then we saw the roadside pond and the ducks. Just the thing for two tired and restless children in the back of the car. I pulled onto the grass verge and we all piled thankfully out. Even these ducks were amazing to us. Special Norfolk ducks – they were all wearing a kind of beret set at a rakish angle with a little 'bobble' on top. We four laughed, the children most of all.

Refreshed, we climbed into the car and continued eastward, sometimes at sea level, then up a short sharp rise to look across grassland to the sea. Past Kelling on tight bends then up a sharp rise round a sharp bend and down steeply, going slowly owing to the nature of the roads, into a village called Weybourne. On the right was a fine, late-Victorian pub/hotel, 'The Ship Inn'; ahead, the road took another insanely sharp bend past a lovely church attached to a ruin. A shop was in front of us on the left beside a narrow lane that obviously led towards the sea. It was around teatime. The children needed to eat, and we needed to find somewhere to park up for the night. I pulled in by the shop. Susan bought food and we drove down the narrow lane, with a stream flowing on one side along to the beach car park at the foot of a shingle bank that hid the beach.

The primus stove was fired up and Susan concocted an inventive meal. Afterwards, with Rebecca and Connie keen to look at the sea, we went up over the pebble bank, down steeply through the fascinating boats and rusty caterpillar-tracked tractors to the water's edge. The pebbles went for miles east and west backed by very low cliffs of sand eastwards. A wartime pill box sat askew in the pebbles to our right, the sandy cliff it had been built on having been washed away. I was in the lead, luckily, because the sea's edge advanced, just an ordinary ripple, and undermined where I was standing. The pebbles became like ball bearings and I went forwards and down, only a couple of feet, but it was a shock and I had only just scrambled backwards before the next ripple came in. We retreated.

The moon came up, full, over the eastern horizon, and we settled down in the car to sleep. Rebecca slept on two suitcases, suitably

313

padded and covered, across the front seats. With the back seats down, it was six feet to the hatchback door. Susan and I laid out in the back on foam mattresses with Connie between us. Stove and provisions were stacked outside. Under these conditions we all slept surprisingly well, but we were awake at six next morning.

The children managed their situation very well. We had some breakfast, wandered about, looked at the tractors, and eventually rearranged the car for driving, setting off in plenty of time to see the house in Helhoughton. At the T-junction with the main road I took the lane to the right, through Weybourne with its pebble-fronted cottages. After a couple of ninety-degree bends the road now led strongly uphill. We faced a high ridge, forested over the top half extending east to west for miles in each direction. What was all this about Norfolk being flat? The road would soon be rising at 1 in 4!

A mile uphill, a *railway station* came into sight. The forecourt gateway was open to welcome us. It was a handsome station, dated by a terracotta panel '1901'. The sound of hammering from a newly built brick barn close by showed it was not abandoned. Rather it was a 'work in progress', a preserved steam railway. How exciting! We certainly had to find a house somewhere around here.

The house at Helhoughton was a washout. It was single-storey, in a courtyard with little privacy and the garden was tiny. From there we drove through lovely farmland to Dersingham, passing the Queen's holiday home on the way. Our friends from Kerry, Anna – Agnes's niece – and Vincent lived in Dersingham. There we all had badly needed showers and were well fed, but we slept in the car that night. Next day we saw two terraced cottages in Dersingham; one was far too small and the other smelled strongly of damp. From there we went to a house at East Winch. That was a three-storey middle-of-terrace house at the end of a lengthy gravel track. Barking dogs greeted our arrival. It was red brick, tall and narrow with a long narrow garden. That was no good either. That night we slept in a wood nearby.

Next day we thought we would look for estate agents in Norwich. We got through Fakenham and onto the Norwich road.

There had been no conversation for miles. We were tired. After Guist the A1067 skirts Bintree. As we went up the rise past the village I recognised with a great shock: the water tower! I swerved into the side of the road and stopped the car.

Susan said, 'Whatever are you doing? What's the matter?'

I shouted, '*Look*!' and pointed at the waterworks tower. There it was exactly as I had dreamed it, even to the yellow front door. We sat there and stared. Susan recovered more quickly. She reached for the envelope of estate agents' particulars and pulled out the very last sheet.

'Look, what about this house? We've not liked the look of it but we ought to go and see it. Get the map out.'

The house was about six miles away from where we'd stopped. We drove back to Spalding's in Fakenham to get an appointment to view. The house was empty, so they gave us the key. We drove into the village of Barney. It was a semi-detached house, gable end on to the road. Nearest the road was an ugly 'Post-war reconstruction' extension to what was originally a very old cottage. The 1950s extension was joined to an old flint house. Both parts had ugly 'Crittall' windows.

There was a wooden garage plonked in the middle of the front garden and a row of home-made sheds, filled with the debris of years including some rodent skeletons and a rusty crankshaft from a car engine, up against the roadside wall. We unlocked the front door and went inside. I looked under the stairs, to look for damp at the base of the wall. There was none. I went upstairs and, using some furniture left behind in the carpetless rooms, I got into the loft. The rafters were sound. The capping tiles on the ridge of the roof were perfectly horizontal. I told Susan I liked what I saw. She liked it too. It was a strong, sound house that had been seriously neglected. The asking price was £15,950. We drove into Fakenham and offered £15,000 for the house. The offer was accepted, but afterwards I thought we could have got it for less. I learned later that it had been up for sale for two years. I still had not learned to *haggle*! I'd pledged, as I had done over Meanus, more or less every penny we had.

315

It was very exciting to find the house. The children thought so too, and rampaged around the rooms. They obviously felt at home. It was not exactly the place of our dreams but we thought it had potential. We could change the windows, put a little porch on the front and grow some ivy up the walls to disguise the ugly Fletton bricks of the extension. It was a good size too, about twice the size of the Meanus cottage, and it had three bedrooms. It was filthy, but apart from that, liveable-in straight away. We could renovate as we went along. The biggest downside was the small garden, but we thought we might find an allotment or some land to rent after we'd moved in. We liked the rural situation of the house, with its back to the village and overlooking fields. The setting couldn't be more different from the dramatic backdrop of the mountains at Meanus, but we liked the gently rolling countryside and the vast Norfolk skies. It seemed very prophetic that we had been stopped on our way to Norwich by the appearance of the water tower that Adrian had seen in his dream. It was only then that we had seriously considered looking at a house that we had initially rejected as too ugly, yet here we were buying it!

Back in Ireland, we had a few days turnaround before my sister's wedding in Limerick. Karen was getting married to a lovely African guy called Ben. He had come to Ireland from the former Biafra, in September 1970 nine months after the end of the brutal Nigerian/Biafran war. Karen and Ben had met in 1979 when Karen was bridesmaid at her friend Sinéad's wedding and Ben was the photographer.

Rebecca was to be a bridesmaid at Karen's wedding. I had made her outfit in the summer, a pretty dress in petrol blue taffeta, the pattern inspired by Princess Diana's wedding gown. For Connie I had sent away to 'Woman's Weekly' for a pretty kit dress in white, with a tiny printed flower pattern. The parcel was waiting with Agnes when we got home. I made up the dress. In England I had found a pair of nearly new, burgundy-coloured, T-bar shoes that fitted Connie perfectly. Trying them on with her newly made dress, she was ever so pleased and, as there was no one else around apart from me, she showed them to Baby

Cat. 'Look puzzy, dere mine,' sticking her foot out, but the cat, fearing a kick, scooted fast out of the room.

Karen and Ben got married in Our Lady of the Rosary Parish Church on the Ennis Road in Limerick. They made a very handsome couple. Karen looked gorgeous in a calf-length cream lace dress and a flower-bedecked cream straw hat, which suited her pretty face. The two bridesmaids, Rebecca and Siobhán, in their petrol blue dresses, provided a wonderful contrasting foil to the bride in her creamy lace.

The reception was held at Katy Daly's overlooking Lough Derg in Killaloe. The guests were an eclectic mix. There were the Irish uncles and aunts of course, my mother's relatives from England, and numerous Irish and African friends. The atmosphere felt very cosmopolitan. The meal was a sumptuous banquet, beautifully laid out with a fabulous decorated whole poached salmon centrepiece. It had been prepared by the head chef at Jury's Hotel, where my sister and father both worked at that time. It felt a million miles away from the Scotch eggs and vol au vents of my own wedding buffet. It was a truly special occasion, not least because it was the last extended family gathering before we left Ireland.

One evening shortly after the wedding, Adrian was doing the washing up and I was in the sleeping loft settling Rebecca down for the night when I was suddenly startled by a noise like the sound of meat splatting on a butchers block. I looked down from the loft – Connie was lying on the floor. We were suspended in the silence. Then she screamed. I leapt down in an instant, but Adrian had already picked her up. A fleeting thought passed through me – was that the right thing to do? We looked at each other with fear in our eyes. He handed her to me. My baby was barely conscious. My heart contracted, I almost passed out. We needed to get her to the doctor.

We dropped Rebecca off next door with a garbled explanation, and Adrian drove us into Killorglin. I was sitting in the back of the car with Connie in my lap. She was semi-conscious. I thought I needed to keep her awake and tried to feed her, but she wouldn't respond. Such terrible thoughts were going through my head. We had neglected to look after her properly, and she had followed me up the ladder without either of us realising. She had fallen possibly six feet onto the quarry tiles, hitting the left-hand side of her face flat square on the floor. I couldn't imagine her surviving the impact without brain damage. We knocked up Dr Billy and he immediately sent us to Tralee Hospital. It was a nightmare journey in the gathering gloom. Adrian and I spoke not a word, but the atmosphere was thick with our unspoken fears. The journey went on and on. My baby had fallen into a deep sleep. I was beside myself with worry.

In the hospital Connie was examined and X-rayed and we were told to wait in a reception area for the results. After an age of anxious waiting with Connie still sleeping on my lap, she suddenly stirred, woke and sat up. She gave me an enormous smile and, pointing to a full-sized statue of 'Our Lady' in a corner of the room, said, 'Look at the pretty lady.'

I was flooded with relief. Miraculously the X-ray showed no sign of skull damage. Happily there were no after effects at all, not even a bruise. Adrian had a pain on the left-hand side of his head right up until four o'clock the next day.

We spoke to Connie about what had happened and she said she would not go up the ladder again but, to be safe, we barricaded the bottom of it. Adrian and I both felt terribly guilty mixed with relief that somehow she had survived and appeared quite her normal self.

Rebecca started school. It would only be for a couple of months, mornings only, but she was keen to go. She was so proud of her new satchel and looked forward to going every morning. One day she came home and said, 'Mummy, aren't those pagans in England awful?'

We were horrified and tried to reassure her that people in England were not awful. She didn't know who had put this idea into her head. We presumed it was another child, but we had no way of knowing. We didn't discuss it with the school as we were about to leave, but it was an unsettling incident. A sad thing to happen so close to the end when almost our whole experience of living in Ireland had been without prejudice or fear. On the contrary, it had been full of welcome and warmth, kindness and good friendships.

The final few months at Meanus were busy with work and getting ready to move. I got the final chapter of *Signalman's Twilight* written and sent it to John Murray at the end of September. Also written and posted was another article for the magazine *Steam World*. In October I drove the school bus for a week, then went into Killarney to a job – found for me by Timmy the plasterer – working on a new pub in Killarney. I worked there for three weeks. I got jobs requiring simple carpentry and house painting. So all our debts were paid off. Royalties from my books went straight into our bank account in England. Zero pounds was transformed into £800 to start us off.

Thanks to Eugene, the very kind second-hand furniture dealer of 'The Castlemaine Emporium', the cost of moving furniture to Norfolk would be cheap at £400. He had moved Stan and Helen's possessions from the Black Valley, which is how we found out that he did removals to England.

We were booked to leave Ireland on Wednesday 8th December. Henry and Linda called in to say goodbye. Kathleen organised a farewell party for us at her house on the Iveragh Park estate. Pat and Agnes came, Anne and Timmy, some of Susan's friends from La Leche League, Kathleen's children and some of her wider family were there too. We had all grown into each other's lives and now leaving did feel a bit like emigration.

The Iveragh Park party broadcast our imminent departure. The following evening, about ten o'clock, I was having a bath and Susan was in the kitchen when there was a thunderous knocking on the front door. I leapt out of the water, grabbed a towel and shouted, 'I'll get that.'

Susan called back, 'No, it's OK, I'm going.'

I got into the kitchen as Susan came in through the inner stable-door with Donal close behind her! He was a bit drunk and very agitated. 'I hear ye're leavin',' he said loudly. 'Who's been intimidating youse? Just tell me and I'll go and see them.'

'Donal! Donal! It's OK, no one's intimidating us. We're leaving to go to England. I can carry on my work better over there. Here –

319

sit down,' I said, and offered him a glass of Susan's blackcurrant wine. So we sat around the table and drank a glass of wine for Auld Lang Syne. Donal was very appreciative of the wine and likened it to a 'delicate cherry brandy'. After a while he got up to leave, and I got up to see him to the door.

'All the best people leave Ireland!' Donal wailed, and fell on me, arms around my shoulders, weeping this farewell in his strong Derry accent. 'On behalf of the Republicans of Killorglin, I wish you all the very best of luck and I'd like you to have this.'

From his overcoat pocket he produced a roll of drawing paper. He turned and hurried out of the cottage. Susan and I sat down, astonished. That 'Republican' was a very emotional softy. I unrolled the paper. He had made a good drawing of a boxer, in the ring, down on his knees, gloves on the canvas. The other boxer was standing over him. There was a caption. 'Down but not out.'

On 7th December Eugene came and our furniture was loaded into his lorry. Pat and Agnes came round in the evening to say goodbye. We set out early the next day for Cork with Baby Cat in her homemade cage in the car with us. We left the Cork main road at Macroom and took the road through Coachford to Blarney. Our little family entered the castle, climbed the steps to the roof of the tower. There, with the help of the tower's assistant, Susan and I in turn laid on our backs and inched forwards to the slot where, bending the back backwards and going down into the slot, we kissed the Blarney Stone. Our thanks and affection for Ireland and the freedom Ireland had given us to improve our fortune.

Éirinn go Brách!

Epilogue

We finished writing this book during the first Coronavirus lockdown. Nearly every day I walked, either on my own or the two of us together: across the fields at the front of the house, down the green road, across neglected pasture land where cows once grazed and where mushrooms grew in abundance long years ago when we first moved here, up onto the old Midland & Great Northern Joint Railway embankment from where we could admire the view of the gently rolling Norfolk countryside. Quiet and contemplative in the sunshine, cold and harsh when the east wind blew. As I walked I began to reflect on the story we were telling and our subsequent life in Norfolk. I realised to my astonishment that, although it was a wrench to leave Ireland, we didn't actually shed a tear, so eager were we to move on to the next episode in our lives. Looking back now at our leave-taking, my tears flow freely.

When Adrian walked with me he would nearly always reflect and wonder and talk about the M&GN Railway, how it had been built, who had built it, what trains had run across it. Stories about the railway were like an adjunct to my life, constantly present, constantly told. I sometimes wondered whether my husband lived more in those stories about the past than he did in his life with me! And yet I knew that wasn't true because we have lived this life together, fully and lovingly. The foundation of our partnership and our philosophy for living, laid down and developed as we rebuilt that little cottage in Kerry all those years ago.

Our good fortune was sealed when our third and last child was born in Drayton Maternity Home just outside Norwich in September 1986. I still wasn't brave enough to give birth at home, but felt this was a compromise and close to the hospital if anything went wrong. Learning from my birth preparation classes, I laboured in an upright position – walking, kneeling, sitting, allowing gravity to help my body prepare –

and this time round I did manage to give birth 'naturally'. I can honestly say I stayed in control and 'breathed through' my contractions, not feeling any pain apart from the actual pushing out of my baby's head. I felt so proud of myself and so in love with this new babe, whom we called Beatrice: 'Bringer of Joy'.

Acknowledgements:

Writing this book would not have been possible without the foresight of our dear friends Paul and Susie Dye, who sadly are no longer with us. They gave us copies of all the letters we wrote to them whilst we lived in Kerry which along with letters written to Adrian's parents and our own records, enabled us to write our story. It is hard to thank everyone as so many friends and family members have encouraged and supported us in our project but we must give special mention to Dr. Lynn Preston who was our first 'reader' and gave many helpful suggestions for improvement. Professor George Huxley also read the manuscript and we are grateful to him for his expert knowledge of Irish affairs and language as well as his encouragement and support.

Our thanks also go to Will Adams who kindly edited the manuscript and gave us much needed confidence. We would like to thank our daughters Rebecca Vaughan, Connie Vaughan and Beatrice Hodson for their support and enthusiasm and Rebecca's inspirational input on the cover design. We are grateful to Susan's mother Pamela O'Sullivan, and her sisters Karen Okoro, Bernie O'Sullivan-Meaney and Siobhan Breen for their helpful input and encouragement.

We would also like to thank Susan's cousins Bernie O'Sullivan, Kevin O'Callaghan and Seán O'Callaghan for answering our questions about family affairs. Thanks also to Anna Sobolewski, Linda Scott, Mervyn Scott, Helen Moore and Stan Moore who answered our questions and helped to revive our memories. We would also like to thank Stephen Thompson of the Killorglin Archive Society and Danny Morrison, Secretary of the Bobby Sands Trust. Finally, we would like to thank the team from 3P Publishing for making our dream a reality.